"Ted Perry's fascinating memoir is both a love poem to movies by a lifelong cinephile and a detective story in which a middle-aged man investigates the parents he knew intimately and not at all. Interspersed with memories of growing up in New Orleans and going to movies with his father, the author reconstructs the lives of relatives, tracks down clues to the past in that elusive, colorful, past-haunted city, and recalls movies and scenes that elucidate significant moments in family history. The interweaving of fiction and reality, the unreliability of memory, the various guises with which people, real and cinematic, present themselves, all play off each other in this richly textured narrative."

MOLLY HASKELL
Film critic and author of *Holding My Own in No Man's Land:
Women and Men and Film and Feminists*

"An eminent teacher and scholar of film here shows causes and finds ways of recounting movies and of telling journeys of his life by articulating each in terms drawn from the other, lending to each the touch of strangeness that insight thrives upon. The result is continuously surprising, moving, meticulous, and—a still rarer thing—illuminating, both about movies and about lives."

STANLEY CAVELL
Professor of Philosophy, Harvard University, Emeritus

"Ted Perry is one of America's most respected film teachers. For decades his analysis and interpretation have made him a distinguished cinematic scholar. Now he tells us the tale of his childhood—where family ties were inexorably linked to movies. His relationship to both his father and movies planted the seeds that blossomed into his devotion to the cinema. *My Reel Story* is eminently readable, insightful, and moving. The flickering lights of the projector shine through the painful layers of the childhood that gave him his love of cinema, radiating on every page of his tale."

JEAN PICKER FIRSTENBERG
Director and CEO, American Film Institute

"Not since Walker Percy has a moviegoer ruminated so poignantly on his passages in and out of the theaters of New Orleans. Food, art, sex, death, and the cinema itself—these great mysteries are touchingly, unpretentiously evoked in a style whose reveries and shifts in mood owe much to the cinema. The eccentrics we meet in Perry's obsessive pursuit of a secretive father might come straight from the movies (scores of them and of all sorts) that transform this personal search for meaning into a cultural probe, as well as that quest for 'transcendence' that every filmgoer will recognize as his own."
DUDLEY ANDREW
Professor of Film and Literature, Yale University and author of
Film in the Aura of Art

"*My Reel Story* is a remarkable reflection on the art of film and its power to shape the human imagination. Ted Perry takes the reader on an evocative journey through painful and joyful memories captured and retold through the power of the movies. He brings us to the heart of life and film: a brilliant achievement!"
JOHN G. HANHARDT
Senior Curator of Film and Media Arts, Guggenheim Museum

"Ted Perry understands the tides that flow between art and audience. His students are fortunate to have a teacher for whom honesty in the art that is taught is matched by honesty in the teacher. The movies are not a dry object for Perry, they carry emotion and history, and so does his book."
MICHAEL TOLKIN
Author of *The Player,* and writer/director of *The Rapture* and *The New Age*

"A sumptuous matinee of a book. Ted Perry's lustrous prose ushers you into a nonesuch movie palace of words and memory, where the triple feature—a son's time-journey back to the side of his movie-addled father, a gorgeous disquisition on film-making and human consciousness, and a sly deadpan comedy about a daft New Orleans family in the 1940s—somehow dissolves into one unbroken celluoid dream. I can't wait to see it again."
RON POWERS
Author of *Dangerous Water: A Biography of the Boy Who Became Mark Twain*

MY REEL STORY

Ted Perry

My Reel Story

Middlebury College Press
PUBLISHED BY UNIVERSITY PRESS OF NEW ENGLAND
HANOVER AND LONDON

Middlebury College Press

University Press of New England, Hanover, NH 03755

© 2001 by Edward S. (Ted) Perry

Printed in the United States of America

5 4 3 2 1

New England Review previously published selections from this book.

Library of Congress Cataloging-in-Publication Data
Perry, Ted, 1937–
  My reel story / by Ted Perry.
    p. cm.
  ISBN 1-58465-076-1 (alk. paper)
  1. Perry, Ted, 1937– 2. Film critics—United States—Biography.
I. Title.
  PN1998.3.P457 A3 2000
  791.43' 092—dc21
                                          00–009336

    For

Melissa, Megan, John, and Thad

Contents

	Acknowledgments	vii
	Introduction	1
1	The River	14
2	Secrets	21
3	Texts	48
4	Window-Shopping	73
5	Journey-Proud	99
6	Who's Who?	121
7	Better to Remember	146
8	No Touching	172
9	Memento Mori	194
10	Crossing the River	222

Acknowledgments

Without the efforts and encouragement of Paul Baker, Gene McKinney, Ray Roberts, and Gerald Gross, as well as the generous support of Middlebury College, this book would never have been undertaken, nor finished, and I am very thankful to them. My gratitude extends also to Michael Collier, Jaime Grechika, Patricia Hampl, Don Mitchell, Scott Russell Sanders, and Alec Wilkinson, who read parts of early drafts and offered perceptive comments. Courtney Palmbush, Rich Gallup, and Sean Vawter gave vital help, as did Ralston Cole, whose memory of our childhood is better than mine. I am especially grateful to John Bertolini for his expertise and assistance. Those who read the final drafts of the manuscript—Stephen Donadio, Miriam Perry, and Ron Powers—responded with thoughtful insight and constructive guidance; to them I am extremely indebted. I want to acknowledge with much appreciation the competence, enthusiasm, and support of Phil Pochoda and the staff of the University Press of New England, who oversaw the publication of the book.

MY REEL STORY

Introduction

This book will make more sense if I suggest something of what it's been like to spend a lifetime writing, teaching, thinking, speaking about, and looking at movies. They created me, or I conceived them; I'm not sure which.

My grandson and I were watching on television the Japanese science fiction film *Gamera: Guardian of the Universe* (1995), which was a remake of one of the Gamera films from the 1960s. Even more than the original, the 1995 version was very camp. Gamera, a flying turtle who can spin around like a saucer and move at astounding speeds, is the good monster, trying to destroy the bad monster, Gyaos, another airborne creature who looks like a flying turkey with a flat plate on top of its head. I chuckled repeatedly at the dialogue, rendered even worse by bad dubbing from the Japanese.

Surely the filmmaker was deliberately spoofing Japanese science-fiction films of the fifties and sixties—yet I wasn't always so sure. One conversation was particularly funny. A woman who is a doctor of ornithology, having discovered that Gyaos can reproduce by itself, says to a man, "Gyaos is capable of destroying mankind!" Acting as if he's just come home from a hard day and his wife has told him the children have been misbehaving, the man turns his back and walks away, saying, "What do you want me to do about it?" I almost fell out of my chair with laughter until I saw that my eight-year-old grandson looked perplexed; he didn't understand why the dialogue was so funny to me.

How very different it was going with my father to the movies in the early forties when I was my grandson's age. Thinking back to some of the films we loved—the Dead End Kids, Hopalong Cassidy, the Road movies with Bob Hope, Bing Crosby, and Dorothy Lamour—I recall that we always had the same reactions. We agreed on what was supposed to be comic. And what was tragic. Or unhappy. We shared what feelings there were to be had from a movie, or at least that's how I remember it. Some sons unite with their fathers over fishing, baseball, or hunting. For my father and me it was the movies. Whether it was being absorbed by powerful images on the screen, or the sense of being bonded with my father, I don't know, but something wonderful happened to me in that movie theater with him.

I thought about my father and movies the other day when I was sitting in my doctor's waiting room, thumbing through magazines, and came upon a photograph of Humphrey Bogart that startled me. The actor was wearing a fedora that threw a slight shadow over part of his face, and around his neck was a scarf on top of what looked like an overcoat. What surprised me was that the photograph was almost identical to one of my father taken in the early forties. That posed, studio image of him had always confused me because I couldn't imagine why my father would have worn a hat, an overcoat, and a scarf when he went to a photographer's studio to have his portrait taken. Thinking about how hot the lights must have been, I was sure my father must have been burning up in his outfit, waiting for the photographer to take his picture. It had made no sense to me, but seeing the photograph of Bogart, I realized that my father had tried to copy the look of a star he liked so much. He may even have brought a copy of the same Bogart portrait with him and said to the photographer, "I want to look like this." Movies, and movie stars, meant that much to him.

I know a little about that feeling. There have been times when I have met my movie heroes and been so starstruck I could hardly speak. Not long after I started teaching film at the University of Texas at Austin, I had a chance to meet Michelangelo Antonioni, the Italian filmmaker I most admired. We were both at a conference, and I got up the courage to ask him if we could meet the next morning for breakfast at an outdoor café. He arrived on time, looking a little like the last thing he wanted to do so early in the morning was talk to a young academic.

I tried to smile and appear at ease, but I was shaking a little and my mouth felt like it was full of white paste. Antonioni made me even more uncomfortable when I pulled out my tape recorder and he said, "No, don't turn that on. I don't like my voice, and I don't want any recordings of it around." Now what? I asked myself. Having left behind paper and pens, I would have to try to remember what he said.

Some details of his life were unclear to me, but when I asked, he refused to answer my questions. "My biography has nothing to do with my movies," he said. Now I was feeling really uneasy, but then I remembered how much he was supposed to like the Bolognese painter Giorgio Morandi, who mainly painted still lifes of bottles. I asked Antonioni why he admired Morandi's work. The filmmaker looked at the sky for a very long time, and I couldn't tell if he thought the question was foolish or if he was trying to formulate an answer. Finally, he said, without looking at me, "Because he was after the truth of the bottles."

Antonioni's answer seemed to end that line of thought. Hoping I might impress him with an observation, I said, "I don't think you ever show a couple starting a relationship—for instance, when the man asks for a date and the woman says yes. In *Eclipse* there's no scene of them agreeing to meet at a certain street corner, but they show up at the same time. The moments when a man and a woman break up, that's not in the films either. One minute they're a couple and the next minute they're not." Thinking I had really offered a unique perception, I asked, "Why don't you show a couple getting together or splitting up?"

Antonioni furrowed his brow, looked skyward again, and said, "Because it's hard."

I wanted to ask, "Because it's hard to show on film, or hard to do in life?" but something about the way he answered my question made me feel he didn't think much of my insight, which now seemed silly to me, so I shut up. His tweed sport coat began to interest me. The color—a dark leafy green—was what struck me the most. Monica Vitti wears a coat of a similar shade in the opening and closing sequences of *Red Desert* (1964). The color of her coat sets her apart from the gray industrial site she is walking through, as if she is a refugee from a natural world of rich vegetation. Antonioni's jacket was also the color of the park that the photographer enters during Antonioni's *Blow-up* (1966)—a park that the Italian director spray-painted to make the green richer and more saturated.

In Antonioni's film universe, from what I had seen, green was the color of Eden and of those connected with that innocent world to which we all once belonged. When, not too many months after our breakfast, I saw Antonioni's next film, *Zabriskie Point* (1970), my impression was confirmed because the dress of one of the protagonists, Daria, is almost the same green color; and she is the kind of spontaneous, innocent creature who would have been at home in the London park of *Blow-up*. A few years later, in *The Passenger* (1975), the green reappears as a realm that surrounds Jack Nicholson as he walks along Barcelona's Ramblas and also as he sits quietly in the Umbraculo garden—tropical vegetation, as the script calls it. Nicholson comes to this bowered world just as he is beginning a new, carefree life.

A film director often identified with the harsh manmade colors of the modern world, that day at breakfast Antonioni had worn an earthy green jacket. He didn't have to answer my questions about his life; I understood who he was, and what his sentiments were, by the color of his sport coat.

* * *

Reading the entertainment section of *The New York Times* today, which was previewing the fall cultural scene, I was very aware of what it's like to live in Vermont. I usually don't miss living in New York City. Vermont has many virtues, and I get to New York often enough that I can satiate my desire for movies. But this morning's *Times* listed about a dozen movies that I would like to see—new foreign films, silent films being played with a live orchestra, independent films by new directors, avant-garde films and videos, a restored version of Fellini's *Nights of Cabiria* (1957), and a new version of Orson Welles's *Touch of Evil* (1958) that's been edited to conform more closely to Welles's intentions. Most of these films will appear in New York only a few times, at most for a few weeks, which means that when I get to the city again, I will have missed them. For someone whose life has been involved with movies, there's a strong feeling of deprivation in being away from major cities like New York. Much of the most interesting and adventurous work gets shown there.

The positive side of being in Vermont is that I get to stand before hundreds of bright college students, point at the screen, and say, "Let me tell you why I think this movie is important." What I wish I could also do for them is re-create the excitement surrounding movies in the sixties, when film was such a crucial element in the culture, and every new film by a Godard or an Antonioni or a Fellini or a Bergman played to a packed house. That's impossible, but if anything I say helps to make the students into better viewers, tomorrow they'll demand better films, or so I tell myself

Teaching film at any college or university has its problems, though. Walking across my campus recently, I passed a professor from the literature department who asked, "Hey, how about that *Titanic*?" The question really irritated me. I almost responded, "Hey, how about that new Jackie Collins novel?" What I really wanted to be was a smart aleck and ask the professor if he knew that James Joyce opened the first movie theater in Dublin, and that *Ulysses* probably wouldn't have been *Ulysses* if Joyce hadn't seen a lot of movies where subjective and objective are mixed, where the point of view shifts, and where space is manipulated. Why, when the phrase "pixilated doodler" shows up in *Finnegans Wake*, don't you think Joyce was remembering a scene in the Frank Capra film *Mr. Deeds Goes to Town* (1936)? Fortunately, I contained myself and didn't make any rabid claims about Joyce and movies. Mumbling instead something about how impressive were *Titanic*'s special effects, I went on my way.

What almost prompted my outburst about Joyce was the feeling that my work is diminished by the perception that what I do is show films like *Titanic* and talk about them. Only a few people at my college have this attitude about movies, thank goodness. Yet it's still true that the study of film, even though there is more and more serious film scholarship, often has about as much standing as the study of English literature had when it was first introduced at Oxford and Cambridge.

It's heartening to realize that now my English department colleagues don't have to justify what they do; perhaps someday the study of film will have the same aura. Years ago the professional society for academics in film study was called the Society of Cinematologists. No doubt that pretentious title was invented by some academic who was trying to convince his dean that film study was a serious field. When I first asked that we start teaching filmmaking at my college, a dean said, "No, we're not a trade school!" Teaching creative writing was okay, but not how to make and put together images to tell a story. That was years ago and the situation has steadily improved. Now the problems are very different: too few students, or even film teachers and scholars, care passionately about movies. My other fear is that all the significant movies have already been made, but then I'll see a film like Kusturica's *Underground* (1995) or Angelopoulos's *Ulysses' Gaze* (1997), and I'll know the medium is still powerful and alive.

* * *

To visit me, my wife, and our children, my mother came once to New York City, where we lived. She asked to have lunch with me, which I knew was not a good sign. Her timing couldn't have been worse. That morning there had been a very unhappy scene with the Museum of Modern Art's film staff. Because more and more interesting work was being done by artists using videotape, I wanted to add video exhibition to the film program, but everyone in the department was absolutely opposed to the idea. At the meeting that morning, one person stood up on a table and yelled at me, "We're a department of the *big* picture!" He meant everyone was committed to exhibiting films on a large screen and that any showings—whether video art or feature films—on a small television monitor were anathema. It was hard to disagree with such dedicated people. They were the film department, and without their devotion to the "big" picture its importance would have waned generations ago. They were right to defend the big picture, but it was also true that work of consequence was being made for the small screen. The meeting did not end well, and I then had to rush off to meet my mother.

I can't remember for sure where we ate, or what we ate, but the gist of our conversation is still clear. My mother made small talk until the food arrived and then she abruptly said, "We need to talk."

I waited. What I had learned after years of conversations with my mother was that it was best to say as little as possible. However innocent, almost any answer could provoke a sudden furor.

"If I remember, you went to Iowa to study playwriting, but the first thing I knew you were teaching about movies."

Instead of saying, "It was the only job I could get to make enough money to pay for school," I nodded.

"Then you suddenly started working on a Ph.D."

I almost said, "I needed the Ph.D. to get a teaching job, which would leave me time to write."

"But then you didn't write plays."

"Correct." It's important to agree with my mother now and then. What I'm thinking is that I wish I had ordered the shark.

She said, "I don't understand."

I wanted to say, "Me either," but I concentrated instead on making an elaborate effort to use my knife as a scalpel to perform microsurgery on a piece of chicken breast. The body of a chicken and the head of a woman—that was a creature in Tod Browning's *Freaks* (1932). A lady trapeze artist is turned into this freak by the friends of her midget husband, whom she has tried to poison. How was the scalpel used to turn her body into a chicken? I had wondered. Only after I had pondered the question for a moment did I remember I was watching a movie. On the screen the chicken-woman had looked absolutely real.

My mother interrupted my thoughts by saying: "Now to make things worse, you're not teaching; you've got a job at some museum."

Her belligerent tone provoked me, and before I realized what I was doing, I raised my knife, pointed it at her, and said, "I'm not just working at some museum; I'm directing the best film department at the best modern museum in the world."

"So you say, but it doesn't seem to make you happy."

I pushed some peas from one side of my plate to another, then back again.

"You're not teaching, that's for sure," my mother said.

"I fly to Boston one night a week and teach a course at Harvard."

Mother said, "That doesn't count."

"Harvard doesn't count?"

"New York is not a safe place to live and raise a family."

So that was it. She wasn't concerned about my job or my happiness; she didn't like New York City. I continued eating; if I were to take her on about New York, we would soon be at each other's throats. I pretended not to have heard her.

"You need to figure out what you want to do, Son."

Instead of disagreeing with her, or telling her I might be fired after the defiant meeting with the film department staff, or letting her know that there were times when I hated movies and wished I never had anything more to do with them, I said, "Yes, Mother," and turned away. On such a day I needed something sweet, so I looked for the waiter to get a dessert menu, but I couldn't find him. I did see a couple near me being served a small bowl of caviar, and it reminded me of something that happened just a few months earlier.

I was in Moscow at the railway station, about to board a train for Leningrad. It was midnight in January and the snow was falling, although I don't remember it being cold. Blackness was everywhere, but along the walkway that ran parallel to the train tracks there were tall lamp poles. In the cones of light they created, little snowflakes were visible, floating slowly down on their trip toward the ground. Standing beside me were Larisa Shepitko and her husband. Just a year before, a film of hers, *The Ascent* (1977), had won the Golden Bear Award at the Berlin Film Festival. The film astonished me because it dealt with a subject universally forbidden in the U.S.S.R.—the collaboration of some Russian peasants with the Nazis during World War II. I could only begin to guess at the enormous struggle Shepitko must have gone through to get the film made and released. I admired her.

Larisa and her husband had been my salvation during a month in Moscow, where I went to look at films for a Museum of Modern Art series on the history of Soviet documentary. It was an agonizing time. After the first week or so of seeing again the brilliance of early Soviet documentarians—Vertov, Shub, Turin—I had to endure three weeks of watching propaganda films: paeans to the glories of the U.S.S.R., tributes to the building of great hydroelectric dams, endless celebrations of Stalin, Khrushchev, and Brezhnev. Now and then I would catch a glimpse of real talent—some filmmaker who actually understood the medium and wasn't just making one more commercial for the Soviet state. I ached for these people, so constrained by the kinds of films they could make, and I admired Shepitko even more.

In the midst of this boredom and frustration, Larisa and her husband, a filmmaker who had had one of his films banned, invited me to their home several times, which made Moscow more bearable. They helped me arrange a weekend trip to Leningrad for a few days of vacation before my last week of viewing films. As we stood beside the train, Larisa handed me a brown paper bag. "For the trip," she said. We embraced and I got on the train. I waved to her and her husband as the train pulled away, then opened the bag. Inside were a bottle of vodka and two sandwiches, made of dark bread and filled with caviar. I put part of one in my mouth. The bread was so thick that I had to bite hard and tear a piece off. A sweet and salty taste of caviar hit my palate so hard I winced. I took a long slug of vodka and swirled caviar, vodka, and dark bread around inside my mouth. Life was good. For two days I could walk the streets of Leningrad and forget about movies, especially bad movies.

Shepitko and Antonioni were just two of my many heroes in the world of film. If I had to pick out one group of people for particular praise, it would be the older generation of film scholars and archivists, especially the people who felt so passionate about movies that they saved them. I remember one of these men, James Card, who was the film archivist at the George Eastman House in Rochester, New York, telling me once how he brought a print of *The Scarlet Letter* (1926) into the United States so he could have it for his archive. At the time, it was illegal to bring the print in, or so he said. I can't remember why exactly, and he may have made the story up, but I'm sure it was either true or based on something that he actually did. To get the print of *The Scarlet Letter* into the country, Card told me he changed the title to *How Hester Got Her A*. Under that title he easily brought the film through customs. It was that kind of ingenuity and daring, and love of movies, that led to the preservation of films that otherwise would have disappeared.

I remember once watching the German Expressionist silent film, *The Cabinet of Dr. Caligari* (1919), with Jay Leyda, one of the early film scholars, who wrote the first history of Soviet film, and of Chinese film, in English. He was a friend of Sergei Eisenstein's and the first translator of that filmmaker's essays. At a point in the film where a title card was showing some of the dialogue from the film, Jay said, "My hand was shaky that day." I looked again at the title card and recognized Jay's handwriting. When I asked him why he was the one who made the title cards, he told me the story of how he acquired the film in Germany and brought it back to this country for preservation and, eventually, for exhibition. People like Leyda and Card were collecting and preserving films when hardly anyone else in the world was saving movies. Even producers were destroying negatives and prints after they had made the circuit of theaters, believing that the movies no longer had any commercial value—or any other importance.

One of the collectors I most admired was William Everson, who, like Leyda, was also a film scholar and teacher. Going to his apartment on the Upper West Side of Manhattan was like going to a film vault. Every nook and cranny, including his bathroom, was filled with cans of film—hundreds, perhaps thousands, of them. To walk down some hallways I had to turn sideways because huge stacks of film cans lined the walls. Everson's living room had a film projector, a screen, and several rows of movie seats. There was no popcorn, but prominent in the space was a refrigerator half full of Hostess Twinkies. In Everson's living room I was shown films I had never heard of, but that often were masterpieces.

Everson and Leyda were both on the faculty of New York University's cinema studies department, as was I, so it was sometimes the case that we were on the same doctoral committee, examining a Ph.D. candidate. I can't imagine a more daunting experience than to be questioned by Everson and Leyda, who, between them, seemed to have seen almost every film ever made. One such oral examination stands out in my mind. More than once, the candidate was stopped by one of the men, who pointed out mistakes and asked for clarification. Everson interrupted the student several times, referring him to other versions of a film, versions the rest of us had never heard of. After the meeting was over, Leyda and I were walking out of the room, and he turned to me and said, referring to Everson, "He's so intimidating." This said by a man who probably was, at the time, the most respected film scholar in the world. I wanted to say to Jay, "How intimidated do you think I feel, being in the room with the two of you?"

Feeling inadequate around people like Leyda and Everson reminds me how complicated is my relationship with films. Spending most of my days and nights involved with movies doesn't mean I haven't had my doubts about what I am doing, nor does it mean that I've only thought about "serious" films. I struggle against going to the most popular movies, sure that they will just anger me with their unsubtle display of murder and lust, their portrayal of unbelievable heroes, and their pyrotechnics, but more often than not I can't stay away. Watching a movie that millions of other people see is very comforting, as if the act bonds me to humankind. My mockery of film, and my admiration, seem inseparable. Even as I think this is so, I can't help getting angry at a popular movie for its pretensions and its lies. The angrier I get, the more aware I am of every bad edit, every shaky camera, poor lighting, inane dialogue. Long since lost is my moviegoing virginity. My students tell me that it's happened to them, too, and they're angry at me for piercing their illusions.

Movies have enriched my life, yet there are days when the work that puts food on my table, and that I love, owns me, which feels very confining. I tell myself that movies, like my home and my garden and the pictures on my walls, are just things, and that I shouldn't get too attached to things. Yet the truth is that they've often been the glue that holds everything together, sometimes even the source of feeling and thought.

Usually, to find out what I think about anything, I have to write down what I think I think and then read it to see if what I've written is true and makes sense. Often the first attempts are stupid and dishonest, and even when they don't seem so that day, they do the next morning when I get up. In order to get at what is true I have to keep writing until what I write makes sense to me.

It's the same for me with movies. I feel as if I invent them, in the same way that I create sentences. If I look at enough films, I'll know what is true. Most movies are like all the first sentences I write—foolish and dishonest. Some of the movies I admire one day seem juvenile and false the next. Finding a film that I can watch dozens of times means that I have come across a film that has some measure of truth, if not for the world, at least for me. I learn through real experiences, of course, but the movies confirm what I think I detect. For me the task of going to hundreds of films is the same as the task of writing and rewriting in order to make a sentence that is true.

Peter Kubelka, an Austrian filmmaker I admire, took years to edit his short films. When I asked him why, he said it was because he would be asked by museums, archives, clubs, colleges, and universities to screen and talk about his work, which meant he would have to see his movies over and over. The years of editing were crucial to make sure that his films were true and that they wouldn't bore or embarrass him after hundreds of screenings. I look for the same kinds of movies, believing that when I find them, I discover what I really think, which means, who I am.

What surprises me sometimes is that the attempt to clarify my thinking through writing and rewriting sometimes leads to discoveries of something I didn't know beforehand, as if the words and sentences have a life of their own. It's not so much that I write the sentences to clear up my thinking as it is that the sentences reveal some new truth to me. The same happens for me with films. What begins as an attempt to find a movie that clarifies and confirms what I think, winds up being the discovery of a movie that tells me something altogether original. Those movies are the ones I hunt for, and when I find one—like Scorsese's *Raging Bull* (1980), or Kieślowski's *Decalogue* (1988), or Mekas's *Reminiscences of a Journey to Lithuania* (1986), or Tarkovsky's *The Sacrifice* (1986)—it turns upside down all my conventional notions about movies, and about life.

Sometimes I don't want to watch a film that shows me something new. Sometimes I don't want the screen surface to act like a mirror and make it possible for my eye to do what it most often wants to do— see itself. Sometimes what I dearly want is a movie that reinforces my illusions—not the petty ones but those that I need to survive, a belief that will get me out of bed in the morning. I need a movie that sustains these necessary deceptions, even as the facts of my experience tell me otherwise. I want to believe that if I just keep plugging away, using my abilities like Buster Keaton, Julie Andrews, John Wayne, or Katharine Hepburn, I can survive and overcome.

When a movie reinforces an illusion that I need, when a movie helps me look within by looking out, when a movie reveals a truth I did not know, then I recall clearly why it is that I have spent so much of my time with films. While my attachment to movies then makes sense to me, what is not clear is how I came to be so involved. But that is the story of this book.

1 The River

I HAD BEEN IN AND OUT OF NEW Orleans a dozen times since I moved away forty years ago, but I hadn't gone back to my old neighborhood, and I wasn't sure why. I suppose I thought it would be sad to be reminded that I was no longer a little boy, that my parents were dead, and that nobody I knew lived in the area anymore. So it came as a surprise when a few years ago I felt a desire to see my neighborhood again, but I guess that urge comes to a lot of people in their fifties. Realizing that I had to change planes on the way to Houston for a meeting, I asked the travel agent to arrange a long layover.

As the Checker cab left the airport and moved through the streets, the weather rushed in. It wasn't that chilly, only around freezing, but the air was very damp, and I felt colder than I would have if the temperature were the same at home in Vermont. Asking the cabdriver to drop me at the corner of Broadway and St. Charles Avenue, I intended to walk uptown toward my old house. Watching the taxi pull away, though, I felt I wasn't ready. Because my neighborhood was like an unrequited love that had taken me years to get off my mind, I wasn't anxious to be reminded once again of something irretrievably lost, at least not yet. I decided to walk in the other direction, and, after a few blocks, came to Audubon Park. It seemed to be quite peaceful, the live oak trees so beautifully shaped they reminded me of huge bonsai. The landscape felt very familiar; Audubon Park was the place where I went swimming as a kid, where I played catch and flew kites with my father. Most of our kite-flying was done at the very back of the park, on the Mississippi River levee, because it was free of trees and a good wind was usually coming off the river. I liked to watch my father put the kite together and make the tail out of an old pillowcase that he tore into strips. His hands were broad and strong, and I thought he could do anything with them. While my father prepared the kite, I would sometimes turn and look across the river, which made me feel as if I were standing on the very edge of my known world. In front of me was the Wild West, and to my right, upriver, was that other strange land, the North.

The memory of kite-flying with my father made me want to go to the river, which meant walking through the zoo. Strolling in that direction, I recalled quite a different experience with my father on the levee. Now and then he would get an urge to help people, but he didn't usually carry through because my mother would say, "We don't have enough money ourselves," or, "Why don't you take care of your own family first?" She disliked his doing anything that wasn't her idea, yet she also accused him of being too passive.

The Thanksgiving when I was seven, he just ignored her and bought a few cans of food and a small turkey to give away to one of the families who lived on the *batture*, which is what New Orleanians used to call the land on the river side of the levee. Because it wasn't clear who owned this ground, some people had built shacks on the *batture* to avoid paying any rent or taxes. We would call them squatters now, but I don't remember that word being used at all when I was a kid. The families were just people who lived on the *batture*. I had never been in one of these houses, but I had seen them when my father and I flew kites.

Resting on stilts, the homes sat high above the water at the river's edge and were reached by piers that extended from the crown of the levee straight out to the houses. The structures were built from driftwood and from windows, siding, and roofing scavenged from junkyards. I remember one home in particular because the top half of an exterior wall had brown boards that ran vertically, and the bottom half had yellow siding that ran horizontally. The roof was a mixture of gray asphalt shingles and shiny tin; an outside wall had one window that was round, one that was square, and several that were rectangular. To live in a dwelling perched above the river, what could be more exciting? To my child's mind, the houses had been built by fairy-tale figures, like Hansel and Gretel, and I always wanted to live in one.

Thanksgiving morning, carrying the box of groceries, my father approached one of these houses on the *batture*. He started out the walkway with me following, and, as we stepped along, the levee gradually dropped away beneath us. The walkway swayed a little, and I began to feel scared, but my father said, "Don't worry, it's okay." He shifted the box of food to one arm and took my hand with the other. No one answered his knock right away, and I became uneasy; maybe these people weren't friendly. After what seemed like an hour, a large man about my father's age came to the door and opened it. He didn't smile or look as if he welcomed us; the T-shirt he wore was covered with grease stains. My father said, "Happy Thanksgiving. We had some extra food and thought we'd share it with you." A long pause followed as the man looked at my father, then at the box, then at me. Finally, my father spoke: "My name is Ed Perry and this is my son, Teddy." The man smiled a little, then opened the screen door and reached out for the box of food. Catching a glimpse of the room inside, I was surprised to see that the same linoleum was on the walls as on the floor.

As he took the box of food, the man started to say something, but a small boy pushed forward, under the man's arms, and spoke. "Who is it, Pop?"

I was surprised. "Hi, David," I said. The boy looked at me for an instant and then turned quickly and disappeared.

"Thanks for your kindness," the older man said, as he took the box of food inside and closed the door.

My father and I started back up the walkway toward the levee. "Somebody you know?" my father asked.

"I think it was David Buras. He's in my class at school." My father didn't say anything for a few steps, and then I asked, "Why did he run away, Dad?"

My father said, "Did you know he lived on the *batture*?"

"No."

"I imagine he was embarrassed," my father said.

"Embarrassed about what?"

"You saw his house, Teddy, it's just a shack. If they live there it's because they can't afford rent or taxes."

I wasn't sure I understood my father. The house David lived in didn't seem like a shack; in fact, I liked the place because it was so different. I thought David might have been embarrassed for another reason, and I said, "His father's clothes looked pretty dirty."

"He's dirty because he works with his hands, Son, there's nothing wrong with that."

Now I felt ashamed, reprimanded by my father.

I entered the Audubon Park Zoo, fifty years later, still thinking about that scene at David's house on the *batture*, and walked quickly through the zoo to the train tracks that ran parallel to the river. I crossed them, then climbed up the levee which seemed much lower than I remembered.

When I stepped onto the crown, the view was so unlike what I had expected that I looked right and left, wondering if I was at the right place. Instead of an expanse of grass, there were now pine, oak, and magnolia trees. Downriver I saw a soccer field. Upriver some tugboats were pulling out from a dock at the old Walnut Street ferry landing. Where once the levee had sloped down to the river, I saw a parking lot and a concrete walkway lined with wooden benches. Only the river itself seemed familiar, with flashes of light like sparks on the tops of some waves, and whitecaps bouncing around. Across the river the sun was setting. Certainly the word *"batture"* was not used to describe this area anymore. Where were the shacks? Where was David's house? Even the large weeping willows, which had shaded a few of the shanties, were gone.

These discrepancies stunned me. On the way from the airport in my taxi I had passed a dozen other changes in the landscape. Why hadn't I been as disturbed when I saw that the old Pelican Baseball Stadium had been replaced by a motel? Perhaps I had held on to this memory of the incident on the *batture* as a way of idealizing my father. It was a little unlike him to buy food for poor people and to take it to them; maybe I had invented the whole experience to have an excuse for admiring my father. To have a questionable memory is not so unusual, but something about this one seemed to threaten me, as if the scene in my memory and my identity were linked. If I had made up that scene, what others had I invented?

It was lonely standing there on the levee, finding my memory so at odds with what I was seeing. In *Singin' in the Rain* (1952) Gene Kelly tells the story of his past, but what he says is different from what is seen on the screen. While he remarks, "I used to perform for all of Mom and Dad's society friends," the image is something else—a boy singing and dancing for pennies in a pool hall. No better at narrating my past than Gene Kelly, standing on the levee I couldn't say which was true—what I remembered or what I was seeing in front of me.

I'd always loved films that caught me up in intellectual puzzles about memory, but the difference now was that I felt personally threatened by a suspicious recollection. Encountering movies was not the same as standing on the levee, experiencing my emotions firsthand. Films were letting me down. I would have to feel what I was feeling, without benefit of a movie to ground and label the experience. Now I was really lonely.

Turning around and starting back toward the zoo and Audubon Park, I kept hearing my father say, "My name is Ed Perry and this is my son, Teddy." I saw David at the door, the sudden surprise on his face, then him running away. My mind would not think about something other than that Thanksgiving morning many years ago, even though now the cold was really coming through my clothes and I was shivering. Which disturbed me the most, I wondered, my inability to free my mind of the memory, or the way in which movies had let me down, or the fear that the memory was a total invention?

Even after getting back to the airport and taking my plane to Houston, I still couldn't free up my mind. My sleep in the hotel that night was fitful, and I finally got up and sat on the couch. I knew I had to visit New Orleans again and see my old neighborhood, my childhood home, the shops and stores and movie theater near where I had lived. To reassure myself that I had the childhood I remembered, I needed to go back.

Because it would be months before I could leave my home in Vermont and get back south, I tried to begin satisfying my curiosity by digging up information in our library that would clarify old memories. When exactly did the azaleas bloom? What about the magnolias? Did the mimosa have long seedpods, like huge string beans, the way I remembered? What was the real name of that tall woody plant labeled a "misbelieve" tree, which had a delicious fruit we called a Japanese plum? The answer, loquat, satisfied me only a little. I decided to look at movies set in New Orleans. Most were a joke, using the city as if it were exotic wallpaper, the background for baroque excess—of shadows, behavior, emotions. I recognized a little of my New Orleans while watching Malle's *Pretty Baby* (1978), especially when a preadolescent Brooke Shields cries and laughs after losing her virginity in the New Orleans whorehouse where her mother has abandoned her.

A particular moment in a Jim Jarmusch film, *Down by Law* (1986), grabbed my attention. The three protagonists, fleeing jail and pursued by men with bloodhounds, have just come to a bayou outside New Orleans. Only two of the men, Jack and Zack, can swim, and they leave Bob, who can't. Having exited the right side of the screen, Jack and Zack can't be seen, but we hear them swimming in the bayou. Bob begins screaming their names, hoping that they will stop swimming and come back for him. The camera holds on Bob's face as he looks offscreen and rambles on in Italian. Behind him the bayou is partially visible, and in the distance we hear the barking of the dogs who are pursuing the three men.

Suddenly, a few twigs snap, Zack enters quickly from screen-left, grabs Bob, and they both disappear screen-right. The camera doesn't move, holding on the water in the background. We hear a splash and see some small waves in this bayou, but the men are not visible. Since all we now see is the water, we have to imagine that Zack came back for Bob and is now pulling him across the bayou. What's more, Zack entered from screen-left when he was grabbing Bob, but he had earlier exited screen-right when he first dived into the bayou. How did Zack get around to the other side of the screen? Did he walk behind the camera? At what point did he stop swimming and return for Bob? We have to imagine what happened because most of the action is offscreen.

That's it, that's my New Orleans, I thought to myself. Everything important was hidden offscreen. All the consequential matters about New Orleans, all its secrets, were offscreen, and as long as I was sitting in the audience, I would never be able to see what was out of sight, hidden by the rectangular border of the movie screen. If I wanted to find out what was offscreen, I would have to mimic Mia Farrow in Woody Allen's *Purple Rose of Cairo* (1984), and, like her, walk up onto the stage, step through the screen, and enter into the world of the movie. In my imagination I could do that, and if I did, maybe I could then look offscreen and see what was there.

* * *

To see what is offscreen I imagine a movie of myself going back to New Orleans. My footage begins with me getting off the plane. Then I go into the airport rest room and change into some old, dirty clothes. It will be easier to get around in my old neighborhood, I tell myself, if I pretend to be a homeless person. A cab takes me to the corner of Cherokee and Hampson, near the house where I lived as a child. I take an Ace bandage out of my pocket, then wind it on my arm as if my arm is sprained. Slowly and methodically, I cover and uncover my arm dozens of times. Pretending that I simply can't get the wrapping right gives me an excuse to stand in one spot and turn slowly around. People walk by, but they pretend not to notice me. I observe, remember, smell, but the more I bandage and unbandage my arm, the more crazy it feels.

This movie scene won't do. The footage is underexposed, the angle makes no sense, the camera is too far away, and the action is stupid. I will have to go back to New Orleans as myself.

2 Secrets

ALMOST A YEAR LATER I WAS FINALLY able to visit New Orleans again. Driving in from a Mississippi town where I was staying for a month with relatives, I thought about the old neighborhood where I grew up during the 1940s and early 1950s. Within two blocks of my home there was a grocery, a florist, a restaurant, a barber shop, a bar, a movie theater, a gas station, a hardware store, a pharmacy, and a cleaners. Six blocks away was my elementary school. During Mardi Gras, some of the parades on St. Charles Avenue came within a block of where I lived. Three blocks away I could get a loaf of hot French bread in the morning, or, even better, fresh potato chips made in the basement of an old home nearby. During World War II, cars were almost nonexistent, even for those who could afford them, which we couldn't. Travel was by the St. Charles Avenue streetcar; we used it to go downtown to shop for clothes and appliances, or to see a doctor or a dentist, but every other place we needed to go was within a few blocks' walk.

Not everything was perfect. We had our share of mean people, like Ol' Lady McGehee, who would sometimes come running out of her house, screaming, "Get your filthy little feet off my monkey grass!" We didn't mind what she did because she had lost a son at Pearl Harbor, so anything was forgivable, and to our eyes she was a hero, even if she was mean. One of my friends had an older brother who wasn't allowed to leave the house, but none of us ever thought twice about the fact that he was too crazy or stupid to be let out. I came to understand that it was not a flawless world, and my home may have been the least perfect part, but I loved it.

After parking in my old neighborhood, I walked an eight-block grid with my house as the center. It appeared that almost nothing was different. No new houses had been built, and most of the neighborhood stores still existed. X-Ray Cleaners was still X-Ray Cleaners, Bruno's Bar was the same, and Mr. Louis' Barber Shop was there, too. Before the days of air conditioning, a summer haircut was torture. As satisfying as it was to see that the houses, sidewalks, even the trees and shrubs, were the same, everything still seemed remote. The appearance of reality, yes, but none of the emotions connected with reality. I had the same feeling when I first saw the de Kooning painting *Excavation*. Supposedly it was inspired by the film *Bitter Rice* (1948), particularly a scene of women in a rice paddy. I knew that film, and that scene, very well; if there was one moment I associated with my own sexual awakening, it was the sight of Silvana Mangano standing in the paddy, her pants rolled up high on her thighs, her sweater pulled tightly across her breasts. But none of those erotic feelings came forth when I looked at the de Kooning painting. There were forms and lines that vaguely resembled the women in the paddy, but missing were all the emotions that I had experienced watching the movie. That's how I felt walking around my old neighborhood.

Something was holding back any connection between me and the landscape. It made me feel as if I had never belonged to the one place I thought I did belong. My old haunts seemed mysterious, full of secrets that I could not fathom. I'm usually drawn to secrets, especially to films that have some kind of secret. The pleasure for me in *The Wizard of Oz* (1939) is knowing that at its heart there is a dirty little secret, which is that grown-ups—all authority—are incompetent and unreliable.

Walking around my old neighborhood, I began looking for details that were different, hoping they would restore some sense of reality to what I was seeing. The biggest transformation—and the biggest disappointment—was that our movie theater, the Mecca, had become a ballet school. The Mecca, the very epicenter of my childhood, was just two blocks from my house, and the place where my father and I spent most of our time together. The important films played downtown, and sometimes it was years before they reached the Mecca, but we didn't care. My dad loved the movies and took me with him two or three times a week. Let everything else change, but not the Mecca.

Near the end of my walk I stepped into Phillips' Restaurant, which, when I was growing up, was our local "joint," a term New Orleanians use for the neighborhood restaurant and bar. Walking inside, half expecting my parents to be sitting in one of the booths eating crab gumbo and drinking Dixie beer, I was startled to see that the place was mainly a bar and that the only food was pizza. Close to Tulane University, Phillips' had become a hangout for students, and the walls were covered with banners for various colleges and universities, as well as for their fraternities and sororities. At three o'clock in the afternoon the place was empty, except for a man who was reading the newspaper in a booth. "What'll you have, baby?" he asked. In New Orleans "baby" and "darling," even "sweetheart" and "Captain," are common terms, even among strangers.

"A glass of beer." I had no idea what was on tap, but it didn't matter. The man walked over and drew me a glass, then went back to sit down and finish his paper. I looked around. One of the happiest moments of my childhood took place in Phillips'. My mother and father were sitting on either side of me on one of the benches in a booth. During dinner, for no reason, they leaned over to kiss one another, squeezing me from both sides. As I looked up at them touching lips, I felt safe and comfortable.

The memory was so vivid that suddenly I felt very ill at ease, sitting alone, wallowing in the past, drinking beer in the middle of the afternoon. In Coppola's film *The Conversation* (1974), Gene Hackman, a professional eavesdropper, is full of remorse when he realizes that his spying has caused a murder. I felt guilty, too, for eavesdropping on my own past. It was time to get out of Phillips'. Calling across the room to the bartender, I said, "How much do I owe you?"

"I got it, baby," the man said, and he waved, keeping his eyes on his newspaper. Because bartenders don't usually give free beers, Phillips' suddenly felt very unreal. I had accidentally wandered onto a movie set and met a bartender who was really an actor. My parents kissing in the booth, that must have been a flashback in the same movie.

* * *

New Orleans held so many secrets for me, it was hard to know where to begin. Perhaps with the one I had never confronted. After my mother's death her sister—my Aunt Leontine—claimed that my parents had been divorced, which was surprising news to me. I suppose every family has an Aunt Leontine: the relative who keeps the family lore, the one who knows the genealogy back several generations, and the only one who can recite who is married to whom, as well as the names of their children. Her kitchen had a bulletin board that was so full of family snapshots that new ones had to be stapled to the bottom of old pictures, making lines that reached down to the floor like kites' tails. I didn't know who most of the people were, but she knew their names, where they lived, and how they were related to her. Much to the dismay of other family members, my Aunt Leontine didn't mind telling the family secrets either. She filled my visits with hours of tales about our family, most of which my mother repudiated.

If I was going to be honest about uncovering New Orleans's secrets, I had to try to find out if what my aunt said was true, so on my next visit to the city I drove straight from Mississippi to the New Orleans Civil District Court Building, anxious to see if there was any record of a divorce. Parking across Loyola Avenue and walking the two blocks toward the courthouse, I heard a familiar crunch and looked down to see acorns underfoot, dropped there by a few small live oak trees that hung over the sidewalk in front of the public library at Tulane and Loyola. I recalled walking to grammar school on St. Charles Avenue sidewalks—banquettes, as New Orleanians call them—that were so thickly littered with these nuts that it was like walking on marbles. Once, when a friend ripped a cap off my head and took off down the sidewalk, I chased after him, but when I stepped on a bunch of acorns, my footing gave way and I fell. When my knees hit the acorns, hard as little rocks, I screamed out in pain.

Walking into the Court Building, I thought of a scene in Welles's *Touch of Evil* (1958) when Charlton Heston is looking up records in the basement of a courthouse. The room is like a tunnel leading away from the camera. On both sides of the screen are long lines of black filing cabinets, receding into the darkness at the rear of the room. Because of the low camera angle, the ceiling and its bank of dim fluorescent lights are visible, enclosing the space more completely. Sitting in the middle of this cave, at a table whose length stretches away from our view, is Heston, making notes about what he's discovered in the basement. The first time I saw this scene, I took real pleasure in the way Welles had created the illusion of a deep, dark cavern. Only after enjoying the deception for a moment did I realize how oppressive and ominous the space was, clearly saying that Heston had found something foul and ugly in the filing cabinets: records that would prove the police captain, Orson Welles, had been planting evidence on people he'd arrested. Welles's deputy, played by Joseph Calleia, comes in and tears up Heston's notes. "Go on, tear them," Heston says, pointing to the long rows of black filing cabinets. "It's all there, in the record!"

Remembering the ominous feel of that scene, I dreaded what I would find in this New Orleans courthouse. "Sure you can smear him," Calleia says to Heston, referring to Welles, "ruin his whole life's work." If my aunt was correct, I was about to smear my parents—at least that's what it felt like—and I didn't really want to do such a thing, but curiosity overtook me.

Inside the Court Building nobody ushered me into a basement room with hundreds of dark filing cabinets, but I did have to look through a stack of musty three-by-five-inch cards, where, surprisingly, I found my parents' names. Then I asked a clerk to retrieve the file. It seemed too easy. When he returned and handed me a stack of legal papers, stapled together, I went to a nearby desk, sat down, and began reading. What I soon realized I was holding was a divorce petition filed by my mother in 1938, when I was thirteen months old, along with subsequent agreements and judgments. Because the pages seemed to be describing an event that was fictitious, at least to me, I read through them hurriedly, but then on the last page I saw my parents' signatures. I stared for a moment, shocked at how familiar the writing looked. Who would have believed that in 1938 they signed their names the same way they did twenty years later? The signatures were like a wax seal that made the papers authentic, so I went back and read the pages again.

While the divorce papers described several confrontations between my parents, which was no surprise, the documents did contain a revelation. Five months after filing her petition for divorce my mother withdrew it and gave custody of her only child—me—to my father. Her lawyer wrote that she released "any right which she has as to alimony both for herself and for her child and agrees to give the custody of her child to her husband." From the papers I learned she would move to Dallas and live with her parents. This information startled me. Mothers didn't just amicably leave their sons in 1938, giving up all rights to alimony and child support, but my mother did, and even left town. Why was she the one who left? Perhaps my Dad had something on her.

For years I had had a memory, which I thought was a dream, about a posse surrounding our house, holding torches. Horses didn't roam around our urban neighborhood in New Orleans, but it was a dream, so it didn't have to make sense. Years later, sitting in a movie theater watching a posse of men on horses with torches circle Joan Crawford's saloon in Nicholas Ray's *Johnny Guitar* (1954), my dream came to mind, and then I began to shudder. While at first I thought I was cold, I realized I was actually frightened, but why? It was just a scene in a movie. Suddenly I knew that the torches in my old dream were really the lights on top of police cars, and the incident was not a dream at all but something that had actually happened. One of my mother's girlfriends had come to our home, and, in some kind of fit, shot out the glass in our front door. My father called the police, and several squad cars pulled up beside our house, their lights flashing. Frightened, I ran to my father and held tightly on to his leg as he stood in his undershirt and boxer shorts during a hot and humid summer night. The police were trying to calm him down, but the more they tried to soothe him, the more angry he became. He wasn't the guilty party! He was the one who called the police! He didn't shoot the gun!

My mother was very quiet, acting as if it wasn't her fault some crazy woman had shot at the door. I remember her face, the cool disdain she showed. What was all the fuss about? Never in her life had the police been called to her home; she didn't come from that kind of family. It was typical of my father to make a mountain out of a molehill, as she would say. Then, without any warning, she turned and pummeled my father's chest with her fists. When a policeman tried to pull her off, she hit him, and it took two policemen to restrain her. Now my father was calm. He took my mother in his arms and held her as the police left.

I imagine this incident happened years after my mother filed for divorce, or I wouldn't remember it, but perhaps something similar happened earlier, and my father threatened to tell the court about it in order to prove that his wife was an unfit mother.

Or my mother may have withdrawn her divorce petition and left home because being a mother was such anathema to her; maybe that was the secret. How she felt about babies wasn't obvious until after my first child was born, when my wife and I went for a visit. My mother couldn't bring herself to hold our little baby girl. She wanted to, I could see that, but some part of her was not willing, or was unable, to hold a baby. My Aunt Leontine used to say that when God was giving out the mothering instinct, my mother ran under the house and hid. She liked the idea of babies, but not up close. "I can't hold the baby," she said to me, "I might drop her."

The unresolvable issue between my parents may have been money; maybe that was the secret. In giving my father custody, my mother's lawyer had written that the alimony and child support were "not sufficient for the rearing of the child in the conditions which she would desire for him." Could it have been that easy? My mother just didn't have enough money to live on, or to fight my father in court, so she gave me up and moved to Dallas? No, nothing is ever that simple, but all the people who know are dead. No doubt it frightened me for her to leave, but I have no memory of how it felt.

She came back in two years, I know, because I remember my fourth birthday party, and she was there. It's not so hard to imagine them getting back together. Dad was lonely, tired of being a single parent; Mother was broke and had no other place to go.

"I'm glad you came home, Gertie," my father would have said. "I missed you, and Teddy missed you."

"Did I have a choice?"

My father said, "Yes, but we can work things out."

My mother started to cry. "I don't know, honey, sometimes I don't think it's in me to be a good wife and mother."

"You're back. We'll manage."

* * *

Finding the divorce petition made me think my visits to New Orleans just created more secrets. I was like Jack Nicholson in the Polanski film *Chinatown* (1974). When he solves the first mystery in the film, which is whether or not a man is having an affair, it leads him to a hidden plot involving the illegal use of water and land. As he unravels that story, he discovers yet another secret—incest. Like Nicholson, I found that every enigma I pursued in New Orleans brought me to a trapdoor that dropped me into some new abyss of mystery. Even so, I couldn't resist driving back again from Mississippi a week later. Returning to my neighborhood, I had the urge to go to my old house, and I did, walking up the steps and ringing the doorbell. But why? The kitchen sink probably didn't have a wooden drain board anymore, the one that made my mother scream when she got a splinter under her fingernail; but I was sure that everything else in the house would be exactly as remembered, so why go in? No one answered the doorbell. Walking away, it hit me that what I really wanted to do inside my old house was to go where I was standing when I was almost eight years old and my father left for Africa. I remembered exactly where the spot was in the hall, and what it was like to watch him walk out through the front door and leave me with my mother.

If there was one great secret I wanted to unravel in New Orleans, it was why in 1945—not too many years after my mother came back home—my father left home to live and work in Liberia, West Africa. He and I were so close, how could he just pick up and move an ocean away? The act made no sense to me, and I thought naively that it should. I wouldn't believe my father was not capable of making a living in the United States, or was too afraid of my mother, or that he didn't know what he was doing, or that he was at fault in some way. There had to be another reason, something yet to be revealed.

Unraveling the enigma of my father's departure seemed impossible, not unlike trying to understand how Wilder's film *Sunset Blvd.* (1950) could be narrated by a character who is already dead when the film begins. My father was just too full of secrets. After his death my mother found in his personal effects, shipped back from Africa, a pair of diamond earrings that he had given her for an anniversary present. They had disappeared years before, when he was home from Africa during one of his brief visits, and she had ransacked the house looking for them. My father even helped her search. I thought she would be furious when she found them in his African luggage, but instead she cried. I have no idea why my father took the earrings. Perhaps my mother did something that angered him, and, to get back at her, he picked up the earrings and took them to Africa. How childish. As much as I wanted him to be, he was not perfect. Like so many of my father's secrets, why he stole the earrings will never be known.

I used to think my father's love of secrets had something to do with World War II. Hadn't he told me over and over during the war that he couldn't talk about what he was doing at the Higgins plant because there might be spies around? "The Axis are listening," he said one day when I was six. I looked around; we were home, and my mother wasn't there, so I had no idea what or who he thought was listening. Then my father laughed. "That's what the sign at my office says." I thought he was talking about "axes," and I didn't understand how axes could be listening, or what axes had to do with spies, but it sounded terribly important, so I didn't question what he was saying.

Only weeks later, when I saw the word "Axis" in a big headline in *The New Orleans Times-Picayune*, did I understand what he was talking about. Yes, the Axis were everywhere; German subs were just a few hundred miles away, out in the Gulf of Mexico, torpedoing ships as they came out of the mouth of the Mississippi River. Sure, and at night I'll bet they came to the surface and sent spies ashore. Now I understood my father. He never offered any information about his work, and I never asked again, so impressed was I that my father was caught up in secret wartime activity. It still puzzled me that he thought I might tell someone what he was doing. I didn't really think there were many spies among my six-year-old friends, but he was my father and I thought he knew what he was talking about.

Now I realize his silence about his work was just part of a larger, pathological desire to hide everything. What he really thought and felt, why he did what he did, was to be kept hidden. I remember once seeing him tear up a piece of paper, shuffle the fragments around, and then deposit them in three different wastebaskets. He didn't know I was watching, and when he wasn't looking, I retrieved the pieces of paper and put them back together. It was a laundry bill, that's all. At the time the act made no sense, but years later I understood. Nobody was to be able to put the pieces together and read what was written, especially not the money figures. No one was allowed to know anything about this man, especially what he thought or felt. Most of his life, and even his death, remained a mystery. Having secrets would protect him from a world that threatened his very soul. Neither to my mother nor to me did he ever say a word about his childhood, about his parents and siblings, about games played, about school. All my mother knew was that he grew up in Indiana and left there when he was in his twenties.

One of my father's greatest secrets was his money, how much he made and what he did with it. All we knew for sure was that from Africa he had consistently sent money every month for us to live on. Everything else was a mystery. He left no financial records when he died, which is extremely odd given that he had been an accountant for years. He was the president of the West African subsidiary of an international construction company, so you would think that he had a little money stashed away somewhere, but all we found was a small checking account at the Irving Trust Bank in New York City. Or at least my mother said she never found any more money, or records. Now and then when she had had too much to drink, she would say, "You think your father left some money and I hid it, don't you?" Yes, I did, but I wasn't going to make, as she would say, a federal case out of it. Yet there were times when I was sure that my father had concealed a lot of money somewhere. I fantasized about finding his fortune and what I would do with it. My fantasies were preferable to the reality of my mother's hiding money and certainly to the reality of my father's secrecy about his money.

His love of secrets wasn't necessarily consistent. He couldn't stand for other people to have secrets, especially my mother. "I was out," my mother would say.

"Out where?" asked my father. "Doing what? Who were you out with?"

When she just shrugged, he would turn around and quickly leave the room, but I could tell from looking at the back of his shoulders and neck how furious he was with her.

Secrets were not something my father tolerated in movies either. *The Big Sleep* (1946), to him the worst Bogart and Bacall film, had so thoroughly confused my father that he left the theater almost apoplectic. We had gone to see it at the end of his first visit back from Africa, and on the way home, he said, "I don't think they know how to make good movies anymore, not since the war." Too many secrets, that was the problem, and some were never cleared up. Who really did all the murders? You couldn't tell who was telling a lie and who wasn't. The story made no sense at all, and certainly wasn't worth the twenty-five-cent admission.

Hitchcock's *Rebecca* (1940) was another film that upset my father, because the whole film seemed to revolve around unraveling who Rebecca was and how she died. All the conclusions that Dad, and the rest of us, made along the way turned out to be wrong. Her husband didn't really love her, as it seemed; he hated her. Rebecca was not such a grand and wonderful woman; she was unfaithful. She was not pregnant; rather, she had cancer and was about to die. No, my father didn't like such movies, not only because there were secrets, but because the truth behind them got revealed at the end and that truth changed everything, devastating some people.

Surprisingly, some deceptions at a picture show seemed okay to him. He loved the secrets posed by the serials we saw every week at the Mecca. At the end of each chapter something horrible was about to happen, and it seemed impossible for the catastrophe to be avoided. Such were the secrets my father liked. How would the hero or heroine escape? How would the plane, or the train, keep from crashing? Our weekly game was to look very closely at the end of the serial and then to compare it with the beginning of the next week's episode. As we walked home from the Mecca, Dad, who rarely talked about a movie afterward, would go into surprising detail about the end of the serial: "Remember, now. Zorro is on top of the train, which is about to enter a tunnel full of dynamite. Zorro is running along the top of the cars, headed for the locomotive so he can tell the engineer to stop. He has to get there quickly, or he'll be knocked off as the train enters the tunnel. Remember, Teddy, when the chapter ends, Zorro is still several cars back from the engine as it is about to enter the tunnel. He can't possibly make it to the engine in time."

Walking to the Mecca a week later, my father would repeat the previous week's ending. Of course, the next chapter always began at a different spot. Zorro would be several cars closer to the engine and he would jump down and get the engineer to stop the train before it entered the tunnel and reached the dynamite. My dad and I would laugh, and people in the Mecca would turn around and look at us with disdain. We seemed to be the only ones in the house who noticed that the beginning of a chapter was so different from the ending of the previous week's.

In one chapter of the serial *Jungle Queen*, the last shot is a side view of a plane about to crash in the jungle. Neither my dad nor I could figure out how the plane would be saved. The next week the pilot's viewpoint is revealed, and he has actually found a clearing that wasn't visible in the side angle we saw at the end of the previous chapter. A few weeks later, in another episode of *Jungle Queen*, a young woman is about to be attacked by a lion. Shown from her point of view, the lion is up in the air, leaping toward her, when the chapter ends. The next week another shot is added and we see that nearby a native is throwing a spear. It kills the lion in midair, saving the young woman. These serials gave me my first lessons in the crucial effects of shots and angles in movies.

My father loved the mysteries of the serials. During the week between chapters, we would speculate about how the tragedy was going to be avoided. Sometimes he even figured out what would happen, but most of the time my father was surprised. So there were some secrets he took pleasure in. These were innocent; they didn't threaten his whole sense of self, and the revelation of the secret actually saved people rather than devastating them.

That my father sat in the Mecca and took great delight in some movie secrets was obvious, which made me love being there with him. After he left home for Africa, I tried to pretend he was still around by going to the movies. My mother didn't seem to mind if I walked the two blocks to the Mecca by myself, so I went there often. Going to the movies alone was very different from going with my father. For the first time I noticed the ghastly smell of rancid popcorn, urine, and old strawberry bubble gum. During the days and weeks after my father left home, every film I saw seemed to have scenes with quicksand, and my heroes and heroines were always slipping into it and being sucked down. When they fell in, I would put my hands on both sides of my face so that people on either side could not see that I was closing my eyes. Watching was frightening, but I was even more afraid that some schoolmate would see me shutting my eyes. The endings of the serials, when something catastrophic was about to happen, at first seemed scary without my father there with me. It took me months to feel safe in the movie theater by myself. Something—anger, or guilt, or hurt—made me determined to survive there without my father. He had gone to movies by himself, so I could do it, too.

What didn't disappear for a long time was the fear that stalked me when I left the movie theater and walked the several blocks home, winding my way carefully among the dark shadows cast by streetlights shining through the huge live oaks. Because the odor of honeysuckle was so thick sometimes, I would halt, certain that a monster was nearby, trying to disguise himself with sweet perfume. Some nights I would run the entire way home. Other times, when I felt really brave, I walked, although I stayed in the center of the street, keeping away from the shadows that covered the brick sidewalks. They were full of little hills and valleys made by the live oak roots as they spread underneath the bricks. I was sure I would trip on one of these, fall down, and be jumped on by some horrible, slimy creature. When I walked in the middle of the street, I whistled, which was my signal to the monsters that I was fearless. Nobody would dare attack me. I hoped.

Movies were not just something to look at after my father left. Within a few months he sent me back a small ivory tusk from Africa. I got on the St. Charles Avenue streetcar by myself, now eight years of age, and rode the thirty minutes downtown to the shopping area for New Orleans. Crossing the main street, Canal, I walked into the French Quarter, sold the tusk, then crossed back over Canal Street and went to Sears, where I bought a 16-mm, hand-cranked, Keystone home movie camera. The films I made with it were filled with everything important in my childhood—my best friends, my old green two-story house, a scene I staged of my mother picking wisteria blossoms, and, a year later, even a sequence of my father that I shot during one of his brief visits home. I had him hide behind a tree and then walk out toward the camera. We shot that one action eight or ten times; I kept telling him something went wrong, and the scene had to be repeated, but really I wanted something else from him. This time he would do what I wanted him to do, and many times over.

I made home movies after my father left, and I went to more movies. I started keeping secrets, too; if my father was going to leave without telling me why, I wasn't going to tell anyone anything about what I thought and felt. I won a contest at my school for the best essay about the Community Chest, a forerunner of the United Way, and I never said anything to my mother. When I made the softball team, I didn't share the news with her. I would be gone for hours, without telling her where I was going, and she rarely protested.

My best secret, the one I treasured the most, the one that saved my life, was not an event or some information, but a location. I made a secret place of my own that nobody, especially my mother, knew about, and I often retreated to it. Our home was built on a pier and beam foundation, three feet above ground, as were many houses in New Orleans. To hide the opening left by this kind of construction, the sides seen from the street were bricked up. When I was eight years old, I crawled under the back of the house, made my way to the front, and, with a table knife, chiseled out one brick. Through the opening I could watch the sidewalk and the street. As each car passed, I would identify it by year and make; people would stop on the sidewalk and carry on conversations, not realizing that I was hiding nearby and could hear them. Once I saw a friend, Clotilde, who was only five or six at the time, secretly pinched by her mother as they were carrying on a conversation with a neighbor. I couldn't tell what Clotilde had done wrong, but I saw her mother's fingers pick up a piece of flesh on the child's back and squeeze it painfully until the skin was white. Clotilde didn't flinch, or even move, and I was so startled I didn't either.

Her mother never stopped talking. The cruel act was hidden from the neighbor, but I saw everything from my concealed location.

This secret place under the house was pitch-black and damp, a dark sanctuary with a window looking out on the world. It was my hiding place and my true home. Not until years later did I realize how like a darkened movie theater it was. The brick hole was rectangular, like a movie screen, and the events on the sidewalk and in the street were like images on that screen. How much less frightening it was to be under the house, peering out at New Orleans, than to be standing on the sidewalk.

Going to the movies, making movies, creating a concealed movie theater under my house, all these activities had something to do with my father's leaving home. The universe seemed to have run away, and I needed to get it back on its leash. After my initial fears disappeared, the movies helped me regain control of my life. In the dark theater I was in charge. Did I command that the good guys win and the bad guys suffer? They did, always. Even when the bad guys threatened, I could handle it. I was strong, so bring on the quicksand. Maybe I didn't always watch everything, but I would endure any terror, absolutely certain that if I could survive the fright inside the movie theater, nothing outside could possibly faze me. I could whistle my way through life.

I was in charge when I made movies, too. People did what I told them to do, and no matter how many times I projected the images, nothing was different. No surprises, no sudden and painful changes; nobody leaving. Always the same, predictable actions over and over. Under my house I may not have been able to dictate what cars drove by, or which people paused to chat, but I knew I was hidden. Because I could observe without being seen, I felt very privileged and in control. All my relationships with movies gave me a heightened sense of power and a special sense of myself.

As much as I liked having my own secret life, it didn't help me understand my father's secrets any better. I began making up things about him. Didn't my father, a self-taught accountant, have exceptional mathematical skills? I swore to my friends that when we went to the grocery store together, my father kept a running count in his head as we shopped. When we reached the checkout counter, he told the clerk what the total would be, before anything was rung up on the cash register. My father loved to play cards and shoot dice, I told my friends, and not only did he never lose, but he had an incredible ability to win and then walk away. Not one of these stories was true. Fearing that I had invested my love in someone who was just ordinary, I did everything I could to paint my father as someone unique.

I also tried to hold on to my father by imitating him. After he left home to work in Africa, I went to the Piggly Wiggly grocery store and lied about my age so that they would give me a job. I would work, too, just like my father. Years later, at the Johns Hopkins School of Public Health in Baltimore, I flirted again with his lonely, work-filled way of life. A friend arranged for me to get an assistantship in entomology, and, even though I hardly knew the difference between entomology and etymology, I took it. My supervisor was in the middle of a research project on malaria, so the lab was full of mosquitoes. For several hours each day my job was to stick my arms inside various cages and watch while the little beasts sucked up my blood. The *Anopheles* and the *Culex pipiens* weren't so bad, but the radar of one species was broken. Each insect would stick her proboscis in my arm, come up dry, pull out, step over a few paces, then plunge in again, repeating the procedure until she found blood.

The more blood I gave, the more annoyed and sad I became, and, like my father, the more movies I started going to see. The little one-room apartment where I lived was a dump. Men knocked on my neighbor's apartment door at all hours, so I was sure that she was a prostitute. My stove was a tiny hot plate. Maybe my father could live alone in some strange place with nothing to do but work, and no friends, but I couldn't. The loneliness and the dislocation did me in. I couldn't be him, couldn't match the way he lived, no matter how much I tried. How my father survived will always be a secret, as unknowable as why he left for Africa.

When, twenty years after his death, and also after my mother's death, I began realizing how many secrets were connected with my father, I felt an urgent need to get at some truth about him. Enough of putting up with what he concealed, I would find out who he was. In his things sent back from Africa, there were letters, a scrapbook, and, best of all, a diary that recorded in minute detail the simple events of his life. In 1932 he had written:

> Fri. Depression is still on. Will it ever end? To P.O. at 5:30 a.m. for job. About 2000 men there. No job. Walked home, only 5 miles. Found two-bits on sidewalk. Made up with GS. Lost my heart for sure. First piece of strawberry shortcake. Date to picture show, Cla. Colbert in "Sign of the Cross." If I only had a steady job. No more by myself.

All the diary entries were like this one, endlessly recounting the same themes: looking for work, finding work, eating, going to the movies, repeatedly breaking up and making up with "GS," who became my mother. I know that diaries are just memory aids, but it angered me that my father said so little about how he was reacting to what was happening to him.

"Lost my heart for sure" was a start, but not enough. How could he watch *The Sign of the Cross* (1932) and not say anything about it? If I had gone to see the film, I would surely have recorded in the privacy of my diary how I had peered constantly at the half-exposed breasts of Claudette Colbert as she took her bath in a huge pool of asses' milk. I certainly would have noted how I stared intently, hoping to see an exposed nipple each time she moved about and the milk sloshed around. My father didn't share my voyeurism, or, if he did, he didn't dare write it down. Certain that I wouldn't learn much about him from his diary, I tried other approaches, like interviewing every person I could find who knew him. He was a good man who worked hard and loved his family, that's all they had to say. Frantic for more insight, I sent his handwriting off for analysis. "Resentment is present. What he resents, we don't know, but it is a negative trait." The analysis was not helping me. "He is basically a loner, and can work well alone. He doesn't need people around him to be happy." No revelation in that statement.

Determined to get at my father's secrets, I asked the FBI for his file. Nothing. I wrote to the Office of Unclaimed Properties in Indiana,

New York, Louisiana, and Mississippi, to see if there were any funds of his that had reverted from some bank. Nothing. Desperate, I called his sister, Grace, someone I knew only by name because she had sent me a Christmas card now and then. Having her name and address in Indiana made it possible to get her phone number from information. She was startled to hear from me.

"You're Ed's son, Teddy?"

"Yes."

"My goodness. What a surprise. How sweet of you to call."

"I should have called sooner, but Dad said so little about you, I was always afraid there was some bad blood, or something."

"No, no, we wrote each other several times a year. He always wanted to tell me about his son. He was so very proud of you."

"He was? I didn't know the two of you were in touch."

"We weren't for a few years after he left Kokomo for the South. It always seemed he blamed us because he couldn't finish college at Wabash."

"Why, do you think?"

"Heavens, I have no idea. We were all dirt poor—me, our two brothers, our dad—hardly able to survive ourselves. None of us ever dreamed of going to college, but your dad was determined. You know how he was when he made his mind up. When he got to college, he found a job cleaning the local Episcopal church, inside and out, and keeping the boiler fired in the winter. They let him live in the basement, which was a big help with finances."

"He never told me why he left Indiana."

"Too embarrassed, probably. I felt so sorry for him. The job just wasn't enough; he couldn't pay the tuition and all the other expenses. It broke his heart. When he got the job offer in Mississippi, he just took off. Didn't even say good-bye. I don't know why he thought it was our fault, but that's what it seemed like."

"What about before that?"

"You mean growing up?"

"Yes."

"He never told you?"

"No, not really."

"I guess you could say Ed never had much of a childhood. As far back as I remember, he looked and acted like a grown man. He never played and laughed like most kids. Everything was always so serious."

"What happened?"

"He was the baby, about a year old, and our mother died. There were four kids and our dad had a terrible time trying to work and look after us. After a few months he put us all in an orphanage—that was the best he could do. Then they split us up and put us in different places. Your dad was in ten different foster homes before he was fifteen, I counted them. I was in six myself."

"Your own dad just abandoned you?"

"No, not exactly. He tried lots of times to bring us all together, sometimes putting us up with relatives, but something always happened. A housekeeper would quit, or a relative would get sick or lose a job."

"I can't even imagine how hard that must have been."

"I guess it was. Now it seems so long ago, I can't remember. Your father did tell me once he never lived in a home where they didn't hit him. Mine weren't quite that bad. I do recall how upset I was once. Our dad was going to get married, he said, and I got my hopes up we'd be a family again. But when he proposed to the woman, she said, 'I'll be your wife, but I won't raise some other woman's children. You'll have to do something about them.' When Dad told me what she said, I was angry and bitter. It was like she was saying we were kittens that had to be drowned."

"So what did he do?"

"He married her. He married her and left us in our foster homes, but not much later, as soon as we were old enough, my brothers and I, we set up house ourselves. Your dad came and lived with us. That's when he was able to finish high school."

I didn't ask any more questions of Grace. Because she'd given me more information than I could absorb at the moment, I hung up, promising to call again sometime. Thinking about how distressing this childhood must have been, how unwanted my father probably felt, how hard it must have been to be shuttled around among various homes, I thought of the young boy in the Duvivier film *Poil de carotte*

(1932). Asked at school for a definition of a family, he says, "A family is a group of people living under the same roof who abuse one another." My father's life may have been, I feared, an endless repetition of the agonizing scenes in the movie where this same young protagonist is called a "dirty brat," a "little thief," and a "blockhead" by his mother, even as his father neglects him. In this atmosphere the young boy tries to hang himself. Was this the kind of world my father grew up in?

Why my father became such a silent, distant person, so full of secrets, was now more understandable. To survive in so many different homes, he must have learned quickly not to reveal his thoughts, fearing he'd be out on the street again. He learned to shut up. He didn't show feelings, especially not anger. Confrontations were avoided. He did what he was told. He said what he thought that month's parent wanted to hear. If he did these things really well, he got a home, sometimes even a big hug. Having mastered these survival skills, my father practiced them his whole life, even when they were useless. No wonder he loved, literally loved, the movies. He worshiped that screen. In the dark and comfortable movie theater, my father found a home of his own, one without abuse and where he felt very alive and special.

* * *

During the month I was in Mississippi, I had made a number of day trips to New Orleans, and they had convinced me that the city was still full of secrets, enough to justify going back. Eight months later I flew from my home in Vermont to New Orleans, this time staying at a bed-and-breakfast on Prytania Street in the city. The location was ideal, about halfway between the French Quarter and my old neighborhood. The first morning there I went out for a run. It was July, and within minutes I was covered with perspiration. About to cross a street, I noticed, in blue and white tiles on the sidewalk, a street name, "Coliseum," that seemed familiar. When I got back to my room, I checked my notes, discovering that my parents had lived on Coliseum Street when I was born. In fact, the address was just two blocks away. I went back quickly to look for the house, but it no longer existed, replaced by an apartment building that faced what New Orleanians call a pocket park, an oddly shaped area created by streets coming together at different angles.

This little park was lovelier than most, with large live oak trees, some of their limbs touching the ground, and crape myrtle bushes. Two round pools, with old fountains in the middle, were empty of water, but people were sitting on the edges as they watched their dogs romp. Three ragged sleeping bags, held together with tape, hung from different tree limbs. Some homeless people must have slept in the park the night before, and they were drying out their sleeping bags because there'd been a little rain. The ground was still moist. I walked about the park, force-feeding my nostalgia. My mother and father must have brought me here as an infant. Under these trees I crawled, maybe ate a fistful of dirt and a bug or two. My parents probably took some delight in their child. In those first months after my birth, was theirs a happy marriage?

At the heart of the secrets about my parents—why she left, why he left—was the secret of their relationship. From 1945 on they did not live in the same house for more than two weeks a year, yet after he left for Africa my father still sent loving cards and notes to my mother, which she kept until her death. On their twentieth anniversary, in 1956, he wrote, "Twenty years—seems like yesterday. Thank you for making them very fine and fruitful." He enclosed with that letter a little clipping that began, "Love is the most wonderful thing in all your world, for suddenly you are complete." What this message really meant was that my father now had my mother just where he wanted her. He could play the devoted sweetheart—sending loving letters and anniversary cards, providing money for her to live on—but otherwise keep his distance.

The only time he let her into his life was when he was home and they fought, which was rarely something he really wanted to do, but it was their grand passion, and, like all grand passions, it was uncontrollable and unpredictable. One time during a visit from Africa, my father came bursting out of their bedroom, slammed several doors, and slept on the couch in the living room. I'm sure he and my mother did some shouting, but I don't remember that, only the doors slamming.

The next day I found out that the furor was over the monogram on some towels. My father claimed that the initial of her maiden name was too big. What they fought over never seemed very significant. The fights were about simple, meaningless things, like who didn't refill the ice tray, or who used the wrong toothbrush. Now and then the fights were over promises my father had made. I remember vividly one evening: My mother was sitting on one set of steps at our house, and I on another, with my father going back and forth between the two of us. My mother was continuously berating him. "You promised me a carport," my mother said, "and you promised Teddy a boat. We don't have the money to do both. How could you be so foolish!" He ran back and forth between the two sets of steps, trying to convince each of us that he could do both. My mother refused to believe him that night, but he did do what he said he would.

As much as my father tried to avoid these fights with my mother, it was no use. To be around each other was to fight. They were like a couple in some screwball comedy, endlessly bickering but somehow deeply in love. In *It Happened One Night* (1934), Claudette Colbert's father asks Clark Gable, "Do you love her?" And Gable replies, "Yes, but don't hold that against me. I'm a little screwy myself." My mother, and my father, would have said the same thing, but with less humor. Their struggles were more like those in Nichols's film *Who's Afraid of Virginia Woolf?* (1966), where Elizabeth Taylor says to Richard Burton, "I swear, if you existed, I'd divorce you."

My mother liked to party; my father enjoyed a game of poker now and then, some deep-sea fishing, and a table piled high with boiled crabs, but he thought life was mainly about responsibility and doing your job. My mother liked to sleep late; my father would come early into my room and throw open the curtains, saying, "Get up; you're going to sleep your life away." I was caught between them, as if they lived on different planets and spoke different languages. Contrary forces seemed to animate each of their worlds. Moving between their realities was like being Dorothy in *The Wizard of Oz* (1939), going back and forth rapidly between Kansas and the land of Oz. Yet in my world, both places were fantasy and both reality.

I do have to admit that I am grateful to them; my love of certain movies today no doubt grows out of the dissimilar worlds my parents inhabited. Not only do I feel at home in those screwball comedies, like *His Girl Friday* (1940) and *The Philadelphia Story* (1940), where the couples divorce, spar with one another, and then remarry, but I am just as much at ease seeing a film that shuttles between distinct modes of experience. Thanks to my parents, I feel at home watching Fellini's *8½* (1963), with its constant confounding of memory, fantasy, past, present, and dream. The ambiguity of Buñuel's *That Obscure Object of Desire* (1977)—the same character is played by two different actresses, one seen in some scenes and the other in different scenes—is very familiar. In my house people were always changing into different people. In *Un chien Andalou* (1928), it seems normal to me when the cyclist, struggling to reach the woman he desires, pulls two ropes on the end of which are two Marist brothers, two pianos, and the rotting carcasses of two donkeys, their eyes slit open.

For the same reasons, I admire Vertov's *The Man with a Movie Camera* (1928). One sequence begins with a shot of several women riding in an open touring car, and then the next image shows the cameraman and his camera in another car beside the first, presumably just having photographed the first shot of the women in the open touring car. The next image is that of a film editor, looking at pieces of film that contain the same shots of women and cameraman we have just seen. In shifting its point of view from what the cameraman sees, to the image of the cameraman himself, then to the figure of the editor and what she sees, the Vertov film replicates what I did as a child, jumping back and forth from my own point of view, to my mother's, to my father's, to those of relatives and of friends. All were true and none of them was. Discontinuity was everything. A stable, single perspective did not exist in my home, so I don't admire as much the movies that pretend the movie screen is a window through which a fixed and univocal reality is seen. While I respect a film like *Lawrence of Arabia* (1962), it doesn't take place in the kind of world I grew up in. For me to feel at home there needs to be more inconsistency, contradiction, and incongruity.

Some of my parents' fights, or my memories of them, pop up unexpectedly. A few years ago, after a sleepless night, I was sitting alone on a couch and I felt a crazy urge to lie down on the floor. I did. Then it felt as if I needed to turn and lie on my right side. How silly, I thought to myself, but after a moment I did switch sides. Then suddenly, transported back to the room of my childhood, I was six years old and lying in my old bed. The light from the streetlamp was making frightening shadows on my walls as it filtered through a large oleander bush outside my window. In the next room my parents were fighting. I had relived scenes like this before; one time my parents were brawling over who would dress me and what I would wear. Another time they were warring over who would get to keep me. This time I heard another fight altogether, one that had been secret, one that now left me breathless.

"You have to stay with him!" screamed my mother.

"No, *you* have to stay with him!" my father shouted back at her.

I had never before remembered this fight. Now back in the present, I cringed, as if I had just heard the wail of some hurt animal.

* * *

Maybe there were still more secrets in New Orleans, after all, so ten months later I flew back to the city. I was more determined this time, walking my old neighborhood once during the day and once at night. During the day I saw new things—houses in disrepair, a blooming cape jasmine, a fence about to fall down. A man had stopped beside his Jack Russell terrier as the dog peed. The stream hit a brown magnolia leaf and started to splash the dog, but the animal jumped quickly aside. "Isn't it a beautiful day?" the man said.

That night, when I went back to my neighborhood again, I couldn't see as much, but I heard different sounds—a wooden screen door slamming shut, screeching crickets, the terrible howling of a female cat in heat, the muffled voices of people talking quietly on their porches as I walked by. I strolled around, I looked, I took notes. I had written ahead of time to "Resident" at my old home address, asking whoever lived there to let me in for a quick tour of my old house. "I'm enclosing a postcard, stamped and addressed to me," I wrote. "If you agree to let me in the house, just write your name and phone number on the card, drop it in the mail, and I will call you to arrange a time to visit." No answer.

No answer seemed to be the theme of the old neighborhood. I might as well have been the journalist in *Citizen Kane* (1941), trying to find out the meaning of Kane's last word, "Rosebud." Whatever secrets I had hoped to uncover were not forthcoming, and, as I walked around, I realized for the first time that I was bored. Why had no one ever made a movie about the detective who gets bored because he can't find any answers? Enough was enough. No more, I thought to myself as I walked the streets, this would be my last visit; yet even as I said it, I knew I would come back.

The old neighborhood had actually changed a lot, although I hadn't wanted to admit it the first time I returned. Phillips' Restaurant was still there, that's true, as was X-Ray Cleaners, Bruno's Bar, and Mr. Louis' Barber Shop, and the houses were the same; but everything else was different. During my first visit I had let my nostalgia cover my eyes, like cataracts, but now I saw the neighborhood clearly. Rohm's Flower Shop was now something called Wintergreen Orchard House. There was a Greek restaurant in the old hardware store, a Chinese takeout across the street in a building I didn't remember, a PJ's coffee shop in a new structure, a real estate office where there used to be a bar, even a little bookstore in a house I used to dread passing. The neighborhood bully had lived there and he never let me pass the house without trying to beat me up. At the corner of St. Charles and Cherokee, my old Piggly Wiggly store was now a deli–bakery–grocery store named Our Daily Bread. Behind the store was a house. I stopped for a moment. The structure looked very familiar, but it was so well cared for, I couldn't tell if it was the same home or one built in the identical style. Studying the porch for a minute, I decided the building was not new; the boards were just a little too warped and thick with paint. Who used to live here? I couldn't remember.

The neighborhood was different, no matter what I thought the first time I came back, and there were no secrets hiding here that would jump out of the bushes and make me see my childhood anew.

* * *

Getting reality to hand over its secrets is as hard as marking the exact moment when being awake turns into being asleep. I will have to make a little movie. The footage begins with me leaving my old neighborhood and driving thirty blocks away to Franky and Johnny's, one of the few remaining joints in New Orleans. I take a table and wait for an old grammar school friend, who is meeting me for dinner. It's been over forty years since we last saw each other. When the waitress comes over, I ask her for some tea, and, as she starts to leave, I add, "*Iced* tea."

"That's all we got, baby."

I sit for a few moments, feeling very much at home. Franky and Johnny's reminds me of Phillips' Restaurant when I was a kid: red-checkered tablecloths, dining room in the rear, a bar in front where black and white men drink side by side. The menu is on the wall near my table—alligator pie, red beans and rice, turtle soup, oysters, soft-shelled crab, and a dozen kinds of po-boy sandwiches.

The waitress returns with my iced tea, and I add sugar, only to notice there is no iced-tea spoon. As she passes by again, I stop the waitress and ask, "Can I have an iced-tea spoon?"

"Baby," she says, "we don't have them. Just use your finger." She reaches over and sticks her little finger into my tea, giving it a swirl. "See?"

"Yes, thanks," I say, unable to resist a little laugh at her audacity.

My friend is late; I have two more glasses of iced tea, then ask for a third. When the waitress comes over to pour the tea, she says, "I hope you have rubber sheets on your bed tonight, baby."

I am so tickled by her wisdom that I want to ask her to come with me and walk through my old neighborhood. I will say, "There's something secret here, I know it, so tell me what you see." Before I can fantasize too much, my old friend appears, accompanied by a woman he's been dating. After they sit down and order a beer, the lady asks, "What aspects of New Orleans are you researching?"

Her question sounds a little stiff, too much like what I said to my friend on the phone when I explained why I was in New Orleans. I wonder if he has coached her. Yet without hesitation I say, "I really don't know. I just keep hoping the skies will open, or a bolt of lightning will hit me, and I'll uncover some secret."

"What secret?" she asks.

"I'm not sure." What I say sounds stupid, even to me, but it is true.

My grammar school friend and I reminisce a little. He begins talking about someone named Peter Watson, but then stops as he sees the look on my face. "You remember Peter, don't you?"

I don't remember the man and I shake my head.

My friend says, "Sure you do. He came back from World War II all messed up. Shell-shocked, that's what we called it then."

"Peter Watson was his name?"

"Yes. How could you forget him? Big eyes, all wide and frightened, a stubble of beard always on his face, a mouth open all the time as if he breathed through it. He was just skin and bones, and his arms were like sticks hanging out of his short-sleeved shirt."

"Was he the one who wore those shoes with the tips cut off, with his toes sticking out?"

"Right!"

I do remember Peter now. "He lived in the house behind the Piggly Wiggly store, right?"

"Yes," my friend says.

"I walked by it today, wondering who used to live there."

"I'll never forget one night," my friend says, "Peter and his father were out walking, and all of a sudden Peter started pounding his fists on the old man, bending him back over that wrought iron fence in front of your house. It was scary. I ran over and pulled him off, but then Peter turned on me. I ran like a bat out of hell."

"I had forgotten completely about Peter," I say.

"One time Peter threw such a fit that Daddy and I had to go to Baptist Hospital, borrow a straitjacket, put Peter in it, and use the old man's car to drive him to the VA hospital in Gulfport. Remember?"

"Yes, now I do. I can't believe Peter slipped my mind."

I realize suddenly that I've been so absorbed in imagining my movie scene that I've forgotten to plan any camera movements or angles. Shot entirely from one position, with no cuts, my movie footage ends after the dinner, with me leaving Franky and Johnny's. I want to film how discouraged I feel about not remembering Peter, but there's no way to show what I'm feeling inside myself. Instead I say out loud, "What else have I forgotten?"

3 Texts

ARRIVING ON AN EVENING FLIGHT, FOR another visit to New Orleans, I wasn't tired enough to go to bed, and I wanted a coffee, so I walked to Magazine Street, which runs parallel to the Mississippi River and stretches from Audubon Park almost to the heart of downtown. The street is well known as an old shopping bypath, its name derived from the French word for a store. For as long as I can remember, Magazine Street has been the home of the eccentric, a long strip of a flea market interrupted now and then with a restaurant, an antique shop, an art gallery, a grocery store, or a coffeehouse. Since my mother had loved to browse it, I knew the street a little. Not much had changed. Certain stores were bigger and fancier, others more run-down. There were protective bars on some windows and doors, and mixed in among the older stores and shops were a few strange new creatures—fast-food places and chic jewelers—but the street was the same mixture of elegance and indigence that it used to be.

What struck me the most now were all the signs. Never before was I so aware of how Magazine Street was full of messages. One communiqué after another beset me. Hundreds said what you would expect, advertising food, services, collectibles, antiques, used books. Almost everything imaginable was available, so said the signs: "Planned Parenthood," "Goodwill," "Keys Made While You Wait," "Comic Books," "The Original New Orleans Snoball," "Oriental Rugs," "Rabies Shots Here This Sunday," "Pottery," "Brass," "Glass Beads," "Package Liquors," "Pets Need Dental Care Too." Thankfully, some of the signs were humorous: "Angels and Gargoyles Made Fresh Daily." I was really amused by one antique store that had, hanging under its main placard, a little notice that said, "Artist Living in the Back." When did antique stores start having resident artists? What was he doing in the back, I asked myself, making fake antiques?

Signs, texts, and more signs and texts. I saw a bright object on the sidewalk, and I reached down to pick it up. On a thin sheet of white cardboard, like one used in a starched shirt from the laundry, someone had written, "I smoked pot here on April 13, 1994." Another message on Magazine Street.

I walked a few more blocks and came upon a store that sold erotic toys. Next to it was an old bar, in front of which stood a man holding a sign that read, "The End Is Near. www.endnear.com/" The words were on a white wooden cross that the man held upright in the middle of the sidewalk. Facing him was a woman, and they were arguing. He was waving his Bible and she was waving back with her plastic cup of beer. One sentence of hers rose clearly above the shouting, "You're totally full of BS, dear heart." I presumed she didn't think the End was quite so near, or else the man was her husband and he spent more time preaching than with her. As I passed the two people, I looked back and saw that the other side of the man's placard said, "The Cross Is God's Pardon Place." I was impressed; in the middle of a street where signs were dedicated to every possible material object and service, this man was trying to make people think about entirely different kinds of texts.

* * *

Not too many years ago, when I was going through a personal crisis, one of my dear friends, a classicist, called to see how I was doing. I gave him a few details, and then he said, "Oh, my God, what texts are you using?" The question caught me off guard, and I mumbled some meaningless answer. After he hung up, I began to think about his query. A card-carrying humanist, he wasn't asking me to cite bumper stickers that meant a lot to me; no, he was asking if there were any books I was reading in order to gain comfort during those bleak hours. I realized that I was not using any texts, at least not specifically. Was he expecting me to say, I wondered, that I was reading the Bible or *Paradise Lost* every morning?

In fact, I have rarely read and reread certain texts to raise my spirits. Once or twice, it was true, something had so impressed me that I memorized it. At the end of Tennessee Williams's *Memoirs*, after describing what was often a horrific life, he wrote, "High station in life is earned by the gallantry with which appalling experiences are survived with grace." I liked the most that last little phrase, "with grace," but I don't think I quoted the line to myself on those days when I was going through appalling circumstances; perhaps I did, and just don't remember. At a party once with some celebrities, my wife kept saying, "Talk to Gregory Peck, go say hello to Jimmy Stewart, go speak to Katharine Ross," but it just didn't appeal to me. On the way out, though, seeing Tennessee Williams, I walked over and introduced myself, and then, with a silly grin, quoted his line back to him. Williams looked at me like I was an idiot, which was how I felt, and then asked me who wrote those words. To this day I wonder if he was putting me on or if he had forgotten that the sentence was his.

What I remember, and forget, about what I have read or written makes it difficult to live according to some text, even an admirable one. Some of my friends often quote to me things their fathers said—texts that they find important and useful. One friend said his father's advice was always "You only go around once, so get it right the first time." As useless as that revelation was, I felt jealous. My father gave me very few instructions. I remember him telling me not to run with sharp objects in my pocket. The nearest thing to spiritual advice he offered was when he gave me a leather-bound church hymnal and wrote inside, "To my son. This world needs more songs like these. Dad." Which ones, Dad, those about sin, or about salvation, or the hymns about the imminent Rapture?

More often than not, the texts I live by are not the pithy moral, intellectual, even metaphysical statements to be found in works that present themselves as philosophy and religion. I'm more inclined to be influenced by the fictional worlds that I experience, encountering there an alternative universe that has structure and meaning. Urges that I can hardly expose are rendered in some acceptable form within these imaginary kingdoms. Many movies entertain me, and the entertainment is like a sugarcoating for a pill that reinforces one of the versions of reality that is floating around in the atmosphere. Entering these enchanting and fabricated realms, I conjure up the metaphors I need and make them into my own experience, like stories family members tell so often that I come to believe the events actually happened to me and that I remember them. The useful texts are the imagined ones.

* * *

My father's texts were usually movies. In 1931, six years before I was born, he had written in his diary:

> *Thurs. Busy day. Helped Doc inventory his drug store. 2½ hours. To picture show. Good. "Dr. Jekyll and Mr. Hyde." Not safe by myself.*

The first time I read this entry, I thought that it was an accurate description of the man I knew while I was growing up in New Orleans. He worked, he went to movies, he spent time alone, he often spoke in such simple statements: "Busy day," "Good," "Not safe by myself." My father seemed to be like the heroes in the Western movies he liked so much. Woman pretty. Hero shy. Bad people rob stagecoach. Hero find robbers and punish them. Diary entries are not supposed to be given in extended prose, but my father's seemed more taciturn than necessary.

His note about the Mamoulian film, *Dr. Jekyll and Mr. Hyde* (1932), puzzled me. What did my father mean by "not safe by myself"? Was he just feeling suicidal or was he commenting on the movie? After several viewings of the film, I thought I understood. No doubt my father was struck by the way in which Dr. Jekyll became a second person, Mr. Hyde, but it seemed a little too pat to say that my father thought of himself sometimes as two people, one a gentle, sweet man and the other a person overcome by rage. If my dad felt that way, I don't think he would have said, "Not safe by myself." What I would guess frightened my father was the way in which Dr. Jekyll's experiment, the one that turns him into Mr. Hyde, makes his life uncontrollable. Once having drunk his concoction, Dr. Jekyll can no longer predict when and where he will turn into Mr. Hyde. It might happen at any time, whether or not he has just swallowed the formula.

Such loss of control would have alarmed my father, who always had to have complete mastery of himself and his environment. No doubt that's why he never learned to drive a car. What if he were out driving and someone ran into him, or he ran into someone else? He might erupt into a rage, lose command of his feelings, hurt the other person or himself. It was safer to let other people drive him around. This obsession with control and order led him to simplify all of life, even his wardrobe. In the winter he invariably wore a navy blue suit, with a black tie and white shirt, and in the summer always a white linen suit with a black tie and white shirt.

As often as possible he ate the same food every day. Basted eggs, biscuits, and bacon for breakfast. Lunch was always potato salad and a braunschweiger sandwich with mayonnaise on white bread. When there was no braunschweiger, he would eat a tuna sandwich, but it was not his first choice. At supper he wanted chicken-fried steak with boiled dumplings, a small green salad with Roquefort dressing, and a piece of Dutch apple pie with a slice of Cheddar cheese on top. Some substitutes were allowed on Sundays, when he required fried chicken at lunch—dinner, as it was called on Sunday—and pork chops at supper. The weekend also was the time for a treat late each afternoon—strawberry shortcake or watermelon in the summer, lemon ice-box pie in the winter. In the best of all possible worlds, he ate precisely these items every day, with no deviations. One of the joys of working in Africa was that the company furnished the food and the cooks, so he could get them to fix him the same dishes at every meal. The more he could simplify his life, the less likely he was to be carried away in some firestorm of choices and urges. Knowing how much he wanted to be in command of his life, my father must have been frightened to see Dr. Jekyll out of control.

Having films for texts was complicated for my father because there were some films he clearly didn't like. As he wrote once in his diary:

Tues. Date with GS to show, Charlie Chaplin in "City Lights." No good.

My dad was never a great fan of Charlie Chaplin. *City Lights*

(1931) particularly bothered him because it was such a grotesque mixture of comedy and love story, and my father didn't like combinations of any kind. The film would be moving along as a love story, and then there would be these little comic asides, sometimes taking several minutes. My father wanted the love story to be the very center of the movie, but instead it was just an excuse for the little comic moments: Charlie swallowing a whistle, Charlie the Street Sweeper trying to avoid the trail of manure left by the horses, Charlie in a boxing match, Charlie drunk. Worst of all, the love story didn't come to some clear conclusion. Did Charlie get the girl or not? No, *City Lights* was not a good film.

The kind of film my dad preferred as a text was simple, its cards on the table, so to speak. He loved Westerns with Ken Maynard. When I looked at some of Ken's films a few years ago, I wanted to laugh. The plots were just an excuse for Ken to show off his riding, his unwavering enthusiasm, and his perfect compass for deciding what is good and what is bad. When the riding took place outdoors, the audio was so phony I couldn't help seeing men in a sound studio faking the noise of horses' hooves. My father liked Ken because the actor had once been a real cowboy, competing in rodeos. It was easier for Dad to identify with someone who was a little older than most cowboys, a little stouter, and who had made silent Westerns that my father had seen as a young man.

More than anything, Dad liked the uncomplicated morality that Ken, and other movie cowboys, followed. No doubt that's why he memorized the ten rules of the cowboy as given by another Western movie star, Gene Autry:

1. *A cowboy never takes unfair advantage—even of an enemy.*
2. *A cowboy never betrays a trust.*
3. *A cowboy always tells the truth.*
4. *A cowboy is kind to small children, to old folks, and to animals.*
5. *A cowboy is free from racial and religious prejudice.*
6. *A cowboy is helpful and when anybody's in trouble, he lends a hand.*
7. *A cowboy is a good worker.*

8. A cowboy is clean about his person and in thought, word, and deed.

9. A cowboy respects womanhood, his parents, and the laws of the country.

10. A cowboy is a patriot.

As far as my father was concerned, those rules were the perfect texts, and they might just as well have been written by the Archbishop of Canterbury. To know them meant having the key to living a good life. Yet I think that these ten principles were in some ideal realm where he could believe in them and yet not expect to follow them perfectly. I'm not surprised that my father would have memorized the cowboy's rules. They provided direction for his life without having to rely on feelings, which were too unpredictable and changeable. Having done everything he could to minimize emotions in his life, my dad's attitude toward feelings was often formulaic. He believed in them, but he didn't feel them. Better to stick with Gene Autry's code. Movies where the hero violated these rules, whether Westerns or not, were poor movies.

At significant times in his life my father repeatedly turned to the movies as texts, not only for solace or understanding, but also to celebrate, the way some people would take a drink, go out to eat, or light a cigar. He went to a movie by himself the evening I was born in New Orleans. Not to the Coliseum, a local theater just two blocks away, but to the Orpheum, a grand movie palace downtown. He was celebrating. He told me he went to see *Kid Galahad* (1937) because Humphrey Bogart was in it, playing a gangster, which was the Bogart my father preferred.

Since he said he loved the film, I looked at it years after he died, and because the couple in the film start their relationship by fighting with one another, I knew immediately why my father liked the movie. The man leaves the woman only to discover that he can't get her out of his mind, which is true for the woman, too. My father must have felt comforted by a movie in which there was a relationship so much like the one he and my mother had. They were engaged for six years, constantly fighting, breaking up, and getting back together again, and they married because they thought that making the commitment to one another would stop all the brawling. The fighting couple in the movie finally admit they love one another, too, and settle down to a life together. Having a son would have the same effect, my father hoped. He and my mother would have something that would bind them together.

I want to be there in the movie theater with my father, watching *Kid Galahad* and telling him he is wrong, that having a son will not make things better, but he is too absorbed in *Kid Galahad* to hear me.

* * *

Unconsciously, I think, my father also wanted movies to be my texts. Either that or he didn't know what fathers said to their sons, so he took me to the Mecca with him instead. So happy was the experience that I felt as if he carried me to the movies, held me while we sat there, and carried me home, cradled in his arms. He was more my father at the movies, and during the walks there and back, than at any other time. Now and then he would summarize the ending of a serial, or make a terse statement about what we had just seen, and I waited anxiously for these comments, but I was supremely content just to be with him at the movies.

My father preferred Westerns, the Hardy Family series, and, sometimes, war films. He had a very uneasy relationship with the war films because he had wanted badly to be in the service. When World War II broke out, he was thirty-six, which wasn't all that old, but he had kidney problems and the Army just wouldn't take him, nor would the Navy, the Merchant Marine, or the Coast Guard. He went to work at Higgins, a factory that made PT boats and landing craft, which was as close as he could get to the war, except in the movies. I think he worried that people thought he was a coward, unwilling to go into the service and fight. One of the few times I ever saw him cry, or at least have a tear well up in his eye, was when we were at a movie, Renoir's *This Land Is Mine* (1943), and Charles Laughton, on trial in a country occupied by the Nazis, says, pointing to his heart, "I'm not a coward *here*!"

When I screened this film again to remind myself of this moment, I was struck by another line in the movie. Arrested and about to be taken away by the Nazis, a man says to his son, "You go home and comfort your mother. You're the man now." Those were the exact words my father spoke to me when he left for Africa in 1945. I remember because it seemed strange to me that my father was saying "Go home and comfort your mother," when we were actually standing in the front hall of our house.

One of the war films that my father treated like a text was *Bombardier* (1943), with Pat O'Brien and Randolph Scott. Looking at it recently, I could hardly imagine what he saw in such a potboiler, which celebrates bombardiers and their high-altitude precision bombing. Obviously a piece of propaganda, it was designed to impress the folks back home with this new instrument of warfare, along with the bravery and skill of the men who used it. No doubt my father could imagine himself as a bombardier, working a bomb sight the way he worked an adding machine in his job as an accountant. He couldn't see himself with a rifle, getting shot at and shooting other men, but he could see himself adjusting a bomb sight and yelling, "Bombs away!" Watching the movie, my father would also have liked the camaraderie among the men, who seem bound by one purpose, as well as the fact that the film is about one thing, high-altitude bombing. Simple was always best. The little love story seems an afterthought, as a few men struggle over one woman in a sexless manner. Why my father admired the ending of *Bombardier* was clear. Captured by the Japanese, Randolph Scott ignites a target on the ground, knowing full well that he is calling the bombs down on his own head. That was bravery, the kind my father understood. "A cowboy is a patriot"—at any cost.

* * *

Whenever my father quoted one of Autry's rules, delivering it as a text to live by, my mother would roll her eyes. She thought that the rules were inane, so my father rarely spoke one of them in her presence. My mother had texts of her own, so she didn't need Gene Autry, or the movies, to help her live. She liked a movie now and then, but she wasn't dependent on them the way my father was. The text she lived by was, "If you can't eat it, drink it, or catch it off a float, it doesn't exist!" The "float" was a reference to Mardi Gras, where trinkets are thrown from floats to all the revelers standing along the parade routes. My father resented her text, my mother was sure of that, but she repeated it in front of him whether he liked it or not.

My mother's statement also revealed the importance of New Orleans to her. She was the one who had persuaded my father, after their marriage, to move to New Orleans from Jackson, Mississippi. Her instincts were right. It was indeed her city, a place that valued many of the things she valued—food, drink, fun. Work was much less important, or at least any talk about work. Never discussed when I was growing up was what my friends' fathers did for a living. I knew what food they liked, their favorite restaurants, whether they sailed or fished or went duck hunting, but I had no idea what their work was. The topic was considered in bad taste; the priorities were what you did for pleasure, not what you did to earn a living. "The town that care forgot," my mother used to say, quoting one of the clichés about the city.

I envied the way she owned New Orleans. If there was a restaurant that served fine food, she had been there and likely had her own table and a waiter she called by name, one who knew her palate. In the early days, when there was no money, she would have to save for months to be able to afford such a meal, but she was glad to skimp if it meant she could celebrate with a grand feast. She had her own salespeople, too. As soon as we walked through the door of a place where she shopped, a woman would come over and say, "Hello, Mrs. Perry, how are you? What can I help you with today?"

"Helen [or Ruth or Jane], I'm just wonderful, darling, thank you. I need some new dress shoes [or a hat or a sweater], please."

"I'll be right back. The perfect thing just came in." Invariably the saleswoman knew exactly what my mother would like.

New Orleans was my mother's text. She had it completely memorized and knew its every nuance. She worshiped at the feet of the city, adoring its delights. I rarely experienced New Orleans the way my mother did; for me it was mostly a place where I went to movies with my father.

Each parent had texts to live by, but I don't think they had one for their marriage. I wish they had studied some of the diary entries that my father wrote during the 1930s:

Tues. Date with GS for show. Saw Lew Ayres in "Iron Man." What a swell time we had. Crazy about that girl.

Sun. Up late. Broke with GS. Over nothing. Walked around town. To my own church in eve. Lonesome as hell. To midnite picture show, Marx Bros. in "Cracked Nuts."

Sat. Good day. Date with GS. She's a Peach. It's getting serious. To show "Mata Hari."

Wed. More of my bad luck. GS off to Washington D.C. for inauguration of Pres. F. D. Roosevelt. Just when I needed her. Sure miss that gal.

Mon. Out to GS's. On a high horse. Left mad. Seems like we've come to the end of the rope. Shame, too. Nice kid. Late to bed.

If my parents had read these entries carefully, they might have realized ahead of time that their marriage would be a mistake. The themes were clear: my father was depressed, he was alone and poor, he went to movies, he was in love with GS, my future mother, they had fights, they broke up, they made up, my father missed her.

I want to be there to tell them, "Stop, don't get married!" but if I were there, I wouldn't be so bold. Instead I would probably say something awkward like, "Dad, there's not even a Marx Brothers movie called *Cracked Nuts*." He must have confused *Animal Crackers* (1930), which is what he probably saw that day, with *The Cocoanuts* (1929), an earlier film of theirs. I'm not surprised he mixed up the titles, but I am surprised that he couldn't see the pattern in the courtship with my mother: fight, make up, fight, make up. Why would the marriage be any different?

My father's views on marriage now and then led him to misremember, or mis-see, a movie, almost as if the film had to fit a text that he already held dear. At the end of *Edge of Darkness* (1943), Ann Sheridan and Errol Flynn, who are in love with one another and who have led Norwegian villagers in a successful attack against Nazi occupiers, go into the mountains to fight in the Resistance. Not so, said my father. He claimed they got married and set up housekeeping. It was one of the things about the film that pleased him. These two brave people, very much in love, who fight the Nazis and win, deserved to get married. My father thought of marriage as the way to solve life's problems. If he was married, he had a home, and if he had a home, then there was one place in the world where he could go and be accepted for what he was. My father, the foster child, had a dream that he had a home somewhere. That was not true, but he believed it, so when he saw a film in which the people deserve to get married as a reward for their love and bravery, he saw them married, even if it was not in the film.

Now, at a distance, I look with incredulity at my parents' marriage. That they lived through the thirties, forties, and fifties, when not that many people got divorced, is true, but what kept them together? Was it simply a matter of economics? My mother needed the money he sent every month. Or she needed the stability he offered. When she had partied herself to exhaustion, she could go back to my father, and he would take her in, like some lost traveler, just as he had done when she came back after several years away, living with her parents in Dallas. Doing so was his duty; after all, he was her husband.

My father thought his marriage should be like a lot of the relationships he saw in films, involvement without passion. Love seemed very simple in the movies. You found someone, you persuaded that person to marry you, and then you lived happily ever after. Rage was rare, as were lies. I think my father went to his grave thinking that love and marriage were something you put on, like a cloak, and, once done, everything was fine. It worked for him. He did have to live apart from my mother in order to love her the way he thought he should—sending letters and gifts and cards and money every month—but the irony of that seems to have escaped him. Compared to growing up in ten foster homes, his marriage must have seemed like an improvement.

My dad's idea of romance was Greta Garbo and Clark Gable, the way they fall in love in *Susan Lenox*, an early thirties film my father remembered fondly. When they meet, Gable says, "Well, you're a girl, aren't you!"

"Yes," replies Garbo, and from that moment on they are locked in the up-and-down, back-and-forth dance called love. They meet, they fall in love, eventually they kiss a few times. My father wasn't aware that the Production Code prohibited displays of passion; he just thought that love was that way. You clinched now and then, and you sent nice cards and gifts, but you didn't rip each other's clothes off or ever abandon love. Garbo is devoted to Gable even when he rejects her, and she follows him halfway around the world until he relents and acknowledges how he feels. Love is forever, no matter what.

Given my parents' very different attitudes toward movies, particularly as texts to live by, they rarely went to a movie together, or at least I don't remember them doing so very often. One of the few films I remember my mother and father seeing together was Huston's *In This Our Life* (1942), which came to the Mecca several years after being shown downtown. With me between them, my parents sat in the theater and looked at the same screen, but they saw two different movies, or so it seemed to me as I turned my head from one to the other. When my father smiled, my mother was frowning, and when my mother laughed, my father was scowling.

Not long ago I watched *In This Our Life* again. It was not that hard to understand what each parent liked, or disliked, that night at the Mecca. No doubt my mother enjoyed seeing a woman, Bette Davis, who loved to dance and have a good time, who followed her instincts for pleasure and self-preservation completely, no matter what. Perhaps Davis went a little too far, but her attitude toward life was correct. My father saw another movie, one in which Davis got her comeuppance because she mistreated and manipulated everyone around her.

Dad would have liked the conversation between Bette Davis and her father, who says, "In my day we didn't talk much about happiness. If it came, we were grateful for it, but we were brought up in the belief that there were other things more important."

"What things?" Davis asks.

"Oh, old-fogey, fantastic notions, such as duty and personal responsibility."

I don't think my mother heard this exchange. What she probably liked was the conversation that Davis has with Dennis Morgan, the man she has just stolen away from her sister. Morgan says, "We've got to be happy, we've got to be happy."

"But, silly," Davis says, "we are happy. Or aren't we?"

Morgan responds, "Sure, of course, we're happy."

I imagine that both my parents liked one exchange of dialogue, but, again, for different reasons. Bette Davis's sister, after her husband has run off, says to her father, "I've got a life to live and I'm going to live it."

"Don't let yourself get hard," the father replies.

"Be soft, like you? No, I'll go out and get what I want. . . . I'm going to be like the Fitzroys, they know how to live. I'm going to be just as hard as they, that's the way to be happy."

My father became hard by leaving home and working in Africa. My mother became happy by playing hard and getting what she wanted. Their gift to me was seeing life as two totally different movies. I'm not perfectly comfortable with either one. When I play, I want to get back to work, but once I'm settled in to work, I feel cut off from life. I try not to let myself enjoy the pleasures of movie comedies, even as I laugh. When I see a movie that is a tragedy, I love it, but then I leave the movie theater feeling despondent. Who wants to go to a movie that leaves you feeling sad? Transcendence is the only thing that should arrive on the wings of resplendent shadows.

* * *

I didn't often think about movies as texts until I saw an Antonioni film, *Eclipse* (1962). In the scene before the ending, a young man and woman much in love promise to meet each and every evening forever at a particular street corner. The last sequence of *Eclipse* then explores that corner and all the activities that occur there and nearby as a day draws to its close. A water sprinkler is turned off; a bus stops and people emerge; the sky darkens. Finally it is apparent that an evening has come when the man and woman fail to meet. The first time I saw the film, I was deeply affected by its final moments. "In your work, never ignore the libidinal instinct," one of my graduate school professors told me; so I spent some time thinking about *Eclipse*.

Only after several years of being moved by the ending, for reasons that were never clear to me, and even after publishing an essay on the film, did I realize that I was gripped by the last moments of the movie because they replicated my own experience with a father who left home to live and work in Africa. One day he was there, loving and attentive, the very center of my life, and the next day, like the lovers in *Eclipse*, he didn't show up anymore. Being so captivated by that last scene in *Eclipse* helped me to understand how I had felt when my father left. As odd as it may seem, I learned something from *Eclipse* that I didn't know I knew. Realizing how a movie had revealed some old feelings, and knowing how desperately I wanted to understand my father, I resolved again to look carefully at the movies that he had cared about; after all, they were his texts.

My first thought was about the Hardy Family movies that Dad loved. I don't recall seeing any of these films with my father, but his diary is full of unusual—for him—exclamations about them: "Swell picture show!" "Wonderful!" "Great fun!" Starring Mickey Rooney as the son, Andy Hardy, the whole series was given a special Academy Award in 1942 for "representing the American Way of Life." The films had been extremely popular in the late 1930s and early 1940s, when my father was in his thirties, so I started looking at them to find clues.

Andy is a young man interested in girls and cars, who lives in a house with a loving mother and a father who is a judge. Everything is perfect—home, family, town, parents, children. Nobody ever makes any mistakes, at least not any that can't be fixed by a "man-to-man" talk between Andy and his father. Andy is such a perfect son that, even at age twenty, dancing cheek to cheek with his mother in *Love Laughs at Andy Hardy* (1946), he says endearing things like, "Somehow a fellow never gets around to realizing that his mother was once the belle of the ball; he always thinks of her as something more wonderful, like she is now." And he means it.

The father in the series, Judge Hardy, provides sage advice, saying uncommonly sensible things like, "There's no shortcut to success. You've got to eat crow before you can appreciate the taste of chicken." The Hardy films have an intact family, loving parents, and strong relationships between young and old people. My father idolized and idealized that state. In one episode, *Love Finds Andy Hardy* (1938), when Andy's parents are apart because Mrs. Hardy goes off to be with her sick mother, Mom and Dad Hardy write each other daily, sending telegrams and special delivery letters. My father did almost the same when he went to Africa.

When I looked at several of the movies in the Hardy Family series, I was amazed that my father liked them. Andy's sentimentalized affection for his mother—how could my dad identify with that, since his own mother had died when he was a year old? How could someone who lived in ten foster homes and orphanages cherish these movies, which were so different from his own experience? That's the answer, of course; he needed badly to believe in such a childhood, one nothing like his own. The Hardy films were never true, not even in the 1940s, but at least my dad—and millions of other people—could still believe that they were.

* * *

The closest I came to understanding something about my father through his texts, the movies, was in realizing how many of his favorite films avowed a sense of duty. Learning to read his reactions to these movies, and others, was not easy. Today I have his diaries, but back then I often had to interpret something—a laugh, a twitch, a movement in his seat, a grimace, stillness and silence—to know what he thought of a movie, or some scene in the movie. It took me a while to realize how important to my father were all the forties films that presented men for whom duty was paramount, particularly the kind of duty that required them to leave their women and families. In *Action in the North Atlantic* (1943), Humphrey Bogart, as an officer in the merchant marine during World War II, is about to leave with his captain to help sail a convoy across the ocean. His new bride says to the captain, "He can't go. He just can't."

"Baby, look, I gotta go," says Bogart.

The bride insists: "Please!"

Then Bogart speaks. "Baby, there's one thing you gotta understand. Maybe we guys know more about what's going on than most people. We've been hanging around Axis ports for a long time and we've seen what they do. What we've seen ain't nice. So we can't sit around holdin' hands with all that going on."

Hearing these words, how could anyone not believe that brave men left their women in order to do their duty? Dozens of films depicted men leaving their loved ones; it was the signature act in the early forties films. Men were always leaving home to do the right thing. Going off and fighting in World War II had been denied to my father, but he would find some way to make a comparable sacrifice. To fulfill his duty he went to Africa. Since it was the U.S. Navy that was building a West African port at Monrovia, Liberia, the work was surely a part of the war effort.

He couldn't live with my mother, that was obvious, but he wanted to be married, to be a good husband and father, so he went away and sent money and letters and cards back. What began as an act of self-sacrifice, one that gave his life an essential purpose, became a suicide mission, but he couldn't, or didn't know how to, back down. He started eating and smoking more, became obese, and developed heart trouble. About to die in the African bush, my father probably thought he had done the noble thing with his life, too, like the men who had gone off and died in the war. That he might have run away probably never came to mind.

His single-minded devotion to duty was just another aspect of the simplicity and clarity that were so important to my father. After the war, when he came back home for his two-week visits, and I was older, I became more aware of movies Dad did not like. Either he told me outright, or he jerked around as if his behind itched, or he sighed a lot. I thought I could detect some similarities among these films; they were almost always movies that were unbelievable to him in some way. A Bogart and Bacall film, *Dark Passage* (1947), was one my father particularly disliked, and I think it was because he found the movie so filled with impossible coincidences and people whose motives made no sense at all. A taxi driver picks Bogart up, figures out he's an escaped convict, and then takes him to a surgeon to rebuild his face. What taxi driver would do such a thing? Another taxi driver is the same man who gave him a ride when he broke out of prison. Who could believe such a fluke? Only an idiot could make a movie like that.

Thinking a lot about my father's reaction to films like *Dark Passage*, I've come to believe that what he didn't like was the anxiety level that all the nonsense and coincidences created in him. He didn't want to be aware of himself being stirred up at a movie; no, he wanted to sit in his seat and lose himself in the film. It was okay to get caught up in the characters and the plot, but the involvement should be bloodless, without passion. To my father, I'm sure, the great appeal of the movies was that you could experience something but not be overwhelmed.

My mother's response to movies was different, or so it seemed during the few times we went together. Once in a while she even carried on conversations with the actors on the screen, something my father never did. At Tourneur's *Cat People* (1942), my dad said, she shouted "The girl's a panther, idiot, don't go near her!" During DeMille's *The Story of Dr. Wassell* (1944), she giggled out loud a few times, much to the embarrassment of my father and me. It was a film I loved. When Dr. Wassell received the Navy Cross for his bravery, I cried. On the way home, my mother poked fun at the movie because Laraine Day made herself too available to Gary Cooper, and my mother had no affection for women who put a man first. Always appalled when she made fun of a movie he liked, my father suddenly became enraged, turning around on the sidewalk and blocking my mother's path, flailing his arms. She paid no attention, walking into the street and going around him. As my father's voice grew louder and louder, and it seemed he might even strike my mother, I became frightened and fled, running the two blocks home. I was in bed before they came in, but they had stopped fighting anyway. My mother came in and tried to kiss me good night, but I wouldn't let go of the covers that I had pulled up over my head.

* * *

The movies seemed so much to be my father's texts that to see one of his favorite films was like having him back home again. Although away in Africa, my Dad seemed present with me at the Mecca when I saw one of the characters he loved. It was really my father on the screen as Lash La Rue, using his whip to relieve a bad guy of his revolver, or as Fuzzy St. John, reading his poetry to Lash in their film *The Fighting Vigilantes* (1947):

> *A cowhand oughta stick to what he can do.*
> *He shouldn't oughta go trying something new*
> *He oughtna fool around with females nohow*
> *On account of a cowhand was made for a cow.*

How my Dad could love Fuzzy's poetry, how he could double over in laughter listening to words like these, how he could treat such films as texts, seems utterly incomprehensible to me now. Listening to Fuzzy today I want to give up entirely the task of understanding my father. For my own sanity I have to believe that Dad was more complicated than the movies he took delight in. It's also important for me to remember that sometimes the movies he liked, or disliked, contradicted everything I thought I knew about him. To say that movies were his texts was not always helpful. I never understood why he didn't love *The Wizard of Oz* (1939); it seemed like the kind of charming film that he would have admired, but he dismissed it as silly. On the other hand, he worshiped *Bambi* (1942), which to him was the greatest movie of all time. From my father's stories about taking me to the movie, I feel that I remember the experience. To see it we went downtown to the Orpheum Theater—a palace with thick carpets, statuary, and crystal chandeliers over the balconies.

It was summer and my father wore his white linen suit, his black tie, and, because it was a special occasion, his Panama hat. Air conditioning didn't exist in those days, but happily the Loew's was "air-cooled," which meant, I imagined, that fans blew air over huge cakes of ice. Outside a banner hanging the full length under the marquee announced, "20 degrees cooler inside!" The same man who liked Fuzzy St. John's poetry, but who hated the Tin Man, in fact thought Thumper the funniest screen character since Will Rogers, or so my dad said. And when the forest fire seemed about to kill everyone, including Bambi, my father grabbed my arm and dug his nails into it, as if I were supposed to reassure him. That's the part of going to see *Bambi* that I do remember.

How did my dad use his movies as texts to live by? He didn't watch *Action in the North Atlantic* with a pad in hand, taking notes, and afterward act on what he had written: "Men do their duty by leaving their families." Far from it. My father felt this way, I'm sure, before he went to the movie, and the movie reinforced this nascent belief, gave it the force of authority, something like the way a firing in a kiln makes a shaped mass of clay into a piece of pottery. Whether movies were real or true was not the question; what was important was that they ratified some version of reality he was already leaning toward, or some belief my dad needed to be true. Like the rest of us, he had illusions that he was quite ready and willing to believe in, and the movies authenticated those illusions.

The more I contemplate the movies that were my father's favorites, the more aware I am of how fatuous it is to think he believed movies were texts to live by; yet it feels true. While it seems easy for me to improve on his texts, that is probably only because I live by a different set of illusions. Would that I knew my own movie illusions as well as I recognize my father's. Or that I could convince my students of the illusions fostered by their movies. I should be grateful for the fact that I now see his movies as naive, but another part of me wants nothing more than to be at the Mecca again with my dad, sharing his enjoyment. He might also point out that Roy Rogers and Trigger had just ridden by the same boulder four times. That's the kind of discovery you expect from a father, and such a terrible revelation is probably a lot easier to handle if your father is there with you.

* * *

My father's love for the movies as texts has even reached out to me in movies that I saw but he did not. Looking again at David Lean's *Lawrence of Arabia* (1962), some years after it had come out, I recalled that one of my father's favorite books was Lawrence's autobiography, *The Seven Pillars of Wisdom*. I had read it some years before but learned little about my father. This time I decided to look instead at a book written about Lawrence; in the middle of it I found myself reading a description of the famous soldier's masochism, how he liked to be beaten. One of his ruses to get someone to beat him was to say that he had done something quite terrible to an uncle, who was furious and wanted to pay someone to punish his nephew. After beating Lawrence, the accomplice was then to write the uncle and give details of the beating. Lawrence never mailed those letters, but he would compose an answer. As the biography reported, one of these fake responses from the imaginary uncle said, "From what you tell me, and from the reports of those who have examined Ted since, it is clear that he had a sound thrashing." The "Ted" surprised me until I realized that Lawrence's middle name was Edward.

My father had named me Edward and called me Ted. Lawrence died in 1935; I was conceived in 1936. The connection seemed more than accidental. Suddenly a movie, and a biography, had allowed me to reach back through time and read a message from my father. Lawrence, the masochist, was his hero. I don't know if my dad liked being beaten or not, but I do remember that he treated his sinus infections by sucking salt water up his nose and into his sinus cavities. He never cried out from this painful ablution, but afterward, as tears were still streaming down his cheeks and his eyes were red, he would smile.

The more obvious way in which he punished himself was how he lived. If Lawrence was his hero, that truth was most apparent in the cell of Dad's that I visited in Africa. I don't call his place an apartment, or even rooms, although there were two of them, because these two small rooms were so sparsely furnished that I thought "cell" the first time I saw them. Among his things when my father died were several photographs of his quarters, but I didn't really need them; my memory was precise. There was a chair, where my dad sat and read, and next to it a bookcase, on the top of which was a shortwave radio and the *Book of Common Prayer*. The books on the shelf were by authors like Louis Bromfield and Zane Grey, and included all the Horatio Hornblower books by C. S. Forester. My father felt about books the way that he did about country-and-western music. Simple and understandable were best.

On the walls he had thumbtacked a few photographs of the house where my mother and I lived back in the States. He was very proud of this house, but my mother had bought it without asking him, and at first he was furious. Also in his cell was a sink with a light above, and, to one side, a towel bar. On a shelf nearby were a few glasses and a bottle of Jack Daniel's. The cell had no closet, just a rack to hang clothes on. Besides the beds and the chair, the only piece of furniture was a dresser, on top of which was a photograph of my mother and one of me, almost hidden behind some yellowed plastic in a faded leather frame. Two adjacent spaces, one a small bathroom with toilet and shower, and the other a cubicle only large enough for two single beds, completed my father's living quarters. No curtains. No rug. No homelike appurtenances. He lived in that room, or one like it, for the twelve years between the time he left home and when he died.

The one anomaly in the room was a picture of himself. For a man who seemed self-effacing, who lived simply and required little of life, hanging up his own picture was probably an affirmation of his desire to be a presence in the world. Here at last he had a home where he was the top priority; that's what his photograph on the wall said. My father's rage with my mother was always that she did not put him first. Her girlfriends came first; I came second. He was way down the line somewhere. They were in competition. If my father bought something for my mother, she would often go to town the next day and trade it, either for something she wanted more, or for the same thing, only at a cheaper price. Anything to prove to him now and then that she was better than he was. He was not better, nor was he more important, in their house. Whether she was right or not, once again he felt he was in a foster home. He had never lived in a house where he was number one, except now, in his cell in Africa, so damn it, his picture would be on the wall.

Because my dad liked depriving himself, his room was sparse, with very few amenities. When he died, everything he owned was shipped back in a couple of suitcases. Besides his clothes, an array of photographs, a camera, some jewelry, and hundreds of nitroglycerin pills, there was nothing but a small key taped to a piece of cardboard. What it fit was a mystery. My father died with most of his secrets intact.

What frightens me about the way my Dad lived is how attractive it is to me. Not long after he died, when I was working in the oil fields just off the coast of Louisiana, my mother and I had a huge fight. I was working a four-and-eight shift, staying at home for four days and then working in the Gulf of Mexico for eight days. While in the Gulf, I lived at the camp that the company had built on pilings in the shallow water near where we were drilling for oil. My mother said I would have to pay room and board for the four days I was at home. Today I admire her for making demands on me, but then, given that I was trying to save money to go back to college, I didn't appreciate the fact that she wanted to charge me. Packing all my belongings into my little Fiat, I moved out, planning to stay at the company camp in the Gulf on my days off.

The first day out at the camp I threw overboard most of my belongings, keeping only those things I absolutely needed. It was a beautiful day in the Gulf, with a bright sun and swells of water that slowly undulated the surface. My clothes and papers and other stuff, things I felt not necessary, floated across the Gulf, and I felt cleansed. Only later did I realize how much I had adopted my father's way of life, paring everything down to bare essentials and living in a small room. I wasn't off in Africa, but I was a few miles away from the shoreline of the United States. I began smoking Camel cigarettes then, too, the same brand he smoked. I wanted him so much to be alive. I don't smoke anymore, but I am still happier away from people and in small uncluttered spaces.

* * *

As a child in New Orleans, I never thought about movies as texts. I did care a lot about whether or not my dad liked a movie. My mother's opinion was not as crucial, but it was terribly important to me that my parents agree about a movie if they went together. What I wanted most, my biggest childhood fantasy, was to see them have fun together.

In my imagination I can make a film about seeing a movie they both liked. My footage begins with the three of us going to watch *I'll Be Seeing You* (1945), with Ginger Rogers and Joseph Cotten, and we go to see it in April 1945, the day after my dad told me he was going to leave soon for Africa. During the streetcar ride to the theater, my mother sings the movie's title song. Dad likes to hear her sing and thinks she means she'll be seeing him everywhere after he's gone. I know different; whenever she walks away from somebody, she always says, "I'll be seeing you!" She's singing goodbye. Going to the movie is the last big family event before my dad departs.

After the film is over, we ride the streetcar back from the downtown theater, Loew's State. It is dark by the time we board on Canal Street for the ride up St. Charles Avenue to our home. Smiling and giggling, my parents sit together on the first seat that faces forward, and I sit near them but on the long bench that runs perpendicular to their seat. We aren't sitting side by side, but we are still squeezed up close to one another. Mother and Dad are raving about the movie. "What a wonderful picture!" my mother says.

"Real swell," my father responds. Surprised and thrilled that they both like the same movie, I am afraid to tell them I didn't like the film very much; right in the middle a big dog attacks Joseph Cotten and it scared me. The streetcar rocks back and forth as it moves forward through the dark night. I look up and count the lightbulbs. There are twelve, two rows of six. I look out the window, trying to see what is going by on St. Charles Avenue. Now and then the lights of a passing automobile make the trees seem to dart around, and reflections from the streetlamps flit about like fireflies over the surfaces of the automobiles. I feel myself in an airship, full of light, gliding through a dark sky. Jumping up from my seat, I run toward the front of the car to watch the motorman, then quickly run back and sit down again. Flailing my legs and kicking my heels on the radiator under the bench seat, I expect one of my parents to reach over and put a hand on my knee, saying, "That's enough," but they are laughing so much that they don't pay me any attention.

I turn and look again out the streetcar window, noticing for the first time that my mother and father are reflected in the glass. I can see through the window to the cars and lights outside, and I can also see my parents, mirrored on the window surface. They think I am looking outside, not watching them, but I am really observing everything they do. Their reflection in the window is like a movie, my own private movie of my parents. My father leans over to peck my mother on the cheek, but she turns her head and they kiss on the lips for an instant. My parents are beautiful; my father is wearing a short-sleeved sport shirt, which he hardly ever does, but it is a warm spring day. Mother has on a simple blue shift and her eyes are glistening from laughing so much. As the streetcar rocks back and forth, moving forward along the tracks, the noise of the wheels is a melody, and I think of the trolley song in *Meet Me in St. Louis* (1944). The words won't come to me, but I remember it as a happy song.

"I admire her," my mother says.

"Who?" my father asks.

"Ginger Rogers. She loves Joseph Cotten so much she won't tell him she's home on a furlough from prison."

"Joseph Cotten doesn't tell her at first that he's been in a psycho ward," my father says. "Too many secrets."

"No, it's fine," my mother says. "When the secrets come out, everyone is okay. They love each other. He'll wait for her until her prison term is up."

"He makes a huge sacrifice," my father says. "People do that."

"Yes," my mother says, "it makes me very proud of him."

Being a person to be proud of meant everything to my father. A week later he left for Africa.

4 Window-Shopping

I KNEW I WAS IN NEW ORLEANS AGAIN when they unlatched the plane door and, even though it was 10 P.M., I felt a rush of fiery air, as if the door of a blast furnace had been opened. It was August. When I reached the baggage claim area and stood still for a moment, I could feel my armpits become damp and a little drop of water roll slowly down my spine. My suitcase didn't arrive with the other bags, so I went to the baggage service office, only to be given my suitcase trussed up with duct tape. The zipper had broken; pieces of my underwear were sticking out, and I was embarrassed.

The next day I went to buy a new suitcase. On Canal Street were several stores with huge signs that said "Going Out of Business Sale." I knew this was just a come-on—they'd been going out of business for years—but I headed toward one anyway, expecting that I could find a suitcase at a cheaper price. I stood on the sidewalk and stared inside. The windows were filled with cameras, watches, sunglasses, and other gadgets, all with little yellow signs that advertised, in large red letters and numbers, huge price reductions: "50% Off!" Starting toward the shop, I could see that the long counter on my right had more watches and cameras, while the one on the left had binoculars, clocks, radios, and other pieces of electronic equipment. On the floor between the two counters various pieces of luggage were laced together with a locked cable. I got to the door and stopped, unable to go forward, as if there was something forbidden within the premises. It was not unlike trying to get up the courage to go into a striptease club on Bourbon Street. The store on Canal Street scared me. I feared they'd sell me a piece of junk with a fake label, or under the pressure of a fast-talking salesperson I'd buy something I didn't need, or pay too much for what I did need. In my ear was my mother's voice, telling me, "You get what you pay for."

Backing up, without entering, I walked three blocks down Canal Street to Maison Blanche, an old department store that had been there since my childhood. I bought a Samsonite suitcase—I trusted the store; the salesperson seemed knowledgeable; the brand was familiar. Yet my father's voice announced itself inside my head: "You paid way too much." So what. At least I didn't leave Maison Blanche wondering if I had bought something that wouldn't last or that my mother would find tacky. She would have been proud of me, that's what I thought for a second, and then, as I stepped outside onto the Canal Street sidewalk, and felt the hot sunlight, it struck me how much I resented the way in which my mother seemed to have reached from the grave and told me what to do. A ghost from the past, she had materialized and made herself felt. I was helpless. My mother had sweet-talked me into buying what she wanted me to buy. She was the salesperson I feared.

* * *

My mother's attitude about shopping sometimes baffled me. Like the rest of us, what she said didn't always agree with what she did. One moment she would get very excited about something she had bought but in the next breath would say, "It's important not to get too attached to material things." When I was thinking recently about this contradiction, I remembered that my mother had laughed at some remarks that Kirk Douglas had made in *A Letter to Three Wives* (1949), and I watched the movie again to see if I could find the speech. It was easy. Asked if he would consider writing for the radio, Douglas rejects the idea by saying, "The purpose of radio writing, as far as I can see, is to prove to the masses that a deodorant can bring happiness, a mouthwash guarantee success, and a laxative attract romance." My mother must have agreed with Douglas that buying deodorant, mouthwash, or laxatives didn't work such miracles. Or so she believed she believed.

My mother contended that she was not a person who went shopping to entertain herself, or to get out of the house, or to make herself feel good by buying something. She convinced herself that she went shopping only to buy what we needed, but if my mother's trips for clothes and necessities were always purposeful, as she claimed, her trips to the grocery store were certainly different, more like exploratory expeditions. While the essentials were bought regularly at the Piggly Wiggly, just a block from our home, the real grocery shopping was done at Langenstein's on Arabella Street, a neighborhood market on the edge of New Orleans's Garden District that carried specialty items, an array of cheeses, and the freshest of produce, meat, and seafood. My mother never bought a lot at Langenstein's, at least not in the war years when so much was rationed and she had little money, so each purchase was carefully considered. She walked slowly up and down the aisles as if she were the leader of an archeological dig that had just unearthed a new layer of shards, utensils, arrowheads, and human remains, and it was her job to inspect, catalog, evaluate, and authenticate each item.

At Langenstein's, pushing a cart over the worn wooden floors, she took cans and packages carefully off shelves, read labels, squeezed fruit, checked the color of fish eyes ("Make sure they're clear and that the fish don't smell fishy"), deliberated slowly over new cheeses, and told "her" butcher, Buddy Hodgkins, exactly what cut and age of meat she wanted. He knew anyway, and, often before she spoke, would say, "Another pork roast today, Mrs. Perry?" Or another sirloin, or rib eye, or brisket of beef. He knew exactly where the meat was to be cut from, and how much fat my mother wanted trimmed. "How's your son doing, Buddy?" my mother would ask. Because she inquired, and remembered, she knew almost everything about Buddy's family. "A good butcher is your best friend," she would say to me, as if that were useful information to a child, but Buddy was still someone I liked. Twice, when my mother wasn't looking, he slipped me a piece of bubble gum, something so rare and precious during the World War II years that I cut mine into four pieces, sharing two with my best friends and spreading the rest out over several days.

* * *

Going to Langenstein's with my mother was agony because she wouldn't let me get a snack there—take a big dill pickle out of a barrel, or buy a stick of sugarcane to chew on. Her cruel refusal to let me eat anything inside Langenstein's came to mind when I went for the first time to a movie at the Public Theater Building in New York City. Inside was a theater run by Anthology Film Archives that was called the Invisible Cinema. Designed by Peter Kubelka, the Austrian filmmaker, the theater held about ninety people in a black room. Seats, cushions, walls, ceiling, and floor were all black velvet, which was also used to cover the partitions that separated the seats from one another. These barriers extended out far enough so you couldn't see or touch the next person, indeed couldn't tell if there was a person there unless you went in early and watched to see if someone came down the aisle and sat in an adjoining seat. Because there was a black lip arching over the top of each seat, you couldn't see behind, nor could you see anyone in front.

When I went to this theater the first time, and dropped back into a seat, I found myself in a black cocoon that made me feel isolated and deprived. It was like going to Langenstein's with my mother. The only thing I could see, except for all the blackness, was the white screen, and the only thing I could touch was the black velvet that surrounded me. My mouth began to water again. I could hardly stand to watch the movie, Rossellini's *The Rise to Power of Louis XIV* (1966), craving instead some salty, buttery popcorn, or a cold Coke, or a Hershey's bar. Sitting there without being able to put some food in my mouth, much less touch or see anyone, was agony. Rossellini's film, alien and uncooked, confounding expectations, didn't help. It was like eating tofu. I knew the stuff was good for me, but it didn't do anything for my palate. The next time I went to the Invisible Cinema, my wife came along, and we sneaked in a bottle of wine. We had to get on our knees to pass the bottle back and forth under the partition that divided us, but the movie, Dreyer's *Ordet* (1954), although just as challenging, was more palatable.

* * *

One time when my mother went to Langenstein's, she asked Buddy for a piece of pickled pork. She was going to make red beans and rice, she said. I remember the first time she cooked this dish because she was so excited. Dad had left for Africa and a new lady-friend was coming to dinner, so Mother was determined to cook something really special. Her new friend was a native of the city, and there's no meal New Orleanians love more. Over the years I have come to love this "home-style" dish that's served in every neighborhood joint in New Orleans. You won't find it on the menu at the great restaurants, like Commander's Palace, because it's a little too home-style, but in my mother's hands, red beans and rice became a feast. Over the years she worked on the recipe dozens of times, refining and improving it, until the thick liquid had a complexity of flavors. The red beans were mushy, even a little sweet, but the Tabasco, cayenne pepper, and andouille sausage balanced the sweetness with a spicy sharpness.

Because my mother knew how much I loved red beans and rice, she cooked it for me every time I went home for a visit. When I came for Thanksgiving break during the fall that I went away to college, I decided I would try to learn how she made her dish, so that year I watched every step. Because this was the first time my father's visit happened to be at Thanksgiving, it was an especially happy holiday. I spent most of two days in the kitchen, while my Dad played gin rummy with my mother's friend, Helen.

The first day, my mother baked a couple of chickens, pulled the meat off, and then simmered the carcasses in water inside a large black cast-iron Dutch oven. After a few hours she strained out the bones and added the red beans, letting them soak overnight. The next morning, in a large frying pan made out of black cast iron, she fried six slices of bacon, then used the grease to baste an egg. After eating the bacon and egg for her breakfast, while keeping the grease warm, she began slowly adding flour to the grease. "The secret is in the roux," my mother said as she slowly stirred the flour with a fork for about twenty minutes. "Make sure the grease doesn't get too hot and don't be in a hurry to brown the flour." When the flour was a golden brown, she slowly added chopped onions, garlic, celery, and green bell pepper, stirring the mixture for quite a while. "Wait until the onions and celery get translucent." Finally, she slowly stirred the roux into the Dutch oven that contained the chicken stock and red beans, then added canned tomatoes, turning the flame low.

"If you really want to learn, you have to do some of it yourself," my mother said. I then sautéed pieces of pickled pork and andouille sausage, using the same frying pan where she made the roux. Mother stood over me and directed every step: "Turn the heat down, you're doing it too fast. Slowly, slowly."

"Hey, let me alone, I can do this."

"Do what your mother tells you!" Having had a few drinks while cooking, we were now getting tickled. "Take the meat out, it's seared just right, darling." As I lifted the meat out, intending to put it into the beans and roux, she purposely bumped into me with her hip, yelling, "Watch what you're doing!" The sausage went flying out of my hand, skating across the kitchen floor until it hit the bottom of the refrigerator. Mother speared the piece of sausage with a fork and dropped it into the pot. "The best seasoning is always on the floor," she said, and we both chuckled.

My father walked in. "What are you two up to?"

"What's your problem?" my mother asked.

"Helen and I can't concentrate on our card game with all the noise, that's the problem." He looked at what we were cooking. "Beans, God," my father said. "I hate the gas. It'll make us all float away, like dirigibles."

"Tough!" my mother said, giggling. She was now on her fourth vodka, and, as she said, feeling no pain. "You'll have to sleep in the extra bedroom."

"Oh, no, you cook it, you take the consequences," my father said, frowning. He turned and left. My mother and I looked at each other and started to laugh, but we caught ourselves, not wanting to disturb the card game anymore.

Mother went back to the big pot of red beans, now with tomatoes, pickled pork, and andouille sausage, and she added a dash of Tabasco, some Worcestershire sauce, thyme, a few bay leaves, salt, some chopped chives, and cayenne pepper. This concoction was put on the back burner and cooked very slowly for a few hours. I had learned what I wanted to learn, so while Mother made corn bread and a pot of rice, and finished several other dishes, I went and watched Helen and Dad play cards. When mother called out that everything was ready, we went to the stove with our plates, spooned off some rice and added the red beans on top, grabbed a piece of warm corn bread, and sat down at the table together. Insisting that we first hold hands and say grace, mother then started eating. That old refrain of hers came out, "The best thing I ever put in my mouth!"

* * *

Shopping for food, and cooking it, were kin to my mother's great appreciation for the articles she acquired. No matter what she said about the triviality of "material objects," she loved what she owned and grieved over anything she didn't have, or lost. She was devastated when, in 1946, almost a year after my father left for Africa, our landlord said he was doubling the rent. After the war, housing was difficult to find, price controls were lifted, and landlords everywhere were increasing rents astronomically. My mother couldn't afford this new rent, so she sold the little furniture we had, even our dishes and silver, and we moved in with a woman who was her best friend. It was a gloomy time. We couldn't stay with her friend for long, and we had no prospects of a place to live.

In a few weeks my father came home for his first annual visit. I don't know exactly what happened, but he talked to our former landlord and soon we moved back into our old place. You would have thought my father had cured my mother of some terminal disease, the way she hugged and kissed him. My parents then went on a shopping spree, buying new furniture, silver, china, and linens. It seemed to me that they were a married couple again, enjoying every moment together. My father even bought my mother an expensive coat with a fur collar, and the purchase thrilled her. Bringing the coat home, they both looked happier than I had ever seen them. After a few turns in front of my father, modeling the coat, mother sat down in his lap and they giggled like newlyweds. "Do you like my fur collar?" my mother asked.

"I love your fur collar," my father responded.

"What do you like most about my fur collar?"

"I like to blow on it and watch the fur fly," my father said.

As young as I was, I knew they were talking about something other than just the fur collar.

* * *

When I go to a movie, I am also shopping, because I can't help but notice what goods appear in the film, and what my heroes and heroines use. Product placement is what the marketers call this practice, and it's big business in Hollywood. McDonald's paid dearly to have its golden arches appear in *The Flintstones* (1994). In *Teenage Mutant Ninja Turtles* (1990), the pizza was delivered by Domino's. Michael J. Fox drank Pepsi in *Back to the Future, Part II* (1989). Companies pay lots of money so the filmmakers will display their wares, and they want their money's worth. Yesterday's newspaper carried a piece about a suit brought by Reebok against the film company Tri-Star. Reebok was claiming that it had paid a fee to the producers of *Jerry Maguire* (1996), and in return the movie was supposed to present Reebok in a positive light. Because Reebok thought it didn't get its money's worth, the company was suing.

Moviegoing is window-shopping.

* * *

My mother's shopping was connected to a desire to have the best of whatever was available. In 1949 she and I took the Southern Railway train, the Crescent, to visit my Uncle Alexis and Aunt Joan in New York City. Married to my mother's sister, my uncle was a White Russian count who had fled after the 1917 revolution, then lived in Europe until the rise of the Nazis. A man whose family once owned a five-story home in Kiev, whose father committed suicide after the czar was overthrown, Alexis seemed to me the epitome of worldliness and sophistication. Because he made his living as a designer—automobiles for Packard and Willys, furniture for Heywood-Wakefield, appliances for O'Keefe & Merritt, watches for Gruen—my mother respected his opinion about what was the "best," a subject they spent endless hours discussing. Some days the topic was fountain pens (Montblanc versus Alfred Dunhill), or stationery (Crane, the only choice), or china (Limoges versus Royal Copenhagen), or crystal (Lalique versus Baccarat), or cutlery (Sabatier versus Gerber), or watches (Rolex versus Omega), and on and on and on. Uncle Alexis didn't seem to enjoy these debates; at best he tolerated them because my mother was his wife's sister. Once during our visit to New York, I overheard him saying to his wife, my Aunt Joan, "Gertrude has good taste, but she takes it a little too seriously."

Most of these discussions between my mother and my uncle didn't interest me because I was only twelve years old, but one day in New York I walked into the living room and the topic was cars. Alexis, talking excitedly, had raced automobiles in Europe before World War II, as well as designed them for such custom-coach-making firms as Vanden Plas of Brussels, so he knew a thing or two about driving machines. I didn't care so much who won the argument, but I was thrilled to hear my Russian uncle, in his thick accent, talk with such enthusiasm about cars. With his rather formal vocabulary and sophisticated passion, he spoke about automobiles he loved the way a parent talks about a first child. Of his father's big Mercedes-Benz touring car, he said, "Our chauffeur was a devotee of the open cutout, and when this monster roared along at sixty-five miles an hour with flames shooting from the cutout, I knew my future would be connected with big, fast, beautiful cars."

"I wouldn't own a German car, I don't care how good they are," my mother said.

"I understand how you feel, Gertrude," my uncle said, "but a car has nothing to do with National Socialism."

"The same companies made tanks and planes that killed American boys."

"That's true, of course, but not really relevant to which cars are best."

"You drive a Buick Roadmaster, so don't talk to me about German cars," my mother said.

"Yes, I do, but only because that's all I can afford. It's as fine a car as they make in the States—nimble handling, spirited response, wonderful cornering grip. For an American car, that is."

"No, no," my mother said, "give me a Chrysler product any day."

They went on, comparing styling attributes, quality of appointments, and ease of driving. At one point my uncle announced, "Gertrude, having a fine automobile is the greatest pleasure life offers. Without exception. The sense of vigor and dominion is euphoric." My mother nodded her head.

Looking back now I find these discussions with my uncle quite ironic. My mother owned none of the things she so hotly defended. How she could be such an authority on what was best is a mystery, since she did not have, nor had she ever had, any of the things she praised so much. It was two years later, 1951, before we owned a car.

When I think about my Uncle Alexis's passion for automobiles, I realize how important cars were to him, to my mother, and to all of us—but in confusing ways. On television, when Donald Sutherland's voice announces, "A Volvo will save your soul," I sense my Southern Baptist relatives flinching, for it's clear that they and Volvo have very different ideas about salvation. It's easy to dismiss an ad that claims a car can save your soul, but I have to admit I was impressed by the commercial that said James Bond drove a BMW Z3 roadster in his latest movie, *Tomorrow Never Dies* (1997).

A friend of mine, a man in his fifties, bought a new Mazda Miata convertible, and I asked him why. He said, "I wanted a car that would turn me on." I had to bite my lip to keep from laughing out loud. Not only was it funny that the car was supposed to turn my friend on, rather than the other way around, but his sentence was almost the same as one that another friend had used that day to describe why she left her husband of twenty years. "He didn't turn me on anymore," she said.

I didn't go see the James Bond movie because I can't afford to buy a BMW, and I didn't want to leave the movie feeling like an inferior human being. Much too much do I want to have all the bright and beautiful things shown in a film. After seeing the movie *E.T.* (1982), I went right out and bought Reese's Pieces. I may even have bought some Reese's Pieces during the movie. Doing so doesn't surprise me since movies and food go together. I consume images and I consume food. I eat what the actors eat, I eat while watching a movie, and I eat the movie.

The connection in my mind between movies and food goes back to the days when as a child I began reading a newspaper, *The New Orleans Times-Picayune*, and saw on the same page with the movie listings a sampling of recipes—shrimp Creole, fruit salad, deep-dish blackberry cobbler. I remember once seeing an ad for some Jack Benny movie, and next to it a recipe for meat loaf. Food and movies went together. Going to the movies was forever linked with candy and soda pop and popcorn, especially at the Mecca, where the concession stand was actually in the theater, fully visible off to the right in an alcove on one side of the screen. Everyone who went to get food was seen by everyone in the audience. Even better, while standing at the concession stand, I didn't have to miss any of the movie, since I could watch it over my shoulder while getting my snack.

I remember vividly where the concession stand was because sometimes I had no extra money, and it would bother me to see my friends and other people go there and buy food. My mouth would water, making me feel sorry for myself, and I would turn back to the movie, concentrating on it as much as possible. My father would give me money to get in to see the movie, but he would never pay for candy, even when we went together. That was my obligation, out of my allowance, he would say. Sometimes I had used up all of my allowance.

I like movies where food is important, particularly *Like Water for Chocolate* (1992), *Big Night* (1996), *Babette's Feast* (1987), *Eat Drink Man Woman* (1994), and the Marx Brothers' *Room Service* (1938), but it is hard to sit still and watch such movies without salivating so much that I have to run out and get some popcorn or a candy bar. I remember W. C. Fields in *The Bank Dick* (1940), ordering an ice cream soda and, in his mock heroic manner, blowing the foam off the top as if it's a beer. The way that Charlie Chaplin eats his shoe in *The Gold Rush* (1925) made me certain that the shoe was delicious. My favorite eating film is Marco Ferreri's *La grande bouffe* (1973). Not only do I get to enjoy vicariously all the dishes that are prepared and eaten in the movie, but I am also able to feel really self-righteous at the end because the four gourmets who gorge themselves for days finally die, and grotesquely.

The master of food in film is Hitchcock, for he really understands the similarity between eating and watching movies, as well as the way food, sex, and violence are related. In the director's *Sabotage* (1936), the bomb maker keeps his incendiary ingredients in food jars and bottles. Describing the making of a bomb, he says he would mix "a little tomato sauce with some strawberry jam." Later, in the same film, the saboteur is killed with a knife his wife has just used to serve a dinner of meat and potatoes. The killer in Hitchcock's *Frenzy* (1972) is always snacking. Before killing one victim, he takes a big bite out of her apple, another mouthful after the murder, and then, walking out the door, he carries the rest of the apple with him.

Early in the same film, in a brief aside about Jack the Ripper and his victims, a man says, "He used to carve 'em up. Sent a bird's kidney to Scotland Yard." Bird is slang for woman, but it very specifically ties together killing and eating. While the killer's appetites for food, sex, and violence are out of control in *Frenzy*, almost the opposite is true for his pursuer, a Scotland Yard inspector who must pretend to like an array of ghastly foods that his wife serves up. While he talks to her about rape, sadism, impotency, and murder, the inspector keeps his feelings in check, trying desperately to find some meat on a tiny bird that his wife has cooked for him. As he tells her about the killer having to break the fingers of one victim to remove something from her hand, the wife breaks a breadstick in half, the sound identical to the one made when the fingers were broken. Uncontrolled lust for murder, sex, and food are all intertwined within the film, and the film's viewer gets an uneasy pleasure from watching these associations. To see is to have, to kill is to eat, to consume is to kill, to watch most movies is to eat them. Only the great movies resist immediate consumption.

* * *

I like to consume things too, especially as a way to escape from whatever is bothering me. In April 1945—a month and a year that are vividly recalled—my dad and I went to the Mecca on a Friday, expecting a Western, as usual, but that night they were showing *Sundown* (1941). Because Gene Tierney was in the film, and since she and Ruth Roman were my favorite actresses, I've never forgotten the title. My dad said he had seen the film a few years before, he thought, and he was disappointed there wasn't a Western. I also recall *Sundown* because it took place in Africa. When we arrived, the movie had already begun, but we never cared much about reaching the Mecca on time, often arriving in the middle of a movie and staying to see the beginning. The long break between the ending and the beginning was a time to relax, a time to anticipate how the film would begin, and, most important, a time to talk. It was the one place my father felt free to carry on a conversation with me.

When *Sundown* ended, we sat in our seats, looking at the numbers on our ticket stubs. It was Dish Night and a man was standing on the stage twirling around a basket filled with ticket stubs. Finally, he reached in, pulled out a stub, and read the number. Neither my father nor I had the winner, but a lady shrieked nearby and ran down the aisle to get her free dinner plate. My dad and I sat a little longer, waiting for the beginning of the program. We expected a cartoon, a newsreel with images of the war in Europe or the Pacific, maybe a Fitzgerald travelogue or a comic short with the Three Stooges or Edgar Kennedy. Then there'd be the beginning of the feature we had just seen end. Dad didn't move; he seemed to want to be quiet, so I was, too. By now he would have usually said a word or two about the last half of the movie we had just seen, or we would have gone to the concession stand for a snack, but not this time. Finally, he said, "I'm leaving for Africa soon."

Wow, I thought to myself, Africa! "Where?" *Sundown* had taken place in a part I'd never seen before.

"Liberia. In West Africa."

I didn't know east from west in Africa, or where Liberia was. "Where Tarzan lives?"

"More like that, yes," my dad said, and then, after a long pause, he added, "if there were a Tarzan."

Tarzan was pretty real to me. To my dad, too—at least we talked about Tarzan as if he were real. "Is the war going on there, too?" For my father to be a war hero was a secret wish of mine.

He shook his head.

I asked, "Then I can go with you?"

He shook his head again.

Now I was starting to get worried. "How long will you be gone?"

My father looked away, then looked quickly back, as if he were determined to keep his eyes on me. He stared a long time before he spoke. "A couple of years." Then he quickly added, "But every year I'll come home for two weeks."

A couple of years? My father turned away and stared at the screen as if the movie were playing. I did, too, looking straight ahead for a long time.

I asked him, "Is this because FDR died?" For some reason I thought that maybe my dad's leaving was connected to Franklin Roosevelt's death, which had happened a few weeks earlier. My father had been very upset and had taken me to a memorial service at the big Christ Church cathedral, which I had never been to before.

"FDR?" my father asked.

I nodded.

"No, it doesn't have anything to do with FDR."

I waited, hoping he would give me some explanation about why he was leaving. Eventually, without turning my head, I asked, "Can I have some money to get candy?" Without looking at me, my father pulled out a half-dollar. I ran over to the concession stand and spoke to Mary, the old snaggle-toothed woman who waited on people. She always wore an apron, as if she were a cook, when all she ever made was popcorn. "I'll have a Baby Ruth, some Cracker Jacks, and a Coca-Cola." Mary served me with about as much display of emotion as the blank wall behind her. It took almost the whole half-dollar to pay for everything, but I didn't think twice about spending all my father's money.

* * *

Much of my love-hate attitude toward shopping, consuming and acquiring things originated a week or so later, on Sunday morning, May 6, 1945. I remember the day clearly. It was a week before Mother's Day; I remember that, too. What happened first that morning was that my father left for Africa, just as he had told me he would. He didn't let my mother or me go with him to the train station because, as he said, "Saying good-bye is hard." It didn't make sense to me, since we were going to say good-bye somewhere, either at the station or at home. I remember him vividly standing in the hall of our house. He had picked me up in his arms, even though I was just a month shy of eight years old, and given me a big hug. When he put me down, he grabbed my head with one arm and, with the other hand, rubbed his knuckle in my scalp until it hurt so badly that I had to cry out, "Stop, Daddy!" Then he grinned ear to ear, chuckled a little, and walked down the hall to the front door, which had a big oval of glass in it that let the daylight in from the outside. Light bathed him as he said, "You go home and comfort your mother. You're the man now." And then he was gone.

Even though I had known that my Dad was leaving that morning, I still felt a huge pain in my stomach, as if someone had punched me, and it was hard to breathe. In my memory my mother is not standing in the hall. Surely she would have said good-bye to Dad, but in my recollection she's not there. As the front door closed, I ran back to my room and got into bed, pulling the covers over my head, but I had to remove them almost instantly to keep from being asphyxiated. The night before, my mother had spread Vicks VapoRub over my chest and the odor was still strong under the covers. Lying in bed was horrible. It wasn't possible to make myself go to sleep, and all the energy had been drained out of me. Caught in some state of suspension, floating, I sensed that I had forgotten something, but I couldn't remember what it was.

Finally able to get out of bed, I went to the living room. My mother was sitting there looking at the Sunday paper, while drinking coffee and munching on a piece of toast spread with fig preserves. I started to ask her for the funnies so I could read "Prince Valiant," but then I saw the front page, which was on the floor where she had dropped it. My father and I had been reading the headlines together every day for weeks, sensing that the war in Europe was coming to an end. I never read the front page by myself, waiting for my father to get home from work so that we could have the pleasure together. Underneath the words there would be war maps with huge black arrows pointing in different directions. In the last weeks before he departed for Africa, my father and I read excitedly every front page. I don't remember the exact headlines, but they were something like: "Mussolini Slain!" "Hitler Suicide!" "Berlin Falls!" My one great hope was that peace would come before my father left, believing that if peace came, he might not have to go away. No matter, he did leave, and later that Sunday morning, when I looked down at the newspaper headlines on the paper my mother had thrown on the floor, I read these exact words, I'm sure: "Patton Attacks to Smash Last Opposition to Allies." Reading that headline all by myself made me feel even more strongly that my father was gone.

I looked up at my mother, who was still dressed in a light blue housecoat over her pajamas. Since she was holding up the open paper, I couldn't see her face. She seemed oblivious to my father's departure, or at least she seemed oblivious to my feelings about my father's departure. From behind the paper, she began reading aloud what she was seeing in the paper, then commenting. "Someday Soon Canned Beer Will Be Back!" she read, then added, "None too soon, that's for sure. I'm tired of everything going to the front, tired of Victory Lemonade made with no sugar, tired of rationing, tired of reading casualty lists, tired of eating oleo, tired of seeing ads for recapped tires. Oh, look, Gus Mayer has a nice seersucker suit on sale." Mother sounded as if she were talking to herself as she continued: "They say they'll start making cars six to eighteen months after the surrender. That's fabulous. Wouldn't it be wonderful if we could buy a car? I know just what I want, a De Soto like Daddy used to have." She turned the page. "Look what nice saddle oxfords. And here's a beautiful bedroom suite on sale at Hurwitz-Mintz."

As I listened to her talk about cans and cars and seersucker suits, a wave of unease came over me. Dad was gone; Mother seemed to be absorbed in ads. She must have sensed something because she put her paper down and looked at me. "Come here," she said, and when I didn't move, she stood up and came toward me, her arms outstretched. Screaming between clenched teeth, I ran outside to a place behind my house that all the kids called the jungle. A swath of land that no one ever seemed to tend—overgrown with weeds, vines, bushes, and trees—the jungle was our playground, and one of my favorite hiding places. I ran to the other side of a tree, sat down, and cried. In a short while, I sensed someone else nearby and looked up. My mother was standing just a few feet away. She looked down with a sad face and finally spoke. "Let's go to a movie this afternoon. I'll take you downtown."

"It's Sunday," I said. "It's wrong to go to a movie on Sunday."

"Just this once it won't kill us."

We went to a movie, but strangely I have no idea what it was. Two days later I wanted to shout when the newspaper headline said, "V-E Proclamations Awaited Today," but I didn't. My father should have been there, reading the headline with me, dancing a jig around the living room, shouting, "Victory in Europe!"

* * *

It's good now and then to realize that some things were not made to be consumed (I try to remember this when I sense some of my students want me to predigest and package information for them). During the last Thanksgiving holidays, I visited again the Philadelphia Museum of Art, making my way to the wing of twentieth-century American art and walking quickly past a Barnett Newman, a Mark Rothko, a Frank Stella, a Robert Rauschenberg. Though nodding briefly at them like old friends, I didn't stop because I was headed for the end of the wing where there was a large room filled with works by Marcel Duchamp. Reaching it, I sat down on the bench that faced my favorite piece, *The Bride Stripped Bare by Her Bachelors, Even*, better known as *The Large Glass*. Very big, measuring about six by nine feet, the work looked as if it had shapes etched on the glass surface. The figures—abstract outlines of a bride, bachelors, a chocolate grinder, and other forms—were actually made out of lead foil, silver leaf, and wire, all squeezed between two large pieces of glass that had numerous cracks. Behind *The Large Glass*, there was a window, and looking through *The Large Glass*, and out the window, I saw a Christmas tree on the museum grounds, large red balls hanging from several dozen dark green branches. I smiled when I realized that *The Large Glass* was a window through which I saw another window, outside of which was a big tree that reminded me to hurry out and start my Christmas shopping. I said to myself, "Window-shopping." The juxtaposition seemed ironic to me; outside the museum was a symbol of shopping and inside was an object that, at least to me, couldn't be taken in and assimilated like some consumer product. I'm window-shopping but there's a piece of glass in the way and the store is closed.

    None of the writing I ever read about *The Large Glass* quite accounted for my experience of the piece. "A 'delay' in glass," Duchamp subtitled the work, "like a poem in prose." I thought most artworks, particularly most painting and sculpture, were a "delay," since they were all still images. Reading what Duchamp had written about *The Large Glass* hardly made the work more accessible. I did know that I liked standing in front of *The Large Glass* because my mind couldn't quite encompass it. The experience was akin to what I felt when I first walked into a great cathedral, the Duomo in Milan, and immediately said to myself, "What mind thought this up?" Most appealing to me was the way *The Large Glass* stayed distant and apart, not capable of being pigeonholed and reduced to an explanatory wall label. The monumentality was close to that of some huge nineteenth-century paintings, like Frederic Church's *Icebergs*, which is as big as *The Large Glass*. I am so used to being surrounded by objects that can be acquired and taken in at a glance, quickly and easily interpreted, that it was wonderful to look at something that remained defiantly Other—like an object in a store window that I can't reach through and have, or like an impossible love. In David Lynch's *Lost Highway* (1997), Pete says to Alice, while they're making love, "I want you." She leans down, whispers in his ear "You'll never have me," then gets up and walks away. Maybe Duchamp's "delay" is what I feel when I can't completely have whatever I want. Desire perpetually postponed: ceaseless window-shopping.

Not that I didn't have other thoughts about *The Large Glass*; I did. I found parts of it hilarious, or at least that was how I felt about some of the things that Duchamp said about his work. How could I not find it funny when he wrote, "The motor with quite feeble cylinders is a superficial organ of the Bride; it is activated by the love gasoline, a secretion of the Bride's sexual glands and by the electric sparks of the stripping." Humorous too was the way that the nine bachelors seemed solely in the service of the bride's desire. Many parts, like the "love motor" and the chocolate grinder, were things that could move, but seemed momentarily arrested.

All my responses to *The Large Glass* seemed inconsequential, thankfully, and it stayed unexplained, which was what I liked about it. Some movies have this quality, too, but it is rare. Dozens of books have been written about Bergman's *Persona* (1966), offering different and complex readings of a film that explores the relationship between a psychiatric nurse and her patient, an actress who has stopped speaking. None of these interpretations quite accounts for the mysterious and troubling power of the film. It stays apart, like *The Large Glass*. Even though I've read that the Stan Brakhage film *Dog Star Man* (1961–65) explores the cycle of the seasons, cosmology, the creation of consciousness, the conflict of humans and nature, sexual daydreams, and the struggle of a stumbling titan, I find myself more involved with the way the film seizes me. It can't be adequately interpreted, or reduced to a one-sentence blurb for *TV Guide*. It is itself, totally itself, not just some libidinal extension of me, my mind, my feelings.

As I sat on the museum's bench, staring at the Duchamp work, two nicely dressed women in their early thirties came into the room. They talked as they strolled around, hardly looking at what was in the space. In the corner, near one of Duchamp's ready-mades, a bicycle wheel mounted upside down on a stool, one woman said, "What a hoax." The other woman chuckled. I didn't want to agree, but in a way I did; Duchamp was a con man—for all the right reasons and in ways that are not obvious. The two women continued to walk around the room, passing in front of me. Oblivious to the fact that I was sitting on a bench looking at *The Large Glass,* and that they were blocking my view, the same woman said to the other one, "My friend Shirley got so tired of her kids constantly yelling, 'Mama! Mama! Mama! Mama!' that she told them she had changed her name to 'Shit.' And that's a word they weren't allowed to say!" The other woman let out a guffaw as the two moseyed out of the Duchamp room. They hadn't taken notice of me or of *The Large Glass.* If the room had been filled with works that were more easily assimilated, like those of a Norman Rockwell, I don't think the women would have been so blasé or told any jokes. They probably ignored *The Large Glass* because it was cracked. How could it be anything worth looking at if it was cracked? No self-respecting consumer buys anything that's cracked.

* * *

Buying doesn't always mean acquiring an object; sometimes it involves buying into a way of life. During the Christmas holidays in 1956, my father was home on one of his brief visits, and I was on break from college. Helen, the woman who usually lived with my mother, temporarily moved out while my father was in the States, but she spent most of her free time at our home. We were celebrating New Year's Eve with a big dinner.

Following my mother's strict instructions, Helen set an elegant table. Down the center, four red candlesticks stood in a line, each surrounded at the bottom by pieces of green holly. Underneath was a cream-colored cutwork linen tablecloth that my father had brought back from Madeira. My mother made a point of telling us that we were using "her" Gorham silver, Limoges china, and Waterford crystal. She said again, when Helen took the plates out of the china cabinet, "What I really wanted was Rosenthal, it's better than Limoges, but I never could afford it." My father ignored the comment.

A New Year's Eve dinner at my mother's house had multiple courses. We had already eaten a chicken and okra gumbo, as well as big plates of red beans and rice, when mother came in with a large tray of marinated crab claws, announcing, "Stop whatever you're doing and get ready to eat."

"I *am* eating," I said.

Mother waved a knife at me. "Eat, or I'll fix you so you'll never have children."

I laughed, which was a mistake. Mother glowered.

"I'd rather have my children healthy than bright!" Dad shouted.

All of us turned and looked at him.

"It's a line from a movie," Dad said.

"What movie?" Helen asked.

"It's from *Our Town*—you remember, Gertie, you always liked the scene where the couple drink strawberry sodas."

Not willing to be distracted, Mother responded, "No movie talk, Ed. Remember the rule at my table? We only talk about the food. Eat, Ted!"

I grabbed a crab claw, broke off the shell, ate the meat, stared at my mother, and said, "It's almost midnight."

"Midnight?" Mother screamed, then ran into the kitchen and returned with a bottle of champagne. "Open it quick, honey," she said as she handed the bottle to my dad.

He took one look and grimaced as if he had a gas pain. "Dom Pérignon? Good grief, Gert, who can afford—?"

Mother interrupted him. "Just open the bottle, or I'll get Ted to do it."

Shaking his head in defeat, my father opened the bottle, then walked around the table and filled each champagne glass. Looking at her watch, my mother announced, "Everybody up! One minute to the New Year!"

Helen sighed. "Gertie, I'm too old for this."

"You're never too old to see in the New Year!" Mother said. "Everybody up, up onto your chairs."

I dutifully climbed up into my chair. "C'mon, Helen, c'mon, Dad. It's the one tradition we have. Everybody has to jump into the New Year."

"Somebody please hold my hand till I get up," Helen said, and Dad helped her as she climbed up into the chair.

"I'm too old for these shenanigans," Dad announced.

Mother ignored him. "Thirty seconds!"

"C'mon, Dad, be a good sport!" I said, jumping down and helping him to squat in his chair.

Dad said, with a smile, "The air's too thin up here!"

"I'm the one who's too old for this, Ed," Helen said. "You're still a spring chicken."

Mother was fixed on her watch. "Get ready to jump into the New Year! Here we come, nineteen fifty-seven! Five-four-three-two-one! Happy New Year!"

Mother jumped from her chair to the floor, spilling a little of her champagne before taking a big gulp. Everybody called out, "Happy New Year!" Helen jumped without a mishap, and so did I, but Dad, standing up to jump, was losing his balance, and I had to move quickly to save him from falling. He forgot about his glass of champagne and spilled most of it. Swallowing what was left, sitting down again, Dad said, "I don't remember the title of the movie, but there was a scene in it where Victor Mature sits down with Richard Widmark and they order a huge bottle of expensive champagne, take one sip, and then get up to leave. I wanted to holler, 'Finish the champagne!'"

When nobody laughed, Dad stood up. "It's late and I'm tired. Good night."

"I wish you wouldn't leave me," Mother said. "Be happy, honey."

"No, I'm tired, really; you stay and have a good time." Dad walked to Mother and kissed her. "Happy New Year, sweetheart."

As he left, my mother said, "We haven't even told our New Year's resolutions," but Dad ignored her and went up the steps to their bedroom. Mother ran into the kitchen and returned with another bottle of champagne and a silver tray with two little bowls surrounded by crackers and lemon wedges. One bowl had diced pieces of boiled egg and the other bowl was full of black caviar. "I have two more courses, so don't anyone else leave."

She handed me the bottle to open, but I put it down and stood up. "It's getting late."

"No!" my mother shouted, jumping to her feet and bursting into tears.

Looking at my mother, Helen said, "I think it's time you went to bed, honey. You've partied enough."

Mother put her arms around Helen and they kissed briefly on the lips. "I don't want to go to bed yet," Mother said, sitting down. "It's a new year, time to make resolutions. I want to make a resolution."

Now I was curious. "What resolution?"

"Lord in Heaven, I resolve to cancel the New Year. I don't want to go forward, I want to go back. Back home."

Helen and I both said, almost simultaneously, "You are home."

Mother said, "No, I mean really go home. Helen, stay here tonight. Sleep in the guest room, please."

Nodding, Helen said, "Let's go to bed, honey." She and Mother walked out of the dining room, their arms around one another.

I opened the champagne and filled my glass, then spread caviar on a cracker, added a few tidbits of egg, and squeezed some lemon juice on top. I swilled a little champagne around in my mouth, then put in the caviar-covered cracker and bit down. A burst of salty, fish flavor hit my palate, and I smiled, letting the taste roam around my mouth a little, filling every corner, then washed it down with a sip of champagne, Dom Pérignon champagne. It was the best—wet and dry, sweet and tangy, smooth and crisp, all at the same time. The cool odor of the alcohol rose into the back of my nose. At such a moment, my mother's way of living was very tempting.

* * *

Although my mother is dead now, I can easily imagine making a film in which she and I go shopping in New Orleans, especially if we are going to buy me clothes. The point of view is very important, so I want to think carefully about the use of the camera. In the opening long shot of my movie footage, my mother and I are entering Canal Place, a new emporium on Canal Street in New Orleans that looks like it has as much travertine marble as the Vatican.

The camera cuts to a shot of the men's department on the second floor of the Saks Fifth Avenue store, where my mother and I appear soon, riding up the escalator. I am heard saying, in voice-over, "This is not a good idea." The hand-held camera follows my mother in profile as she walks erect and determined, like the figure on the prow of a ship, over to a young saleswoman who wears a dark maroon pants suit with a jacket cut like a man's double-breasted coat. "Hello, may I help you?" the young woman says as she looks curiously at my mother in her best Chanel suit, and then at me in my Lands' End shirt, Dockers pants, and Rockport Walkers.

My mother says, "Yes, my name is Gertrude Perry, and this is my son. May I ask your name?"

"Bea, Mrs. Perry."

"Bea? Beatrice?"

"Yes, ma'am."

"We'd like to look at your fall suits, something in navy, a light worsted wool."

"Just follow me," Beatrice says. We walk over toward the suits, but I stop for a moment and pick up a pair of Lorenzo Banfi shoes. With my back to my mother, I turn them over. The price tag says $385. I put them quickly down and turn around.

The camera point of view shifts to what I see: In the distance my mother and Beatrice are talking animatedly, like old friends. When the saleswoman holds up a suit, Mother shakes her head, so Beatrice puts it back and gets another off the rack. Mother reaches out to touch the lapels, the collar, and the shoulder padding. She has to finger clothes, examine the cut, feel the material, run her fingers over the stitching, inspect the lining, squeeze the shoulder pads. There's an adding machine in her fingers, so she can tell immediately what a suit is worth.

I enter the shot from screen-left. Beatrice is holding a six-button, double-breasted, double-vent dark navy suit with a faint pinstripe. My mother has finished the finger test and is now looking intently at the garment. I'm not sure if she's going to buy it or eat it.

"Wool and cashmere, Mrs. Perry. Ermenegildo Zegna."

Mother has a gray shirt in her hand. She reaches inside the plastic to give the shirt her finger test, then places it next to the suit the young woman is holding up.

"Joseph Abboud, a very fine shirt," Beatrice says.

My voice-over is heard: "Banfi, Zegna, Abboud—they sound like a school of guppies. Abboud? A designer whose last name doesn't end in a vowel! I would point this out to my mother, but she would just say, 'Don't be obvious.'"

Saying, "I have a Nicole Miller tie that would be perfect," Beatrice walks over to the ties on a table, pulls one out, and starts back. "These bright ties are very *in* this—" The young saleswoman stops, sensing from my mother's face that what's in doesn't matter to this lady. Beatrice spins around and goes back, returning quickly with a different tie, which she describes as "Robert Talbott." My mother examines this new combination.

"Perfect. Try the suit on, Ted." I leave to put the suit on, while Beatrice and Mother carry on a conversation about food and clothes and a new restaurant in New Orleans.

I return just as a man enters who has a measuring tape around his neck. "Up here," he says, motioning for me to stand up on a little box in front of a three-way mirror. From the expression on my face it's obvious that I don't like the way the tailor snaps his order at me, and I like even less the way he checks my crotch, then pulls and tugs on the coat, marking it here and there with his piece of flat chalk. As he starts to mark my cuff, Mother's voice is heard saying, offhandedly, "A slight break in the cuff, please."

"Turn your back to the mirror," the tailor barks.

I spin around and then look over my shoulder. The camera cuts to what I see in the mirror—the back of my head, as well as Beatrice holding the Abboud shirt with the Talbott tie. In voice-over I say: "My hair is completely gray now, and really thin on the crown. I'm sixty years old and I'm letting my mother buy me clothes that cost several weeks' salary. The tailor is treating me like a baby. It's like the grocery store scene in Wilder's *Double Indemnity*, where Fred MacMurray and Barbara Stanwyck meet to plot her husband's murder. The couple, talking in the baby food section, are like babies, selfish and insistent on getting what they want. Babies and greed. Food and violence. Consumption and murder. Buy food, kill people—what's the difference?"

The camera cuts back to a wide shot. "Be still!" the tailor calls out as I step down from the little box and walk over to my mother. She looks at me in the suit and says, "You look so precious when you wear nice clothes."

I say to her, "I don't want it." Beatrice and my mother look at me as if I've just pulled the pin on a hand grenade.

The outside entrance to Canal Place is shown in the next shot. After a beat I come out the front door, dressed as I was when I went in. Walking forward, stopping, I look down at my battered black Rockports and say out loud, "You should have at least let her buy you the Lorenzo Banfi shoes."

After a slight pause more words of mine are heard in a voice-over: "My mother is dead, she's been dead almost twenty years. This movie was just imagined, made up. I can reshoot the whole thing as the young saleswoman's story—telling what she was thinking while she waited on us, how she felt talking to my mother, what her reaction was watching me leave. If the movie's done from Beatrice's point of view, nobody will realize that I hurt my mother's feelings so much. The episode needs to be redone anyway. The camera is much too static, hardly ever moving; the images aren't striking; and the whole sequence depends too much on the dialogue. It's just talking heads. Maybe Beatrice can dance and sing a little."

5 Journey-Proud

THE NEXT TIME I WENT TO NEW Orleans, I stopped in Mississippi and took the train the rest of the way into the city, wanting to make the same trip that my Grandfather Stevens did in 1890, when he traveled on a train for the first time. I know this about Samuel Rawlins Stevens, my mother's father, even though he died when I was seven, because he recorded his life in an autobiography that he typed himself for his children. What I also have are many letters that he wrote to family members, as well as two books he published himself, one about trees and the other a collection of his poems. I have always been fascinated by Grandfather Stevens, though I'm not sure why. Perhaps it's only because I have so much information concerning the man; but there's something else. I never heard anyone ever say anything negative about him, which has made me suspicious. My mother worshiped her father. It always seemed to me that he was a powerful figure in my family, and that understanding him would yield some crucial insights. He wrote so effusively about his first train excursion that I thought I would try taking the same trip. If New Orleans would not yield up all its secrets directly, maybe I could approach it a different way—along a train track from Mississippi.

As the train moved away from the station, I tried to imagine what his trip would have been like in 1890, but it was difficult to re-create a past that must have once been enchanting, when what I saw along the tracks was decay, as if all the little towns had turned their backsides to the train tracks. There was nothing charming about woods so wrapped in kudzu vines that distant pastures were almost hidden, nor was there much allure in rusting propane tanks, mobile homes, drainage ditches filled with luminescent green scum, and city signs so faded they were unreadable, particularly from a moving train. Now and then I did catch a glimpse of the kind of woods my grandfather loved—tall yellow pines, blooming dogwood, wild honeysuckle vines—but the sights weren't powerful enough to ignite some special connection to my mother's father. Seeing a satellite dish by a home in the woods reminded me of Kieślowski's film *Red* (1994), in which Jean-Louis Trintignant plays a retired judge who is using electronic equipment to spy on his neighbors' phone conversations. He defends himself by telling Irène Jacob what it was like to be a judge: "I don't know whether I was on the good or the bad side." Motioning toward his array of listening gear, Trintignant adds, "Here, at least, I know where the truth is." Would that there were some electronic equipment that I could use to eavesdrop on the truth of my grandfather's thoughts then, as he rode the train through the Mississippi countryside. Without that ability, my own train ride felt like a waste of time.

Then, as the train picked up speed and rushed through the countryside, I began to sense something unexpected, as if I had been picked up by the scruff of the neck and flung toward some infinite destination. I felt like one of the people in the States of Mind paintings by Umberto Boccioni, where furious brush strokes and disjointed images capture the mad frenzy of passengers, trains, and stations. As I experienced my train under, around, and on top of me, I realized in an instant that I was feeling exactly what my grandfather had felt—the overwhelming power of being pulled forward, flung toward something he could not see. Automobiles could be stopped, bicycles could be braked, horses could be reined in, but this train felt totally out of my control, and, in 1890 at age nine, on his first train trip, it must have seemed even more so to my grandfather. He wasn't riding on a train, he was being catapulted helplessly through space. He must have felt overpowered, as if grasped by a will greater than his own, yet also comfortably carried into the future without having to make any decision or any effort.

Imagining how my grandfather experienced the force of the train pulling him through the Mississippi countryside, I was reminded of how much my mother's father liked to be on the move. He was, as my Southern relatives say, journey-proud, which means he loved to travel. Grandfather Stevens was a man who loved anything that moved: horses, carriages, trains, cars. One of the greatest thrills of his life, he wrote in his autobiography, was the time when his father first brought home a beautiful new four-wheeled, two-seated, horse-drawn carriage: "I ran and jumped and laughed, it seems to me, for hours. That beautiful surrey. All around the top—and this was the prettiest thing about the whole vehicle—extended little tassels hanging down about four inches. These tassels would dance and ripple from the movement of the carriage while in motion."

My grandfather's enthusiasm for the surrey was an early manifestation of his journey-proud gene, a love of movement that permeated every cell in his body. Wanting very much to understand this impulse, I studied his autobiography carefully. During his sixty-three years, my grandfather made a home in each of these towns and cities: Magnolia, Starksville, Picayune, Tylertown, Philadelphia, and Jackson in Mississippi; Madisonville, Natalbany, Kentwood, and New Orleans in Louisiana; Louisville in Kentucky; Dayton in Ohio; Kansas City in Kansas; New York City and Long Island in New York; Macon, Atlanta, and College Park in Georgia; Houston and Dallas in Texas; Caddo Gap in Arkansas; and also Washington, D.C.

The long list of cities and states doesn't really do justice to all his moves because he lived in some of these places several times, returning after a venture elsewhere had changed or ended. In many of those years, when he traveled all over the Southeast inspecting sawmills for the Southern Pine Association, he had no home base at all and lived in different hotels. He was, in my mythology of him, like the heroes of certain Western movies—Alan Ladd in *Shane* (1953), or Gregory Peck in *The Gunfighter* (1950)—who lived constantly on the move. Larger than life, these men could never be tied down to one house, or one locale, or one set of conventions. Romantic wayfarers, they stopped now and then in a community to restore order and justice, but then they left, wandering again through the wilderness. They could not be domesticated.

The chronology of my grandfather's jobs and cities was overwhelming, and the first time I read his autobiography I thought, how incredible that he would have been forced to move so often, but then always been able to pick himself up and start over again. Presumably, all his difficulties were the experience of most people trying to make a living in the first half of the twentieth century. Later I began to question this simple explanation, even as I began to understand why his life obsessed me so.

* * *

That first train trip of my grandfather in 1890 was given to him when he was nine years old as a prize for learning his multiplication tables. He went to visit his older brother, Homie, who lived seventy miles away in New Orleans and came home many weekends. One Sunday my grandfather rode back with him. The journey was so thrilling that he recalled it vividly over forty years later when he was typing his autobiography. The wood-burning engine sent soot, and sometimes sparks, into the air, and the smell reminded him of his mother's wood-burning stove. Not everything about his trip to New Orleans was appealing. About the city he wrote:

> *The stench and smelliness of everything made a lasting impression on my childish nostrils. I had been used to the scent of the freshly ploughed ground, the aroma of the pine needles in the woods, the sweet floating perfume of the wild flowers and the invigorating spring air laden with many pleasing odors. These terrible smells of open sewers and rotting garbage and animals left in the streets offended my sensitive nose no little. The only part I truly loved was the ride on the train.*

Reading Grandfather Stevens's account of his first train trip, the visit to New Orleans, I would have expected that he would never leave home again, but in 1896, at age fifteen, he took the train back to the city to visit the same brother, Homie. The next day they took yet another train out to New Orleans's West End, on Lake Pontchartrain. On a pier out over the water was a large open-air concert hall, and there, after the music was over and it was dark, a large booth was rolled out along a track made of two-by-fours. Inside the booth was a projector (if you paid an extra ten cents, you could look inside the booth), and it threw moving pictures onto a big screen with the lake in the background. Watching these little short subjects, my grandfather was amazed to see street scenes of Paris, France, even some kind of a pillow fight, and cowboys riding at a swift gallop. Everything was so real he kept looking back at the projector booth to make sure there was actually a light coming out of the apparatus. A man eating and drinking appeared on the screen next, and then, as if by magic, the food and the drink came out of his mouth and went back onto the plate and into the glass! My mother's father had never seen anything like it, and he was stunned. Was this the kind of fare that was available in the city all the time?

Then my grandfather saw a couple kissing on the screen, and it startled him. Never before had he seen in public a man and woman kiss on the lips. He turned to look at his older brother and caught him smiling. So that was the idea—the older brother introducing the younger brother to wickedness. My grandfather put his hand in front of his eyes, so his brother would know how he felt, but the picture was too fascinating. He peeked through his fingers at the kiss, which seemed to go on forever but really lasted only a few seconds. Picture shows, to my grandfather's mind, were from that day on associated with perversion and magic, in some odd combination. For years, remembering the perversion, he stayed away, but eventually the magic pulled him back into the movie theaters.

* * *

The train trips to New Orleans were just the first of the many journeys for my grandfather. His willingness to travel somewhere and start a new business or job, supposedly in the service of his family, made him seem brave, even entrepreneurial. Yet the more I studied his autobiography, the more I began to realize that there was something else at work in my grandfather's journeys, and after reading and rereading his autobiography, I finally realized what it was. He loved starting something new, yes; on his own and in a new place, yes; and he loved feeling like a special person; but all these ecstasies wore off after a while and then a despair would set in, the black dog, as he called it. When that happened and he could no longer bear being alone, he would bring his wife and children to join him. In a short while—days, weeks, months, sometimes even a year—the job or the business would come to an abrupt end, almost as if he had willed it as a way to flee family life, and he would have to move on, alone, and start again. There were exceptions—I can't blame my grandfather for wars and armistices, hurricanes, panics, and depressions—but more often than not the stark reality of family life, having his wife and children actually with him, led to the end of a job or a business and a move to a new place.

Thinking about the contradictions of my grandfather's life, caught as he was between his love for his family and the difficulties he had living with them, I realized that his dilemma has been echoed again and again, although more dramatically, throughout the history of film. Within the past fifty years the happy togetherness of the family in the Hardy Family series of the thirties and forties evolved into the turmoil of the families in several Douglas Sirk films of the fifties, and then into the chaos of the warring, cannibalistic household of Hooper's *The Texas Chain Saw Massacre* (1974). Traditional family life has come to look more and more problematic in films.

Michael, in *The Godfather, Part II* (1974), speaking to his mother about his father, asks, "By being strong for his family, could he lose it?"

"But," she says, "you can never lose your family."

Michael's response, "Times are changing," suggests that he has an inkling of what his strength for his family is actually doing to them. As if he has not heard himself, he keeps on being strong, but the end result is that he destroys his marriage, alienates his sister, and kills his brother. My grandfather also must have thought he was being strong for his family, ever moving on to new situations in order to make a living, but the fact is that my grandfather fled family life, always asserting that he was doing so to provide for his wife and children. Who is to say if he did them more harm or more good?

Yet I am bothered by my willingness to accept such a simplified view of my grandfather's motives and personality. My bias usually is to see people as very complicated, but here I was, in the interest of understanding my mother's father, making him into a one-dimensional character. It made me think of a time when my dad and I were both home, he from Africa and I from school. While away at college I had seen a few foreign films, and I wanted my dad to watch one with me, so I asked him to go to Fellini's *La strada* (1954).

We went to the Civic movie theater on Baronne Street, a place we had never been before. My father was restless through the whole movie, squirming about in his seat and clearing his throat, so I knew he didn't like it. At first I was a little ill at ease myself, but I think it was because the film had subtitles, and I wasn't used to them. Within a few moments I stopped noticing, so caught up was I in the story of the character, played by Anthony Quinn, who makes his living by putting on strongman acts in one Italian village after another. Giulietta Masina is a young woman Quinn has bought from her mother to be his assistant. A young innocent, Masina seems to be thrilled by her role, but Quinn treats her badly, and when she slips into crying and deep remorse after Quinn has killed her friend, Richard Basehart, she is hardly able to function. Quinn abandons her, but the film ends with him discovering that she is dead, and he, once the insensitive brute, weeps over what he has done. Maybe the story is a little melodramatic, but it touched me so deeply that at the end of the film I was startled to find myself in a movie theater.

While I wanted to tell my father how much the film impressed me, I hesitated, seeing that he was not happy. As we stood up to leave, he said, "I saw a foreign film once, *Godzilla*. It was a lot better, and it didn't have little captions on the screen. It's like reading a comic strip. I couldn't concentrate on the picture."

"I saw *Godzilla*, too, Dad, but the people talked funny. What they said didn't go with the way their lips moved. The English was dubbed in."

"I'd sure as heck rather that than have to read words on top of the picture."

After a pause I said, "I don't like dubbing."

"They ought to make them all in English in the first place," my father said.

I didn't respond. I did not want to hear or say anything about *La strada*, good or bad. It had moved me too much. My father seemed to be miles away, even though we were walking side by side toward St. Charles Avenue to catch a streetcar.

After a block my father said, "The movie is ugly, and it's about ugly people. Whatever happened to truth and beauty?"

Although silent, I was thinking that my father was incapable of appreciating a movie where the characters were more complicated than Ken Maynard. It wasn't true, but I took some pride in thinking that way, if for no other reason than to justify a belief that I would never again like my father's kind of movie—simple, with one-dimensional characters. I would forever reject such films, even when they were allegorical and deliberately uncomplicated in order to make a point.

Yet, thinking about my Grandfather Stevens, reading his autobiography, I was creating an explanation of his behavior that was so simple that I would scoff at it in a movie.

* * *

Grandfather Stevens had a passion for wood, being on the road, and starting something new in a different place. He also liked "picture shows"—so said my Aunt Leontine, his daughter. Knowing my interests, she told me often about her father and the movies. His first experience, at the West End of New Orleans, was unpleasant, my aunt said, so he vowed never to go again. For years he refused to set foot in a theater where moving pictures were shown, and he wouldn't let his children go to one either. When he first moved to Dayton in 1915, and was so lonely there, he did try to watch a show called *The Cheat* (1915), but, as my Aunt Leontine told the story, when a woman agreed to give herself to a man in exchange for $10,000, he left the theater. It disgusted him. Even worse, until that moment he had found himself absolutely enthralled by what he was experiencing. The people on the screen seemed so totally at home in their surroundings, so self-assured, and my grandfather was jealous. Something bad should happen to the woman, he found himself wishing; she was so frivolous, spending money foolishly, undermining her husband's attempts to be prudent about their finances. Not only couldn't Grandfather Stevens stand the way she sold herself for money, he didn't like feeling such anger toward the woman, and he also didn't like being so caught up in what he saw on the screen.

Yet he knew that ministers and educators in Dayton and elsewhere were endorsing some moving pictures, and he felt that he should try again. Though his family had joined him in Dayton during the closing months of 1916, he still went to the next picture show alone, not at all sure that this form of entertainment was suitable for his wife and children. "Clean Films for Clean People" was what the banner said outside the theater he went into, but my grandfather didn't trust the sign and had to see for himself. The film that he went to see in Dayton was called *Civilization* (1916), and it moved him deeply. His heart was thrilled by the way in which one man, an inventor of munitions and the captain of a submarine, refuses to fire on a ship that has innocent women and children aboard. This submarine captain is literally transformed into someone who will not make war and who preaches peace.

According to my Aunt Leontine's story, one of the other images that touched her father was that of a horse pawing its master, a soldier who had died in battle and was lying on the ground. Eyebright, a little mare my grandfather loved so much and rode everywhere as a child, came to mind, and he felt more for the horse on the screen than he did for the dead soldier. The images of war were horrible and they reminded him of his own father's Civil War stories. The fires that broke out in the forests, the trees embedded with grapeshot, the stench of the corpses, the screams of the dying men, these were all things his father had described in graphic detail. Grandfather Stevens left the movie theater in Dayton a confirmed pacifist and the next day he brought his whole family back to see *Civilization*. Less than a year later his worst nightmare became reality as America entered the war in Europe. Not too many days afterward, he was passing the same theater, and some men were burning an effigy of the Kaiser out front.

Remembering my Aunt Leontine's story about her father and the movie, I looked at *Civilization* again and found it quite remarkable, even today. Its antiwar message is about as profound as that of any film ever made, but its religious sentiments are a little strange, and I'm surprised that my grandfather didn't react differently. Because a fight broke out when the submarine captain refused to fire on the other ship, he lies dying. Christ enters this officer's body, brings him back to life, and comes back to earth in the person of the man, preaching peace. I don't think most Christians believe such a thing can happen, and I don't see how they could have accepted it then, except that the experience of the film was so powerful that nobody stopped to ask any theological questions.

A year or so later my grandfather took his eldest son with him to see another picture show, and one of the shorts was a Charlie Chaplin comedy, *Shoulder Arms* (1918). My Aunt Leontine remembered this event, and what her father said, because she was so jealous that her brother got to go. Grandfather Stevens expected that he and his son would laugh, and his son did laugh, but my grandfather was upset by the images of war, however innocent they seemed to be. In the film Chaplin tries to go to sleep in a room half full of water. A man is floating in the same water, with only his face and hands visible, and nearby on a raised cot several men are huddled haphazardly on top of one another. They looked like stacked corpses to my grandfather, and they made him think again of his own father's descriptions of the dead after the Civil War battle of Shiloh. The water in the film, too, made him think of that conflict, where the soldiers had been out in the open during a fierce thunderstorm the night before. The accounts of the Civil War battle had been so vivid that my grandfather recoiled at thinking of them again; he didn't like remembering the stories or being reminded of his father's foot, crippled so badly by a bullet at Shiloh. Later that year, when the great influenza epidemic hit and soldiers were dying by the hundreds, Grandfather Stevens thought again of the Chaplin film. Soldiers dying by a bullet or with influenza didn't seem so funny.

My grandfather rarely said much about the movies that he saw, but, as my aunt said, his infrequent verbal accounts were quite vivid. One memory was of a film that seemed to take place in a little rural community strikingly like his own. How could the people who made the picture have known what his life was like as a child? What seized my grandfather's attention was a scene in which a woman—Lillian Gish, he thought—is baking apples in front of an open fire, and popping corn in the same fire, much as he did in the home outside Magnolia. That much about the movie my grandfather remembered clearly, although he couldn't recall many more details. What really impressed him about the film was its great promise: everything turns out for the best, so long as you work hard and wait. All his life he remembered this film; and not just because he shared its sentiments, but also because he had, as he said, a "special affection" for Lillian Gish.

In Kansas City, where he lived by himself for almost a year in 1924, my grandfather went to several movies. One show in particular, called *Sherlock, Jr.* (1924), with Buster Keaton, stood out in his memory. My grandfather used to tell my Aunt Leontine about one moment in the film, when Buster is trying to get rid of a piece of paper that is stuck to the bottom of his shoe. He tries to use the other shoe to hold it down, but of course the paper gets stuck to the other shoe. He peels it off with his fingers but then he can't free his fingers. Just when it's certain that Keaton may never be able to rid himself of the sticky paper, the comedian suddenly wheels around and kneels down, just in time to place the piece of paper right in the path of a man who emerges unexpectedly from a nearby door. The paper sticks to this man's shoe, and he walks away. "Buster's action took my breath away," said my grandfather, who was startled and surprised. The comedian had a wonderful ability to find a solution to any problem by using his brain and being quick. My grandfather liked that; in fact, he really admired it. *Sherlock, Jr.,* is filled with moments when Buster finds a wonderfully imaginative way to get himself out of the worst predicaments, always with a straight face, as when his car falls into water and he quickly makes a sail out of the canvas top.

A Chaplin film my grandfather had seen years before had a similar moment. Charlie is running a pawnshop and a man comes in who seems desperate for money. He gestures wildly, acting out his despair and his total destitution. At one point, to emphasize how horrible things are, he puts his hand over his heart. Without hesitation Charlie picks up a phone—the old kind that's in two pieces—and places one part over the man's chest, then holds the other part of the phone to his ear, so he can listen to the man's heart. It shocked my grandfather. Charlie acted without any hesitation, as if it were the most natural thing in the world to use a phone that way. My grandfather realized that for a moment he had actually believed Charlie was able to listen to the man's heart with a telephone.

It was breathtaking sometimes, the way Buster and Charlie had swift and simple solutions to the worst problems. To be that fast and inventive was a secret wish of her father's, or so my Aunt Leontine thought. It was wonderful that a man could face impossible situations and triumph over them, using only his imagination and daring, and to show his appreciation my grandfather typed a letter to Charlie Chaplin on Southern Pine Association stationery. Although the term was never used, it was a fan letter, according to my aunt, who read it. The main point was that he admired Chaplin's ability to deal so well with life's difficult moments. My grandfather said Chaplin reminded him of his own father, a man who lost over $100,000 in the panic of 1874, but who the next day was making plans to start over again. Another time—my grandfather wrote in the letter—when the family house was devastated by fire, his father was at work the next day finding a new home and moving his family to it. My aunt remembered that the letter ended with her own father saying that he was writing simply because he was grateful to Chaplin for the hours of inspiration that his picture shows had provided.

According to my Aunt Leontine, her father never mailed the letter. She thought it was because he didn't want it known that he was writing fan mail to anyone in Hollywood, which was beginning to have a reputation for wild parties and sinful behavior. The more he read about Chaplin's personal life, especially in the late twenties, said my aunt, the happier he was that he never sent the letter. Yet he would always admire Charlie's resourcefulness.

My mother scoffed at the idea that her father had written a letter to Charlie Chaplin, but then she always tried to make me believe that her sister, Leontine, was given to hyperbole, if not lies. I believed my mother, as children do, but more and more I came to realize that this aunt usually told the truth. Her honesty threatened everyone in the family, so they routinely discounted whatever she said. I thought about the story of my grandfather's letter when Chaplin died, and I sent a telegram to the artist's family. For a moment I felt as if I had at last sent off my grandfather's letter, especially when I received a handwritten note back from the comedian's widow:

> *Manoir De Ban, 1804 Corsier sur Vevey (Suisse)*
> *Dear Mr. Perry,*
> *Thank you so much for your message of sympathy and your tribute to my husband. My children and I were very touched by your telegram.*
> *Sincerely Yours,*
> *Oona Chaplin*

In reading over Chaplin's wife's response, I like to imagine that she was actually answering my grandfather's unsent note.

I feel the same way about several letters I have from Lillian Gish. When we first met, I told her of my grandfather's admiration, although I didn't say "my grandfather," but simply "a family member." I guess I thought I would protect her from feeling too old. Nor did I tell her that my grandfather had a "special affection" for her. When I mentioned the movie he talked about, she knew instantly that it was *True Heart Susie* (1919). One of the letters she wrote to me later seemed like her response to my grandfather's love of the role she played in that film, in which everything worked out for the best, as my grandfather wished it to. Seventy years later Lillian Gish sent me a thank-you note for something I had done for her. When she found herself having difficulty finding a way to express her appreciation, she wrote:

> *Oh, it was easier being in silent films—we didn't need words. Somehow we managed to express how much the heart overflows.*
> *Your ever grateful, Lillian, with love and kisses*

These sentiments are not unique to my note; she often expressed them in other letters and interviews, but I take her words as something she might have said to my grandfather, and they are words that he would have believed.

According to Aunt Leontine, my grandfather went only to a few movies after his second heart attack, which was in the spring of 1937.

Confronted by the reality of his own death—she concluded—he found that illusions and fantasies no longer sustained him. The last movie he saw was Ford's *Stagecoach* (1939), and he disliked it, she said. That opinion seemed so strange to me, and I looked at the film several times to try to understand his response. At first I thought it might have been something that offended his moral sense, like the time in New Orleans when he saw the couple kissing on the screen, but there was nothing like that in the film, which portrays a stagecoach journey made by several people. John Wayne makes the trip to another town with revenge in mind; he's going to kill the men who murdered his brother. Along the way he falls in love with a prostitute riding the stagecoach, and after he's killed the murderers—redeeming the town from their evil influence—he and the young woman ride off together to begin a new life. It seemed to me that *Stagecoach* described the expedition my grandfather thought was his life: a journey with an underlying moral purpose that embraces Redemption and Romance. Why, then, dislike the film?

Looking for clues, I read the section of his autobiography for those years, and it reminded me that in 1937 my Grandfather Stevens thought, although he was wrong, that he could finally stop moving and settle down. He was tired of driving, tired of living in hotels, tired of endless numbers of homes in different cities; so he began building a house in the Lake Highland District of Dallas, Texas. While it sounds a little too simple, I can only guess that when my grandfather decided to stop moving, he had to quit believing in movies like *Stagecoach*, which promised salvation to the journey-proud.

* * *

Building the house in Dallas, my grandfather seemed certain that he was building the place he would stay in for the rest of his life, and he threw himself into the work with enormous enthusiasm and pleasure. After finishing the house, he wrote a long letter to my mother, describing in great detail the building of the structure, the size of the lot, the number, as he said, of "bearing" pecan trees on the property. He mentioned with great pride the efforts he had made to use the very best materials: "I had all this lumber shipped in to Dallas in one car from a sawmill in Arkansas. The lumber used in this building is at least 85% heart. That means it will never rot." He described his choice of Schlage hardware; the system he used for keying all the locks; the selection of Cirklair heaters; the choice of a particular oak for the paneling in the living and dining areas; even the kind of "artistic" wrought iron grillwork he had put on doors and windows. He wrote extensively about what he had done to insulate the house with "the very finest insulating materials available," and also about the way he had used louvers and vents to make the attic cool in the Texas summer.

I'm not a builder and don't understand all that my grandfather was writing, but in his careful description of the most minute details I detect a great love for what he was doing. In the midst of his words about the house he inserted a sentence to my mother, "If you were here I think I could hug and kiss you," as if the mere act of describing the house had made him more affectionate.

A long section of the letter was devoted to the home's foundation: "There are 65 piers, and that is about twice as many as the usual builder puts under a house. The concrete foundation is all reinforced with several extra rods, and I saw to it that the concrete work was carefully seasoned or cured." The information about the foundation interested me when I first read the letter, found among my mother's things when she died, because the story in my family had been that my grandfather dug each foundation hole down to bedrock, dropped in a stick of dynamite, poured the wet concrete in on top, and then exploded the dynamite so that the concrete would spread over the bedrock and make an even stronger foundation.

It would seem from his letter that he did no such thing, and even though I know nothing of foundations, the story about the dynamite did sound a little preposterous. Some family member must have made up the tale just to make it clear that my journey-proud grandfather had finally settled down and built a house with a foundation that would never shift.

Reading for the first time my grandfather's description of his foundation, I realized that I had never crawled under his house during a visit. Even though he referred to the house as being built on piers, I couldn't recall if there was much of a crawl space. It certainly wasn't as high off the ground as my home in New Orleans. I had such a fear of rattlesnakes in Texas that I wouldn't have tried to go under the house anyway.

Studying Grandfather Stevens's letter again recently, I thought for some reason of a scene in a Makavejev movie, *WR: Mysteries of the Organism* (1971), that features Wilhelm Reich's Orgone Accumulator, a tall wooden box whose inside is sheathed with metal. It heals the person who shuts himself up inside for a few hours, according to Reich. The way my grandfather described his house made me feel that he expected it to rejuvenate him, as if the home were his own Orgone Accumulator. It didn't work, not for Grandfather Stevens.

Thinking about the Makavejev movie today makes me realize how few films there are about building and furnishing a home, especially ones in which the house-building is meaningful. As important as homes are in movies, there aren't many scenes of house-building. Kane's construction of his palace in *Citizen Kane* (1941) is one exception, but there it's an act of hubris and ostentation, not salvation. In Renoir's *The Southerner* (1945), a sharecropping family takes over an old abandoned house and makes it livable, establishing themselves as a family and creating a new life. Otherwise only a few films, like *Mr. Blandings Builds His Dream House* (1948), deal with constructing a dwelling. Perhaps the act is not dramatic enough, or, more likely, we don't believe, as my grandfather did, that building a house will protect us from our demons. And we certainly don't think our homes are Orgone Accumulators.

One of the ways that I know my grandfather thought his house was to be his final home was that he built most of its furniture himself. I had always thought that he built his own furniture out of a noble love of wood, but the real story is more complicated. His endless moves had made it impossible to hold on to any furniture. Often, because he could not pay the storage costs, or could not afford to move all his belongings, he had been forced to sell for almost nothing some expensive pieces that he had recently bought, and it angered him so much that he once wrote, with unusual passion, "I feel I have worked for furniture dealers all my life. . . . I have bought thousands of dollars' worth of furniture since I have had a family and do not own a dime's worth today. If I ever have any furniture again, and I expect to someday, I will build every piece of it. It will be good furniture, beautiful, I will get a lot of fun out of building it, and I won't owe a cent on it." Obviously his reaction was no passing fancy; he harbored the resentment for several decades, and in his later years he finally built his furniture. Today the bed that I sleep in is one of the ones he made.

The fact that my grandfather built his own furniture, and, as his letter attests, invested himself so heavily in his house, came to mind some years ago when I saw Wilder's *Double Indemnity* (1944) for the second or third time. Fred MacMurray's apartment seemed so dull and lifeless, so totally unlike the house and furniture that my grandfather had built, and I wondered if the rooms were so bland because the filmmakers just didn't have the money to dress the sets very well. But then I realized that Billy Wilder, the Austrian, must have found California apartments, like the protagonists of his story, devoid of personality and history. Everything Wilder wanted to say about the inhumanity of his characters was said with the decor of MacMurray's apartment, just as everything about my grandfather was made clear by the way he built his house.

No matter how well he built his Dallas home, or his furniture, and regardless of how much he thought he had come to a stopping point, my grandfather was not able to stop moving. Fate intervened. The Japanese attacked Pearl Harbor, and the next day, December 8, 1941, Grandfather Stevens sat down at his typewriter and typed a letter to the U.S. War Department, offering his services. Another war had come along, and, like the first, altered his plans, presenting an opportunity, perhaps a necessity, for my mother's father to move yet again. I know that he wrote on December 8, because in a letter addressed "To All My Children," dated December 12, 1941, he typed, "Four days ago I wrote the U.S. War Dept. offering my services to do any job my government may need me to do." They did need him, and within days he was on the move again, traveling all over Texas, Oklahoma, and Louisiana, as the regional lumber adviser for the War Production Board (WPB). Within a year he was promoted and had to spend some of his time in the Washington, D.C., offices of the WPB.

No doubt many men wrote and offered their services to the War Department, but Grandfather Stevens, at age sixty, having finally built a place he thought would be his home until death, could have chosen to sit this war out. But no. The journey-proud gene was just too strong; it had pushed him all his life, and it wasn't going to disappear just because he was older and had built a house. I can't help but wonder if my grandfather stopped to ponder what effect the various wars had had on him and his family. Not only had his father suffered at Shiloh, but, as he wrote to Chaplin, the financial crises after the war had forced his father into bankruptcy. Grandfather Stevens's mother had lost two brothers in the Civil War, and her own father, crushed by the loss of these sons and deprived of much of his livelihood, died before the war ended. The First World War had forced my Grandfather Stevens out of one business venture because the government had taken over the rail lines. Now another war had come along and upset his plans to settle down. I doubt that he thought these thoughts, but I do, feeling even today the ways in which these wars have affected my family.

When World War II ended, my grandfather was no longer alive, so he never again had a chance to stop moving and to live in the house he had built in Dallas, the one with the especially strong foundation. I wish I could say that he died in that house, lying in the oak bed that he had made, but the habits of a lifetime are not easily jettisoned. On a trip from Washington, D.C., back to Texas in October 1944, Grandfather Stevens died in a hotel room in Houston, felled by one last heart attack. A hotel room was more his home anyway.

* * *

I have a copy of that letter my grandfather wrote to all of his children on December 12, 1941, and I've read it over a number of times. I can imagine making a movie in which I am there with him in Dallas as he types the letter. The dialogue in the scene would include questions I want to ask him about what he wrote. My footage starts with him sitting at the table in his oak-paneled dining room, slightly hunched over his little portable Smith-Corona. I'm on a chair beside him, watching each typewriter key strike the paper, watching each word being formed. While he's only sixty, my grandfather looks very old, his skin pale, his blue eyes dull, surrounded as they are by dark circles. Under his white dress shirt, open at the collar, he is wearing an undershirt, and his shirtsleeves are buttoned at the cuff. Starting his letter to his children, five days after the Japanese have attacked Pearl Harbor and war has been declared, he types:

I feel it my duty, as head of my family, to tell you how I feel, and I voice the firm opinion of your mother also.

I say to my grandfather, "Your six children are all grown and married, how can you think of yourself as head of the family?"

"What?" my grandfather says. "I'll be head of the family until I die; some things never change." He seems genuinely confused by what I ask.

"Everything changes," I say. "Everything. I'm not the same person I was yesterday or a decade ago. The wars and depressions and hurricanes and business failures, the dozens of moves, I would guess they've all changed you, too."

My grandfather ignores me and types:

This war is the most serious thing that has ever confronted the American people.... We must be willing to face any sacrifice. I wish that every one of my sons would volunteer their services at once. Two of my sons-in-law are in the service and I would be very proud and happy to have the third offer his services and no doubt he will.

My grandfather's devotion to his country and to his family, and his call for sacrifice, seem foreign to me. I think of Bette Davis in *The Corn Is Green* (1945), deciding to raise the illegitimate child of one of her students so that he, the student, can go off to study at Oxford. Nobody makes sacrifices like that, I told myself, when I saw the movie. Does my grandfather really believe what he is typing or is he just writing the letter he thinks he is supposed to write? He looks at me and seems to sense my thoughts. "I learn better how to do some things," he says, "but the important matters don't change. In a little poem once, I wrote, 'Place thy hand upon thy heart / . . . Conventions are not outmoded, dear; / Matters not what they may say.'"

I would like to believe him but cannot. I want to tell him about a movie, *Wings of Desire* (1988), that at first viewing seemed to me one of those extraordinary films about transformation, even transcendence, in which an angel, anxious to experience earthly pleasures, changes into a human being. I loved the movie, yet not six months later, looking at it again, it shocked me to realize the film was simply a boy-meets-girl, boy-wins-girl story, only this time the boy was an angel and the girl a mortal. How discouraging to admire a movie and then to see it months later and find it inferior to the film I thought I saw the first time. It's not unlike resurrecting the spirit of a dead parent, once loved, only to be startled by the imperfections.

My grandfather seems to read my mind; looking directly at me, he asks, "What's important to you?"

I can only think of platitudes, so I try to avoid the question. "You've changed, too, I'll bet."

"Of course I have," my grandfather says. "I'm not some rock. I move, I change. Even my faith. It's not the same as when I was ten and my father read the Bible every night after supper." I watch as my grandfather continues to type, but after a moment he turns and asks, "Since everything does change, why does that bother you?"

"I don't know."

"You're not in charge of the universe," my grandfather says, "nor am I. The great God Almighty is. If He wants it to change, it will, no matter what you or I want." My grandfather turns back to his typewriter, stares at the piece of white paper for a moment, and then begins typing again the letter to all his children:

> *So far as Mother and I are concerned we are ready and willing to make any kind of sacrifice—take on new duties or do anything that will help our country. This to the limit of our strength and ability. We are buying defense stamps and bonds with every available dime we can save from our actual expenses. This is something we all can and must do. No half-way methods will do this job. We must bend every ounce of our resources to the task of defeating the enemies of America.*

Reaching out to put my hand on my grandfather's shoulder, I hope to absorb some of this unchanging assurance he has, but it doesn't work. While paying attention is easy because it's my grandfather typing these words, I can't bring myself to believe what my mother's father says. It would make more sense to know that he has mutated as much as I have over the years. "I don't want to change anymore," I tell my grandfather.

"Good luck."

He doesn't understand, and I don't know how to make him. Watching my grandfather makes me feel as torn as I did when I first saw Ford's *The Sun Shines Bright* (1953), a film totally committed to tolerance but one filled with terrible stereotypes of black people. I believed it and I didn't; I admired it and I didn't. The same with my grandfather. Would my Grandfather Stevens, seeing again those films he first saw at New Orleans's West End, on Lake Pontchartrain, laugh at them and wonder if they were the same films he saw as a boy? I doubt it. He still believes in his God, his country, even in himself as head of his family. It all seems very sentimental to me, and I feel a huge chasm between us, which I dearly wish were not there. He's finishing the last paragraph of his letter, typing:

Let's be calm and resolute. Let's pray, work, save, and in every way be all we should be and do every possible thing to bring this horrible war to a successful conclusion at the quickest possible moment.

Having removed the letter from his portable typewriter, and put the lid back in place, my grandfather turns and looks at me a long time.

"You still watch old picture shows, don't you?"

"Yes."

"Do you believe every part of them?

"No."

"Is that important?"

"No."

"You're gulled by them."

"Yes, sometimes."

"They're just movies. I'm flesh and blood. Why can't you be gulled by me?"

My thought pops out of my mouth: "I don't want to have a corny grandfather who types hackneyed letters."

My grandfather bursts into laughter, something I've never seen him do. His body pitches back and his head flips up toward the ceiling. Between snorts, he says, "There's an excuse if I ever heard one." When he finally stops chuckling, he says, very seriously, "You've been asking me lots of questions, let me ask you one."

"Okay," I say, a little taken aback.

"It's nice to have a grandson who's so interested in me—I'm flattered—but I feel a little like you've invaded my privacy. What is it you want?"

He's surprised me. I have an answer to his question, but I don't reply. It's too embarrassing to admit what I've come to realize, which is that I have been using him, telling his story in order to justify my own life. All the places he's lived, the multiple jobs he's held, the flight from family, the writing of books, the building of houses, they're all too familiar. Because I can see myself in him, I feel a little justified and a little less inept.

Before I can figure out what I am going to say, my grandfather adds, "I'm not an actor in an old picture show. There's more to my story than what you choose to find."

Before I can even say, "You're right," he interrupts me.

"You've got it wrong, you know; I always liked being at home with my family more than being on the road."

"Really?"

"You try making a living during world wars, a depression, heart attacks, a panic or two, an armistice, not too mention a few dishonest partners, and see how much staying-put you do."

My grandfather fixes his eyes so intently on me that I start to look away, but then I remember that this conversation is imaginary, a part of some footage in a movie I would like to make.

6 Who's Who?

BACK IN NEW ORLEANS FOR ANOTHER visit, I drove to a part of town that I had never been in before, one originally known as Fauborg Marigny because it was a suburb downriver from the original city. Now it was almost in the center. To get there I drove through the French Quarter, went up Elysian Fields Avenue, and then turned right on St. Claude Avenue. My parents lived in this area, known as the Ninth Ward, before I was born. It was very different from the neighborhood I grew up in, which was full of old live oak trees, apartment houses, large homes, and little yards. The Ninth Ward had few trees, and the houses, neat and well cared for, were small, many of them duplexes with no yards, their front steps starting at the sidewalk. I felt that I was not in New Orleans, at least not in the New Orleans I remembered.

I drove around trying to find St. Roch's Cemetery. My father had often mentioned the chapel there, its walls lined with crutches, braces, and artificial limbs, as well as plaster casts of human limbs and organs, all supposedly put in the chapel by the faithful whose body parts had been healed by St. Roch. I found the cemetery finally, but the chapel was closed and when I looked through a window, the walls were bare.

I got back in my car and went in search of Campo's Grocery; my mother and father had raved about this little store, and its owner, Cosmo Campo. "The best muffuletta in New Orleans," my mother said, and even after my parents moved from the Ninth Ward, they would sometimes make a pilgrimage back to buy this New Orleans sandwich, made with Italian meats and cheeses that are spread with an olive salad. Cosmo had given my parents credit when they were broke, too, and they never forgot him. It wasn't likely that Cosmo was still alive, but the store might be run by one of his children.

Maybe they still served his famous muffuletta, and, although I was no fan of this greasy sandwich, I would try Campo's version and see what the fuss was about.

At the corner of St. Claude and Clouet, where it was supposed to be, Campo's Grocery was nowhere to be seen. Instead the site was now the Saturn Bar. Though disappointed, I thought I would take a look inside anyway. Entering the bar by pushing open its plywood veneer door, which was peeling, I had to wait a moment to adjust to the darkness. My eyes, when finally able to see, didn't believe the scene, and I went quickly back out to my car and got my journal to take some notes. Whoever owned the Saturn Bar was part amateur artist, part collector of the useless and odd bibelot, and part taxidermist. The only light came from some red and blue neon circles above. This ceiling, so darkened by age and smoke, was full of painted clouds and spheres, which no doubt were supposed to be planets. The neon circles were meant to be the rings of Saturn, or so I presumed.

Various paintings—a shrimp boat, a swamp scene, horses, cemeteries, a Madonna made of glitter—hung on different parts of the walls, along with old political posters, like "Elect Louis Bezou for Civil Sheriff, Parish of Orleans, Ward Nine." Paintings of a bullfight, and another of a dragon, were nailed to the ceiling, from which was suspended an enormous horn from a longhorn cow, with strips of reddish cloth wrapped around different parts of the horn. The booths in the bar seemed to be covered in a dirty leopard skin. Empty beer cases were stacked around, and the area behind the bar, where the liquor bottles stood, was covered with Mardi Gras baubles—mainly cheap necklaces made of glass beads. Above these ornaments was a picture of Our Lady of the Sacred Heart and a nearby sign that said, "Abandon Everything."

Fascinated by the scene inside the Saturn Bar, I sat down quickly. It was early afternoon, and the place was empty, except for the bartender, who was watching a horse race on television. He looked my way: "You look familiar, Captain."

"It's my first time here."

"My mistake, I guess. What'll you have?"

"A Coke."

As the bartender pulled a can out of his cooler, I made some notes about the bar in my journal, which I was hiding in my lap. Putting the Coke down at my place, the bartender said, "Glass or straw?"

"Straw's fine," I said. Just as he was handing me a straw, two men walked in, one after the other, and sat down at the bar.

"Where y'at, Jake?" the bartender said to one of the men, opening a bottle of Jax beer and putting it in front of him.

The other man announced, "I'm fine, thanks." He reached over, grabbed the bottle of Jax on the bar, and took a long swig. The bartender, without hesitating, opened another bottle of Jax and put it in front of Jake. The other man finished his bottle, then turned and left the bar.

"Not very polite, your friend," the bartender said.

"My friend?" Jake said. "I never saw him before in my life."

"What? You sure came in together," the bartender said.

Jake shrugged. "So? We just hit the door at the same time. I thought you knew him, the way you didn't say anything when he grabbed my bottle."

"I thought he was your friend, so I kept quiet."

"Yeah," Jake said, "me, too."

The bartender ran out from behind the bar, went to the front door, and opened it, looking for the man. The light blinded me for a moment and I shut my eyes. Finally opening them, I could vaguely see the bartender coming back around the bar. He said, "Shit, I thought he was your friend and you'd pay for his beer. He's nowhere to be seen."

"No," Jake said, "I ain't paying. I never saw him before." The bartender shrugged, as if it had all happened a dozen times, and turned back to the television. Jake joined him. Watching them looking at the screen, I was thinking to myself what a stupid charade they had just performed. Jake pretended not to be upset when the other man stole his beer, and the bartender pretended not to care, thinking the other man was Jake's friend.

Before I could feel really superior, it struck me that I was involved in my own deception. Here I was at the Saturn Bar pretending to be just another patron. In my lap was a journal, hidden from sight, which now and then I scribbled in, making notes to use later. I felt deceitful, having turned this bar and the men into objects for me to use. I was also doing exactly what I criticized in movies like *The Big Easy* (1987) and *Tightrope* (1984), exploiting the idiosyncratic aspects of New Orleans. Pretending to be a patron made me feel hypocritical. A large Mardi Gras mask stared at me from behind the bar, but it might as well have been my reflection in a mirror.

* * *

Whether I like to or not, I sometimes wear masks, impersonating whomever I think I need to be. So do others. One of my friends, who is an English professor and a lover of film, was once so upset that one teacher had been fired that he stood up at a faculty meeting and courageously railed against those who had made the decision. When another colleague went in to see him the next day, and asked how he could risk his own career, my friend answered, almost without thinking, "My fear is my concern." That's a line Peter O'Toole delivers as Lawrence in *Lawrence of Arabia* (1962), and my friend loved the fact that he had quoted the sentence. Doing so made him feel partially as if he were impersonating Lawrence and partially as if he were being himself, saying exactly what he believed.

When he told me this story, I thought about impersonation and remembered back to a time in 1947 when my dad was home for his annual two-week visit, the second one after he went to Africa. One of the first things he said was, "After supper, let's go see a picture." Walking along Hampson Street the two blocks to the Mecca, I was thrilled. My dad and I, going to the movies again, it was all that I had wished for since he left, but once inside our movie theater, a pall settled over me and I felt more sad than anything. Nothing like this had happened the previous year when my father was home from Africa, but for some reason this time I realized that things would never again be as good as I remembered, before Dad left.

A Double Life (1947) had already begun, so it took a few minutes to figure out what was going on. The movie didn't interest me very much. At my age, ten, a film about a stage actor, played by Ronald Colman, actually becoming the character he is playing, didn't really grab my attention. I would have long since forgotten the movie except that my father insisted we leave at the end. He didn't want to wait for the beginning that we hadn't seen, and he talked a little about the movie all the way home, something he rarely did. "I wouldn't have taken you to that picture if I had known what it was about," he said. "They shouldn't make movies like that, people might think they're true." I don't remember much else of what my father said, but something about the movie disturbed him, that was certain.

Looking at *A Double Life* years later, I guessed at first that my father's response was like his reaction to Mamoulian's *Dr. Jekyll and Mr. Hyde* (1932). Nothing scared my father more than to think that one day he might suddenly exhibit some strange behavior, as if during the night a vampire had bitten his neck and turned him into another kind of creature—a pedophile, or a ne'er-do-well, or an angry murderer. Yet that wasn't the whole story, I told myself, as I thought more about how angry had been his reaction to *A Double Life*. No, it was even more personal. He had seen himself in Ronald Colman, a man who becomes the person he impersonates. My father, to avoid losing control, had lived his life impersonating someone totally in control. "You must have order in your life" was what he repeated often to me, which was his way of saying that we all must do whatever is necessary to keep chaos at bay. Having order meant eliminating as much as possible those possessions and people—my mother, me, his siblings, his father—who might make demands upon him. Like Ronald Colman in *A Double Life*, and a host of other impersonators, my father worked so hard at his task that he became the person he impersonated.

* * *

My father's reaction to *A Double Life* didn't interest me much as a child, nor that much as an adult, and then one day, watching Frankenheimer's *Seconds* (1966), in which a man takes on another person's identity, I became fascinated with the notion of impersonation. As soon as I began thinking about the idea, of course, I found it everywhere. Not only were there dozens of films—*Tootsie* (1982), *Vertigo* (1958), *Mrs. Doubtfire* (1993), *The Return of Martin Guerre*

(1982), *The Brighton Strangler* (1945), just to name a few—but the idea, so inherently dramatic, turns up again and again in literature, theater, and opera. For a while every work I encountered seemed to be about people pretending to be other people, about doubles, about doubling, about the confusion of identities.

The seventeenth-century French play by Rotrou *Le véritable Saint Genest* is based in part on the Christian legend of Saint Genest, a Roman actor who, while playing the role of a believer in an anti-Christian play, was suddenly converted to Christianity. In Poulenc's opera *Dialogues of the Carmelites,* the heroine, pretending that she is still a Carmelite nun, chooses to be guillotined with the other members of the order. Charles Dickens's *Tale of Two Cities* concludes with the death of Charles Darnay, but the person who dies is actually Sydney Carton, pretending to be Darnay and choosing that man's death.

Wondering if impersonation was just some petty interest of mine, I mentioned it to several of my academic friends. One said, "I do that all the time. I want to have my summers off and to read and to write books, so I put on the mask and uniform of a college professor." The more I thought about the ways in which humans pretend to be other people, and what effect it has upon them, the more fascinated I became, but then one day it struck me that my interest might be just another sign of my own midlife crisis, the middle-aged man's desire to start another life and be someone else. However true this might be, and however much I recognized some of the reasons for my interest, my fascination would not diminish; understanding the obsession didn't rid me of it.

* * *

My Grandfather Stevens seemed like someone who understood impersonation—intimately. His autobiography described a man who lived and worked in so many different places that it seemed obvious he had to play several roles.

He told my Aunt Leontine once about having to impersonate someone who sold rugs, even though his heart was really in the woods or at a sawmill. It was after World War I, and my grandfather, out of work, had taken a job selling rugs in Georgia, leaving his family in New York City. He had his own new car, a 1919 Studebaker. The decision was whether to buy a car that was fully enclosed or one that was open. Either you got dust on your clothes if you drove in a touring car on the Georgia roads, or you died from the heat if you rode in a sedan with the windows up to keep out the dust. He bought the enclosed car, preferring the heat over the dust, knowing he could always roll a window down. Selling rugs to country stores, in small towns, was something Grandfather Stevens had never done before, and it was challenging. To invent a new life did not seem so strange, and he went about it with determination. If there was one thing my grandfather knew how to do, it was this, to become a new person in a new place at a new job. He had been doing just that ever since he left Magnolia, Mississippi.

The story my aunt repeated was about her father pulling into a little Georgia town, Cordelle, parking his new Studebaker, and walking into the little dry goods store on Seventh Street. What happened inside the store was vague in his memory, but for some reason he had a fixed image of the walk from his vehicle to the store that day. As soon as he stepped out of the car, he stood up straight, threw his shoulders back, and felt himself become someone else, as if he had put on a costume. It was a lovely spring day in Georgia, the air unseasonably cool and the sky clear, the dogwood in full bloom. He didn't feel well, but he pretended he did as he entered the building, his book of samples under his arm. He never rehearsed his opening speech, preferring that the words come out spontaneously. It wasn't what he said, anyway; it was his attitude. The right attitude would win anybody's confidence. My grandfather had to look good, to be the kind of man that the store owner would respect and want to have as a partner. Which is what he was, a partner with the store owner in making money.

For his opening words, my aunt said, her father always made it a point to pick out something about the store, or about the owner, to give special notice. "Your display window is very unusual, did you do it yourself?" "You have the best-kept store in Georgia, the customers must take great pleasure in coming in." Grandfather Stevens loved that first meeting, the challenge of finding something to say that would instantly grab the owner's attention. He liked having to think so quickly on his feet, and he felt gratified when he came up with something really fresh and interesting to say—and true. Perhaps he exaggerated now and then, but he never lied to anyone. Once, when a haggard owner had horrible breath, my grandfather took the man aside and, in a whisper, said, "I hope you don't mind if I tell you this, but I thought you might want to know that your breath is a little unpleasant." It was a big gamble. The owner might have been furious, but instead he appreciated Grandfather Stevens's honesty and bought every rug that was for sale. My grandfather loved these visits—entering a store for the first time, making a deal. When he left, he felt good, and the personality he had assumed on entering the store was now in fact his own, not a mask.

The impersonation did become tedious after a few weeks. I suspect that this new person, the one my grandfather invented, even when very successful, began to wear upon him, and after a while he could no longer find the strength to sustain this new creature. Even if no one else knew it, he was all too aware that he was acting. When that realization came, there was no place to hide. Grandfather Stevens said he never knew when it would begin, but one morning, in some little hotel or boardinghouse, he would awaken early, before daylight, and a huge anvil would be sitting on his chest. He couldn't take a deep breath. Sometimes it was more like a fluttering in his breast, like the frantic heartbeat of a dying bird, and his life seemed threatened. When these feelings came over my grandfather, nothing seemed right for days, even weeks; he would go about his business as best he could, his body resisting any movement and his skin now and then smarting with a strange burning. Sometimes his face would flush, as if his blood pressure had suddenly soared. When it came, this melancholy, the world turned weary. Spring flowers would seem to wilt even as they bloomed, and a walk in the woods no longer refreshed him. He would be eager to sit down to eat a meal, hungry to dip some corn bread in a glass of buttermilk, but what he tasted in his mouth didn't seem to match what was there before his eyes. Like paste, it stuck to the roof of his mouth, and he wanted to spit it out; but that was too much of an effort, so he chewed instead and eventually swallowed the food. When the black dog came, nothing was what it seemed, or what it should be.

*　*　*

Grandfather Stevens was not the only one who assumed another identity now and then. While my own father would probably never have admitted it, he also played different roles. He did his best impersonation as his version of a husband. Among my mother's things when she died were dozens of cards that he had sent to her. One was a Valentine's Card from 1951 that on the outside read, *"Heaven's really quite a wondrous place."* I unfolded the card once and the inside read, *"It is shining stairs and pearly gates and streets all paved with gold."* Some of the words were in red, and the illustration showed a little dog with a halo and a harp walking over a golden street and climbing shining stairs. Unfolding the card again, I read, on the next page, *"And I swear by all the angels when my earthly span is through . . ."* I then unfolded the card once more and read, *"I don't wanna go to Heaven . . ."* Unfolding the card one last time, to its full size of two feet by three feet, I saw the words, *"I just wanna be with* YOU!" The "you" was huge, inside an enormous red heart, and below it the card was signed, "Love, Ed." I was aghast as I read this. My father, the "Ed" off in Africa, thousands of miles away, who saw my mother for only two weeks a year until he died, sent her a card that said, ironically, "I just wanna be with YOU!" Where did he get such a card? At a navy PX in Africa? Or did he buy cards for a year ahead when he was in the States? She, in turn, who once left my father, saved the card, and many others like it, for over twenty-five years.

Reading that Valentine card, I wanted my parents present. I would pin them both to a wall and make them explain, word by word, what they meant to each other and why they chose to live the way they did. Yet I know that I would not have received straight answers. They would just mouth platitudes. "I worship the ground your father walks on!" my mother would say, and my father would add, "What are you talking about? I love your mother! I got a great girl!"

"No!" I would shout. "It makes no sense!"

Folding and unfolding the Valentine card, I wondered if there were invisible ink that made it impossible for me to read some explanations written on the card. My first rush of anger disappeared, replaced by curiosity. What really went on between these two human beings? I'll never know. I want to understand the people my parents pretended to be, but most of all I want to take off the masks and see who they really were. Perhaps then I could begin to uncover what lies under my own mask.

* * *

Men like my father, who avoid feelings by impersonating people in control of everything, could make good use of some safe ways to experience emotions. What's needed is a franchise of shops where such men could go in and rent some feelings. "Could I have a little prick of rage, please? Not too much, I don't want to alarm anyone, I just want to remember what it's like." Maybe there are such little shops; they're called movie houses. I am in one now, stocking up for the week. I need to go to the bathroom, so I slip out of my seat and start back up the aisle. Faces look past me at the screen behind my back. I am startled for a moment, realizing how strange it is that I and other humans would gather in a dark room and look at these moving shadows on the screen. We go in for a while and get a little déjà vu of anger and resentment and love and sadness and joy.

Yet often I don't trust what I feel at a movie. Beresford's *Driving Miss Daisy* (1989) moved me, but I was wary. What I felt while watching a black actor, Morgan Freeman, driving for a white woman, Jessica Tandy, might have been provoked by the fond memory of the black man that my grandparents hired as a driver in 1934, when Grandfather Stevens went back on the road for the Southern Pine Association. The few times I was around them, I sensed the two men shared an affection and respect. When the black man married, his new bride joined the other three people in the automobile. So close were this couple to my grandparents that they named their two children for them. It was impossible to watch Freeman drive Tandy around in Beresford's movie without wondering if my grandfather and his driver really respected and loved one another, or if I had invented an intimate relationship to ward off any charges of racism.

My father, though, never seemed to question what he felt at a movie. All that mattered to him was that the films allowed a safe outlet for some emotions. A man isolated from himself and others, he could feel less lonely in a movie theater; for a short while he felt stimulated and part of humanity. In the movie theater he could impersonate someone with anger, compassion, pride, and a host of other feelings that would disappear as soon as he walked out the door. I do what my father did, assuaging my emptiness and loneliness by going to a movie, and I adhere closely to the rule that emotions are to be kept inside the movie theater. An invisible sign on the wall says, "Please deposit your empty drink and popcorn containers on the way out, plus any residue of feelings. They're not allowed outside."

Not only the exit signs but the films themselves remind me often that it's not safe to have strong emotions outside the movie theater. I wasn't conscious of the lesson at the time, but when I went back later and looked at many movies of the 1940s, I realized that they taught me to be very careful of feelings. All the movies with women who jerk men around by their passions—like Welles's *The Lady from Shanghai* (1948) and Cromwell's *Dead Reckoning* (1947)—are beacons, signaling me to keep away from strong feelings; they're dangerous. All the movies that show people trying to act out a desperate yearning are also warning me to be careful; if I feel too much, I'll be destroyed. It's better to impersonate someone without feelings, or so the movies and my father taught me. Knowing now that these movies and my father are wrong is not enough to keep me from impersonating my father, trying often to reduce my circumstances as much as possible. My wardrobe is a little more diverse than my father's, but I have worn the same brand and color of socks for fifteen years.

* * *

I have impersonated other people, and I have friends who have done the same. On one of my trips to New Orleans I found the phone number of a grammar school friend—I'll call him Richard—and gave him a call. We hadn't talked since he was a pallbearer at my father's funeral, forty years ago. He was surprised to hear from me, and we chatted briefly. I asked him if he had children, where he lived now, and what kind of work he did. While he was clear about having three children and living in the same house he grew up in, Richard was vague about his work, which didn't surprise me, since I had heard he had married a woman with money. We agreed to have lunch the next day in the French Quarter, at Brennan's, and he put the receiver down to get a pen and paper to write down the phone number of the place where I was staying. While he was away, I heard his wife ask, "Who is that?"

"An old grammar school buddy," Richard said.

"Does he want money?"

Still holding the phone, waiting on Richard to return, I smiled. It would not be easy to be married to someone who worried that your grammar school friends wanted money. When Richard returned to the phone, he asked me to have lunch at his house instead of meeting at Brennan's.

When we were kids, I liked having Richard as a friend. It was fun to visit his house because it was on the side of Walnut Street where the houses back up onto Audubon Park, so we had the whole park to play in. His father also took us sailing on Lake Pontchartrain a few times. Richard was very intelligent, too. He put me onto Victor Hugo when we were only in the sixth grade. I can't remember anymore why we lost touch with one another.

The next day it was easy for me to find his house, since I had gone there often as a child. Richard met me at the door, but I hardly recognized him. He had grown very fat, his stomach so large that his shirt was stretched across it as tight as a drumhead. As I stepped into the living room of his house, I was amazed at how little had changed. Over the mantel there was still the same oil portrait of him as a child. The pastel colors in the living room seemed exactly the same, as did the furniture. If his wife had money, she didn't spend it on redecorating Richard's home. The only thing that looked new was a huge vase, full of tall stalks of bird of paradise, that sat on top of a glass coffee table. We walked through a set of French doors to the patio that looked out on Audubon Park and then sat down at a white wrought iron table. Scraped and repainted several times, it looked like the one that was there fifty years ago. Richard's wife was nowhere to be seen, and he didn't mention her. In fact, he said almost nothing. I had to pry information out of him. He didn't ask me a single question about where I worked, what I did, what my family was like. That I was the only one making conversation irritated me, and as quickly as possible I began to make sounds about leaving. Why had I wanted to see him anyway? When I stood up and headed for the door, he finally spoke, saying, "Do you want to see the attic?"

"Sure," I said, without knowing why. We walked up the steep steps and emerged into a large room. Richard and I had played there as kids, but otherwise I had no idea what he was trying to show me. We walked around. The space had been newly painted and carpeted, but there was no furniture. I told him that it looked nice, but Richard offered nothing about why he brought me here. He led me back downstairs without any comment.

At the front door, as I was about to leave, he asked me to call him again the next time I was in New Orleans. "We had some good times together," he added, his face a little pensive.

"Yes, we did," I said, backing out the front door. Then I turned and moved as quickly as possible to my car, wanting all too badly to tell Richard, "Showing me the new attic is just your way of impersonating a man who has accomplished something with his life." I couldn't bring myself to say that; it was too fatuous. Besides, I had done too much impersonating myself.

* * *

My fascination with impersonation is really a passion for what I think is an essential movie theme, which is that change is possible. I can transform who I am, the way I feel, the circumstances of my life. Hope is worth having, progress is possible, life eventually makes sense. If we're good, we get to be and to have what we want. I love the promise that movies hold out. Who wants to live a life where everything is the same? It's hard to think of a movie that doesn't have as its core this idea of metamorphosis. How could it be otherwise? Inside the movie camera an unexposed frame is being replaced, twenty-four times a second, with another unexposed frame. Inside the film projector still images are substituted for other still images, again at twenty-four times each second.

Change is inherent in the movie system, it's obvious, but there's a catch. Those are unchanging images that appear on the screen twenty-four times a second. The movement we think we see is a total illusion, created by our eyes and brains. Nothing really changes. Even cartoons like "The Road Runner" and "Bugs Bunny" repeatedly show transformation, as well as its static opposite. A steamroller flattens Bugs, changing him into a two-dimensional bunny, but in the next frame he is normal again. Everything changes and nothing changes. A masterpiece like John Ford's *The Searchers* (1956) is ultimately about a character who changes—yet doesn't change. The Ethan who begins his quest with a plan to kill his niece because she's been "living with the bucks," as he says, becomes the person who saves the young woman and brings her home. Yet at the very end of the film the door of that home closes, leaving him outside in the wilderness, which is where he was when the film began. The narrative of the film—and perhaps all narrative—involves a character negotiating change by meeting a challenge. Crossing a threshold and becoming a different person, Ethan still comes full circle to where he started. Only the melodramatic films escape this paradox.

The idea of change, and its opposite, no change, is pervasive: "People do grow up—barely. You can get a life—perhaps. Those self-destructive instincts can be banished—somewhat. Becoming a better person is possible—more or less. If you work at it, you can stop kicking dogs, hating children, using people—now and then."

The viewer that says a film is bad because "nothing happens" really means it's bad because nothing changes. Most moviegoers ignore the pieces of a film that show no change, preferring to cling to the illusion of change that the movies foster. Me, too. I live by that illusion; I need to believe that I can change, that things can get better, that I can be happier. The message of many films is that even the worst of us can improve and redeem ourselves. I know that my father saw this message in every film he watched, and in some way it sustained him; but it wasn't true. He found that out for sure in the last moments before he died. Having a heart attack in the African bush, when the weather was bad, meant that it took two days before they could fly him to a hospital in a city. As the ambulance arrived at the emergency room door, he said to the doctor who met him, "Better hurry up, Doc." I was told those were his last words, and, in saying them, I'm sure Dad thought "Doc" would indeed hurry up and save him. Things would change for the better, my father believed. The movies told him so.

* * *

Now, after my father's death, and that of my mother, I decide that I will make a movie in which I explain to them what I do. My mother tells me over and over that she would like to know exactly what it is that I do for a living. Teaching about movies at a college doesn't make much sense to her, and she suspects that what I really do is thread projectors. I send her articles and books that I write, but they don't help. She buys a well-known biographical dictionary and puts a bookmark at the page where my entry appears. Now she has something that she can show to her friends, which helps, but she still doesn't really understand what I do. Sometimes she begs for me to tell her in a way that she will grasp. That's what my movie will now do.

It's not easy to get my parents in the same room for any kind of discussion, but they will listen if I buy them dinner, so I imagine film footage of me taking them to Commander's Palace, not only because it's one of the best restaurants in New Orleans—and one of my mother's favorites—but also because my mother's waiter there has died. I want to be the host, not have her show off with her waiter. The trade-off for my parents is that they will have to watch a film with me.

Wanting this to be a really special occasion, I rent a room at the Pontchartrain Hotel, where we spend the late afternoon before dinner looking at Rossellini's *Il Generale Della Rovere* (1959). Watching might be difficult for them, I think, and I say so, suggesting that they get comfortable while I fix drinks. In her slip my mother takes the vodka I offer and sits up in bed, a tin of macadamia nuts perched on her stomach. My father, his coat and tie on, lowers himself into an easy chair and takes a sip of the Jack Daniel's I've poured for him. He nurses one drink as we watch the film, while my mother finishes three.

I ask them not to throw questions at me during the movie, and neither one breaks the silence, but my mother now and then looks at me the way she did when she was dying in the hospital and asked, "What's wrong with you, is it my fault or yours?" I picked this film because it has a strong story that I thought they would like, but I forgot some of its nuances and that it's subtitled. The tension in the room—mine, theirs—gets thicker as the film continues. My father keeps hoping there'll be something to laugh at, or a shoot-'em-up. Putting them through this ordeal makes me feel guilty, but I soothe myself by recalling that they are going to get a great meal. My mother, I know, will delight in her dinner. My father, while he won't say he loves the food, will eat it and enjoy himself.

When the film is over, my mother says, "I don't get it," as she stands up and puts on a midnight blue velour pants suit with a velvet collar on the double-breasted jacket. Adding a string of brilliant white Mikimoto pearls around her neck, she looks beautiful. In the little movie I am making she is a young woman, her hair still dark with no sign of gray, her widow's peak a little less pronounced than it was as she got older. My father has on a new wool suit, navy blue, that he bought at Wallachs in New York, which is where he likes to shop on trips back and forth to Africa. The black tie is knit, square at the bottom. His broadcloth shirt, pima cotton, is white. He has polished his black wing-tip shoes himself. I am filming my father before he put on so much weight, so now he just looks like a man of substance and sophistication, his dark hair combed straight back and shiny from the Vitalis he uses.

Looking at the blue color of his suit and of her pants suit, my mother says, "We're twinsies."

At Commander's I slip a twenty-dollar bill to the maître d' and ask for a table in the patio near the little fountain over which hangs a huge live oak limb. We walk through the restaurant's kitchen to reach the patio, and I have to pull my mother along to keep her from stopping to look in every kettle. As we sit, the waiter comes over and my mother orders another vodka on the rocks, while Dad sticks with his bourbon. His cheeks are a little red and shiny, the way they get when he has any alcohol. Mother shows no sign that she's been drinking.

"What don't you get?" I ask, then realize that I am rushing things for my mother.

"Let me have a few sips of my drink."

My father adds, "I want to eat something first."

As the drinks come, my mother says to the waiter, "I was so sorry to hear about Jean-Paul. He was my waiter for years, starting back when the Morans still owned Commander's."

The waiter says, "Yes, m'am, he was a fine person."

"May I ask your name?" My mother avoids my glare. She can't avoid making it her show, no matter what I say or do.

The waiter, a large man with eyes surrounded by dark circles, looks a little like a panda bear. "Anthony, m'am."

"I'm Gertrude Perry, and this is my son and my husband. This is a very special occasion for us. You've worked here a while, haven't you, Anthony?"

"Twenty years, Mrs. Perry."

"My goodness, Anthony, you must have started when you were ten years old."

The waiter smiles, extremely pleased. "Not quite, Mrs. Perry."

As my mother turns on her charm, my father has a physical response, his shoulders tensing up and his jaw locking. Standing up, he says, "Excuse me a minute."

"Can't you wait to go to the little boy's room, honey, at least until we order?" In my mother's book of etiquette, it's a major offense to leave the table before the meal is over.

"I'll be right back. Order for me, son, you know what I like."

Before my father can finish his sentence, my mother asks, "Do you have any suggestions, Anthony? I want something wonderfully special."

Feeling challenged, and treated like a person with particular knowledge, Anthony snaps to attention. "What do you like, Mrs. Perry?"

"Everything! Crawfish, soft-shelled crab, redfish, beef, pheasant, quail, everything."

"Do you like things spicy?"

"Absolutely!" my mother says.

"Heavy or light sauces?"

"Both," my mother says, with a mischievous smile.

"Trust me, Mrs. Perry," says Anthony.

"Fabulous!" My mother looks right at him, putting her menu down. "Anthony, you seem like someone who knows his way around food; I'm sure I'll be delighted."

Anthony breaks out into a huge smile. Although he does write down the Turtle Soup au Sherry and the Filet Mignon Adelaide I order for Dad, as well as the seafood gumbo and the Crawfish Maque Choux I order for myself, Anthony is hardly listening to me. He's too busy thinking about how he is going to dazzle this lady.

As my father sits down, timing his return so he arrives as Anthony leaves, my mother says, speaking directly to him, "I remember the first time we ever came here. It was our first night out after Teddy was born, remember, Ed? We were broke and couldn't afford it on your Goodrich salary, but you had been saving up all during my pregnancy without telling me."

"The bill was twelve dollars and eighty-three cents, with the tip."

Mother turns and looks at me. "Your father surprised me, you know; he told me we were going to Uglesich's, which was where we usually ate when we went out. It was all we could afford—but the food was good. The walk to Uglesich's was just five blocks, so I didn't understand why your father wanted to take a cab, but he said he wanted to make the night special."

"It wasn't any farther to Commander's," my father says, "so we could have walked here."

My mother frowns. Why doesn't he remember the good things? She goes on talking. "This patio wasn't here then. We ate in the old part of the building."

My father looks at me and winks. "Upstairs used to be a sporting house, I guess you know. A friend of mine lived on the second floor of a home across the street and said he learned about the birds and bees looking through the windows into the private rooms upstairs." My dad snickers a little, like a little boy who just said his first cussword.

Mother acts as if she didn't hear my father. "I was so touched by what your father did," she says. "It was the happiest night of my life. I had a cup of Barataria Bay Oyster Chowder, I remember, and the Crabmeat Imperial. Dessert was a delicious praline parfait."

My father frowns as he asks, "Gertie, how can you remember what you ate?"

My mother fires back, "You remember exactly what it cost!"

I interrupt: "So what is it you don't get, Mother?"

My mother takes a deep breath and a sip of her vodka. "The rule at my table," she announces, "is that we don't talk about anything but the food."

"It's my table this time," I say, surprised at my own firmness. My mother doesn't look at me; one of her gifts is knowing when to pick a fight and when not. "Come on, Mother, you're always asking me what I do for a living."

My father says, "You start, Son. We want to hear what you have to say."

"I'm going to write about the film you saw, and two others I think are like it."

My father hopes he might know the other films. "What are the other two?"

"Antonioni's *The Passenger* and Kurosawa's *Kagemusha*."

"Oh," my father says.

"To say what? I mean what will you write?" my mother asks. I can't tell if she really wants an answer.

I try to be simple. "All three films are about people who are misfits. In the film this afternoon Vittorio De Sica starts out as a con man who cheats people. In the other two films one man is a thief and one is a journalist who is divorced from his own life." I hear myself talking, and I feel like I'm pretending to be an intellectual, but I continue. "All three of the men then impersonate somebody else. What's interesting to me is that in the process they're transformed, or redeemed. From being men with meaningless lives they become men with a purpose."

"That's crazy," my mother said, "who wants to be somebody else?"

"Transcendence," I say, the word slipping out before I know it.

"What?"

"Nothing." I search the table, wishing I had ordered a drink.

After a silence my mother says, "I don't know anybody who pretends to be somebody else."

"We're all like that," I say. "That's why you make all those New Year's resolutions. You want to be somebody else."

"Speak for yourself," my mother says, looking me straight in the eye.

"Gert," my father says, "you are too like that. You just got through pretending to be Miss Charming Madam for that waiter."

"Touché, Dad," I say to myself. My mother gives my father a look that would freeze alcohol. The stare is made more menacing because she has to cock her head back a little to keep her eyes clear of the thin column of smoke that trails upward from the cigarette perched in the corner of her mouth.

I say, "I think most people feel a little fake sometimes, like they're wearing a mask."

Nobody speaks. Anthony arrives, interrupting the silence with the first course. "Here's your appetizer, Mrs. Perry, I hope you like it, and I made a very special suggestion to the chef for your entrée. He's hard at work. I think you'll be pleased, but it will take a little longer."

"Anthony, you're a dear, we wouldn't dream of being in a hurry," my mother says as she takes a bite of her appetizer. Suddenly her face beams, as if she just stuck her finger in a live socket. "My goodness! That's the best thing I ever, ever put in my mouth! What is it, Anthony?"

Anthony beams. "Truffle and wild mushroom stew, Mrs. Perry."

"It's delicious! What are the little red strands on top?"

"Sweet potato hay."

"It's all perfect, Anthony, what a darling you are. I'll have another drink, please."

"I want to order a good bottle of wine," I tell my mother.

"Go ahead, but I want my drink, too."

"Anthony, a red or white for my mother's entrée?"

"A dry red, fairly heavy."

"Then bring us a bottle of the Barolo Cannubi."

"Excellent choice," Anthony says. I don't know if he really likes my choice or if he's thinking about what his tip will be on a $140 bottle of wine.

"Yes, excellent choice," my mother says, looking at me with pride. She's partial to Italian red wines and at the drop of a hat can give a lecture on the virtues of the nebbiolo grape. It's a little niche of wine knowledge she's carved out for herself, mainly as a way to be unique.

My father says, "In your movie, the man who's impersonating the general, just before he's shot by the firing squad, he sends a note to his wife."

"Yes."

"But it's the wife of the man he's pretending to be. When she sees the handwriting, she'll know it's not her husband."

"I think the point is that he feels he's become the general he was impersonating."

There's a long silence that is awkward. All three of us want to say something, but we're afraid it will sound superficial or, worse, stupid. I watch the goings-on at a nearby table, where a young beautiful woman is helping a very old woman with her food. The young woman is patient, lovingly offering the old woman a forkful at a time. She chews each bite very slowly, savoring it and beaming, as if taste is the only sense organ that works very well anymore.

Anthony arrives with three green salads, and says, "I know you didn't order these, but you need your vitamins—and to clean your palates." He lingers nearby and when we are only half through he comes over and takes our plates away, saying, "That's enough vitamins, now for the good stuff."

Returning almost immediately, Anthony quickly sets down the wine and food for my father and me, then proceeds to present my mother with her dish. "What we have here, Mrs. Perry, is a variation on our Roasted Mississippi Quail. It's boned and filled with a Creole crawfish sausage stuffing, served with a sauté of corn and jalapeño, touched with a reduced port-and-quail glaze. Just for you, the chef has changed the seasoning a little to make it more piquant." Anthony looks toward the kitchen, which can be seen beyond the bar and through a large glass window. A man in a chef's hat is looking our way. "That's the chef, Mrs. Perry," Anthony says as he pours me a sip of the Barolo to taste.

My mother is delighted; she puts a forkful in her mouth and breaks into a huge smile, as if she were a child eating her first piece of birthday cake. She waves back at the chef, closing her eyes. Her lips move, mouthing the words, "It's delicious!" I guess she thinks the chef can read lips. He gets the point anyway and blows her a kiss; she blows him one back, then her eyes well up. When she's really, really happy, my mother weeps. "Anthony! I've died and gone to Heaven! What a wonderful thing you and the chef have done. I'll never forget this." She takes a sip of the wine, smiles appreciatively, then dives back into the quail, as if she hadn't eaten in weeks. "My goodness gracious, that's the best thing I ever put in my mouth. Son, you won't believe this; here, take a taste," my mother says, and she holds out a forkful for me.

I take a bite. "That's good."

"Good? Can't you show a little emotion? You don't know what delicious is if that's all you have to say."

Dad and I try to eat our food as my mother continues to hum, sigh, and make other noises of pleasure as she eats.

I can tell that my father is puzzled and finally he speaks. "What's it supposed to represent when the man lets himself be shot, when all he has to do is stop pretending to be this general. Then he'd go free. Getting shot doesn't change anything."

"Maybe he thought he had found a fate that was better than his own."

"He's stupid," comments my mother as she wipes her mouth.

"No, there's more to it than that," says my father.

It seems to me that the two of them are actually getting interested in the conversation, which surprises me. "They're all religious films," I say, and then wish I hadn't spoken. This is dangerous ground.

"It's not any kind of religion I know about," my mother says.

"Now *I* don't get it," my father adds.

I try to explain. "They're all films about men who save their souls by pretending to be people who are living meaningful lives."

My father winks at my mother as he says, "It's not any kind of religion I know about." My mother looks at him and smiles, reaching out and putting her hand on top of his.

I say, "It's not religion with a capital R. I'm not talking Southern Baptist or Episcopalian or whatever."

"I'm talking Christian, with a capital C," my mother says. She turns and looks at my father. "Isn't that right, honey?"

My father, pointing to the huge bite of food in his mouth, signals that he can't talk.

Feeling cornered, I wave at Anthony. "Let's order dessert," I announce, not daring to get into a debate with my mother over religion. If I am going to film a scene with my parents, why can't I imagine other conversations? Why don't I imagine asking my mother why she left when I was eighteen months old? Why not ask my father how he could leave home and go to Africa, and what he really thought of my mother's lady-friends? Those are the conversations I really want to have.

A big smile breaks out on my mother's face as Anthony arrives. "Anthony, the quail was heavenly! Is the Bananas Foster still the most delicious thing in the world?"

"You do know your desserts, Mrs. Perry, but actually, if you don't mind a suggestion, I think the bread pudding soufflé is even better."

"Then that's what I'll have."

"The Dutch apple pie for me," my dad says, "with a slice of Cheddar cheese on top."

Anthony grimaces. "I'm sorry, we don't have any apple pie, but the sweet potato chocolate pie, or even the Creole cream cheese cheesecake, is delicious."

My father is not pleased. "Damn, I could taste the apple pie. Bring me the cheesecake, I guess. I do like Creole cream cheese."

"No dessert for me."

My mother grits her teeth as she whispers, "Ted, you're at Commander's Palace, have some dessert."

"I ordered dessert, Son," Dad adds.

"No, thanks."

My mother rolls her eyes back. "Such a party-pooper. You don't know how to enjoy yourself."

My father interrupts, "It's like *The Man in the Iron Mask*."

It takes me a minute to realize that he's trying to take up the movie discussion again, talking about an old film where Louis Hayward plays two parts, the twin sons of the king of France. They're separated at birth so there won't be any confusion about who is the heir to the throne. When one of them becomes the king of France, and later learns about the existence of the other twin, he has him imprisoned with an iron mask over his face to keep people from seeing the resemblance.

I say, "Yes and no, Dad."

"No? When the good twin is put in the iron mask, his friends get him out and put the bad twin in the same mask. They change identities. Isn't that what you're talking about?"

"I'm trying to write about people who have their souls saved when they impersonate someone else. That's not quite what happens in *The Man in the Iron Mask*."

Neither one says anything as the desserts arrive and they start eating. I feel left out, even a little anxious without something to do with my hands and mouth, and I want to call Anthony over and order a slice of pecan pie. Because I'm too obstinate to do something that would please my mother so much, I resist.

"I hope you're satisfied, Mother, now you know what I do for a living."

"I think it's wonderful. I'm very proud of you."

Dad adds, "Me, too, and I liked the picture. Very unusual."

They light up cigarettes even before they finish dessert. I imagine that Anthony brings me a piece of pecan pie anyway, with a dollop of whipped cream that's starting to melt because the pie is warm. It looks elegant, the top covered with pecans that have been salted, buttered, toasted, and then sprinkled on this piece of pie after it's heated and before it's served. Thinking so clearly about eating the pie, I can almost taste some of the filling, which is thick and sweet, made with dark Karo corn syrup, and also full of crunchy pecan pieces. My fancy taking hold, the lump of filling slowly softens in my mouth until the sweetness invades every corner and every taste bud. I detect a hint of something else, probably a dash of Grand Marnier. For sure I have a huge grin on my face, but at least my mother and father don't know that I am imagining myself eating pecan pie. Because a conversation about movies seems remote and out of place, my parents and I chat about insignificant things while drinking our coffee. Now I feel off the hook and can relax. I've done what my mother asked me to do. I've shown her what I do for a living.

7 Better to Remember

THE NEXT TIME I WENT BACK TO NEW Orleans I decided to take a ride on one of the St. Charles Avenue streetcars, which outwardly looked the same as they did more than fifty years ago. My plan was to board one of these electric trolley cars downtown on Canal Street and to ride uptown to my old neighborhood. When a car finally stopped in front of me, the back door didn't open, only the front, so I had to run forward to enter there. Everyone entered at the back door when I was a child, because that was where the conductor stood to take the fare and to give change. The front door, the one by the motorman, was the place to exit. Now the motorman, who was also the conductor, operated the streetcar from the front, and every rider had to have the exact change to deposit in a little box next to this person. The difference didn't bother me too much because I had made a conscious decision to fight off any nostalgia I might feel in riding a streetcar again after so many years.

It was hard not to get sentimental, though, so little having changed. Above me were exposed lightbulbs, and the seats were the same varnished wood. A little unsightly, the floor was unfinished, weathered gray and easily replaced when grit and grime and water had worn the boards down. Although the motorman's seat was now more padded and comfortable, his controls were exactly the same: a little handgrip for opening and closing doors, a crank for accelerating and slowing, another handle to work the brakes. The clang the motorman made by stamping on a metal button on the floor was as familiar to me as the sound of my mother's whistle. It would have been easier to fight my nostalgia if more had changed inside the streetcar, but almost nothing had. Except, as I looked around, I saw that many of the riders on the streetcar were black. In my childhood there would have been more of a mix of white and black people. Only after I had been sitting for a while did I realize that the "Colored Only" signs were missing. Dropped into metal holes on the backs of seats, the signs used to divide the seating areas, but sometimes, if the conductor was kind and there were black people standing, he would move a sign forward so there would be a larger colored section.

I rode the streetcar again, looking out the window at the azaleas blooming in the neutral ground where the streetcar tracks ran. Joggers were running in this same area—a sight that was new. With metal wheels on metal tracks the streetcar was noisy, and the hard wooden seat was uncomfortable. After a while, even the clanging noise lost its charm and became irritating. What I saw from the window of the streetcar, riding along St. Charles Avenue, was very familiar—a few K&B Drugstores, a florist, many large homes, and huge live oak trees whose branches formed a canopy over the avenue.

As we progressed along the middle of the avenue, I found myself moving not only through space but also through time. Electric streetcars like the one I was riding had existed in 1908 when my Grandfather Stevens moved to New Orleans. Since he lived in an area near the end of the St. Charles line, he must have ridden this same route, in a similar streetcar, and so must my grandmother and the two children they had at the time. From 1936 on, when my own parents moved to this city, they rode the St. Charles cars all the time; it was the way they went to and from downtown, and how my father got to work. As a kid, I rode this same route, and, after my father left for Africa, my mother had let me ride by myself. It was my lifeline, making it possible for me to travel downtown or to go to some part of the city where there was a specialty store, like the one that sold parts for Lionel trains.

Only one person might be driving the streetcar now, and the "Colored Only" signs might be gone, but almost everything else felt the same, and as I looked out the window, I didn't know if I was seeing the trip I was now taking, or remembering what I saw as a child when riding an identical streetcar. Past and present were so superimposed over one another that each seemed to fuse into some new tense. This confusion exists in a number of films, like Angelopoulos's *Traveling Players* (1975) and Bergman's *Wild Strawberries* (1957). In Alain

Resnais's *Last Year at Marienbad* (1961), two of the characters seem similarly confused as they fight over whose memory of the past is true. A man, trying to convince a woman that they had an affair the previous year, visually recalls specific scenes and events for her. We see on the screen the past that he describes: "You stood there, straight, motionless, your arms alongside your body. . . . And you look at me; your eyes are wide open, too wide, your lips parted a little, as if you were going to speak."

The woman's voice, heard in the film's present tense, keeps telling us that what the film is showing in the past is not true. Or "was" not true. Gradually the man begins to persuade her that his memory is the correct one, forcing his past tense on her present tense, compelling the woman to change her own memory. "Yes," she says, "maybe, oh, no, I don't know anymore." The film seems simultaneously past and present, as images from the past are shown as present tense to the viewer.

Films like these are bewildering, deliberately so. I may like to think about my mind thinking, but observing the mental process makes me realize that my mind does not make the neat division between past and present that I would wish, and that language itself doesn't necessarily correspond to experience.

Looking out the window of the streetcar again, I realized once more how untrustworthy my mind was.

* * *

To think about such mental unreliability is to remember some of the tricks my mind has played. Some years ago I went to see an Australian film, *Careful, He Might Hear You* (1983), and, after leaving the theater, I replayed the movie in my head. Having seen so many films over the years, just after a screening I can pretty well recall every scene, even some of the shots. This time there were two large gaps in my memory, which surprised me, so I went back to see the film again a few days later. The first gap occurred just after a scene in which some children at school have been teasing a young boy, who is called P.S., forcing him to take down his trousers in front of them. What followed was what I had conveniently forgotten. It was another scene with P.S., this time in a huge room with his aunt, Vanessa. She is making him sing for a woman who will become his music teacher. Watching this scene, I couldn't help but remember the number of times my mother compelled me, at about P.S.'s age, to sing in front of her friends. It made me very uncomfortable, for I felt too much like the little man my mother sometimes wheeled out to perform. No doubt my mind was trying to protect me from an unpleasant memory by blocking out the section of the Australian film when P.S. is forced to sing.

Realizing why my mind had obscured that part of the film, I suspected that something similar would be at work in the second gap. I remembered seeing P.S.'s father in a conversation with Vanessa, but not what followed. Watching and listening to this scene with Vanessa and the father, waiting for the next scene, I suddenly felt very thirsty. Without thinking of the consequences, I got up and went to get a drink, only to return and realize that the sequence had passed. The second gap in my memory of the film was still there. Curious, I went back to the movie again two days later and forced myself to watch the sequence. What I finally sat through was a scene with Vanessa, P.S., and his absent, wandering father, who long before had abandoned the young boy. The father says he has a gift for P.S., and he opens a piece of cloth to expose what he has brought. "Gold," he says. "I brought you some gold."

Vanessa comments, "Isn't that nice. Your father dug that out of the earth for you."

Staring at the piece of gold in the movie scene, I suddenly recalled that the first gift my father sent me back from Africa was not an ivory tusk but a gold nugget. Until that moment, watching the scene in the film, I had conveniently forgotten that my father had sent me a fragment of gold from Africa. When the little package arrived, it sat unopened for two days. I wanted my father, not some token gift. The gold nugget, not the ivory tusk, was what I had gone out and sold to buy a 16-mm film camera. Because the ivory tusk had arrived months later, when moviemaking had become such a joy to me, it was welcomed as something I could sell in order to buy, not the camera, but a 16-mm home movie projector—which is what I really did with the tusk. A part of my mind wanted me to forget how angry the gold nugget had made me feel, and I had to sit through three screenings of the movie to dig up that old memory.

* * *

Much can be learned from what my mind makes me forget. One summer I visited my father on his job site in Africa. At that time the administrative head of a large construction project, he gave me a little job doing inventories, but I was in and out of his office all the time. Though I was seventeen, it was the first time I had ever visited my dad's office, in the United States or Africa. I found excuses to be there, to talk to the people who worked for him, and to watch my dad effortlessly tap hundreds of numbers across his adding machine—all with his left hand, even though he was right-handed.

My father had an administrative assistant, and I remember a scene that took place one day with this man. He had taken me outside my father's office building, and he was explaining to me very carefully that my father had a very important position, that he was in charge of a multimillion-dollar project, and that sometimes he had to do difficult things. What was strange was that I couldn't remember what had provoked this conversation, or why my father's assistant had taken me outside. My mind wouldn't let me remember. Yet it's easy now to figure out what happened—and what I'd witnessed. My father must have become really furious at an employee for doing something poorly and had fired him. Whether it was the display of anger or the treatment of the employee, I don't know, but whatever it was, my mind was not going to let me remember the event.

The scene is not hard to imagine. My father would have called the employee into his office and said something like, "You only had to add these four columns. When I checked your figures, two of the columns were wrong! That's ridiculous! How can you call yourself an accountant!"

"I must have made a mistake," said the young man. "I'm sorry."

"Sorry? I don't care whether you're sorry or not!" My father's voice got louder and louder.

"I'll be more careful next time."

"You're not capable of being careful," my father said. "Tomorrow there's a plane back to the States. I'll cut you a check for two weeks of severance pay."

"Please, I—"

My father waved the man away.

Getting along well with people was not my father's strength. The only time he was comfortable with other people was sitting in a movie theater. Once I overheard an uncle of mine say to my mother, "Ed's fine as long as you keep him in the back office away from the customers." I suppose I saw that flaw of my father's fully presented in the scene in his African office, the one my mind wouldn't allow me to remember. Numbers were after all my father's domain. At an early age he began doing people's books and taught himself accounting. He must have loved working with numbers; they were like his Western movies. Figures didn't lie or cheat or steal, and they never provoked any unwanted feelings. The pleasure for my father was in seeing accounts balance. If you studied numbers long and carefully, you could understand anything.

Whatever the slight had been that day in Africa when my father blew up, I am sure that it was minor. He only got angry at small things, little ways in which people had not been perfect—misplacing a file, leaving a typo in a letter, forgetting a task, doing personal things during office hours. I think he was jealous when other people made mistakes. Growing up in a dozen or so different homes, he must have learned that you got to stay longer in a foster home if you did nothing wrong. My father had not been allowed to make little mistakes, so he took personally any slipups made by other people. He thought of such errors as an attack on him, on the way he had been forced to live his life, and there was no way he was going to laugh carelessness away or to be understanding. I never heard him say, "I'm just human," nor did he let other people say that without a row.

Because I absorbed some of this unreasonable perfectionism, I can't bear it when other people don't make their best effort. As a teacher, it's been almost impossible for me to accept students who don't work as hard as they might. My belief had been that if I were a perfect child, my parents would get back together and stay at home, and, unfairly, I expect the same perfection from my students. Far too many times my father's words pop out of my mouth when a student apologizes for poor or late work: "Sorry? I don't care whether you're sorry or not!"

* * *

Forgetting a painful moment is just one of the tricks the mind plays. Sometimes it becomes obsessed with something, locking onto it like a Gila monster and not letting go. For me it happens sometimes with movies. Becoming preoccupied with the physical feature of an actor is an example. Clark Gable's ears were always more interesting to me than his movies, and while viewing him in a Huston film, *The Misfits* (1961), I kept wondering if the actor's ears had gotten bigger over the years, like some men's noses. Watching Raoul Walsh's *The Horn Blows at Midnight* (1945), I couldn't take my eyes off the place on Alexis Smith's white dress where her navel creates a little indentation. The film that obsessed me the most was Bruce Conner's *Report* (1967). A short movie made in the aftermath of President Kennedy's assassination, it uses footage of the events that day in Dallas, along with a sound track made up of what was said on the radio before, during, and after the assassination. A film of mourning, it expresses one man's reaction to the assassination.

The first time I screened *Report*, I was overwhelmed, reminded once again of that grim November day. At the moment in the film when Kennedy is shot and the radio announcer says, "Wait a moment, something has happened, something has happened in the motorcade," the screen image is disturbed, showing pieces of film leader that then turn blank. The screen becomes an empty rectangle of light. Gradually the light begins to flicker, faster and faster. At first, thinking the film had torn, I looked back at the projector, but nothing was wrong. The audio track was continuing, so the film couldn't be broken. Looking at the pulsing screen again, and waiting, made me more and more uncomfortable. What was going on? The flickering began to slow down, while the screen grew darker and darker until it was black. The longer this went on, the more anxious I became.

Finally, after what seemed like hours, some images appeared. When *Report* ended, I projected it again and looked at the moment when the screen becomes flickering light. What was the filmmaker trying to do? I felt confusion, even panic. Surely there was something to be understood about this part of the movie, but what? After three more screenings I told myself to stop thinking about the movie. I couldn't. At dinner that night my wife said, "What are you thinking about?"

"What?"

"Your mouth is moving, as if you're forming words and sentences. You're thinking about something. What?"

"If I said it out loud, it wouldn't make any sense right now." That was true. I couldn't make sense out of that part of *Report*. Was the filmmaker trying to depict what went on in Kennedy's brain as he died? Or hoping to create in me the same anxiety and paranoia I felt when I heard that Kennedy had been assassinated? Thinking about the movie, I almost never got to sleep that night, and the Conner film was the first thing on my mind the next day when I woke up. In my office I planned to get back to what I was working on before I screened *Report*, but my mind just wouldn't turn loose of Conner's movie. Going to the library, I read half a dozen articles on *Report*, but nobody even mentioned that blank spot. Had I imagined it? I screened the movie again, but there it was. Phoning a friend, an Ivy League film professor who knows Conner's work, I said, "What do you make of that long blank section in *Report*?"

"Blank section? Where?"

"Right after the announcer says something has happened in the motorcade." My friend didn't say anything, so I asked, "Don't you remember it?"

"No."

"The film's only thirteen minutes long, and you don't remember forty-five seconds of nothing?"

"No, not really, well, sort of, why?"

"If you did remember, what would you make of an interminably long period of nothing but flickering light and then darkness, just as we're learning that Kennedy has been shot?"

After a pause, my friend said, "I'd have to see the film again."

"You're a big help."

He laughed. "I just can't immediately figure out the personal part."

"What?"

"There's always some personal angle in your intellectual interests."

"You make it sound terrible."

"Wait, wait, I get it," he said. "The screen has gone blank. The images have left without any explanation, just like your parents." He laughed again, truly pleased with himself.

"How perceptive!" I laughed, or I pretended to laugh.

We hung up. I went back to the library, this time finding an article that did mention the blank section, claiming that Conner was just depicting what had happened in Kennedy's brain when the bullet hit his head. I didn't agree, but at least somebody else saw the thing.

Late in the morning I realized that for twenty-four hours I hadn't thought about anything else but a flickering, blank screen. It was not funny. My mind sometimes has a mind of its own and won't listen to my remonstrations, no matter how hard I press them. Finally, without any solutions, exhausted from having to think about a movie, tired of having to see a movie screen as a palpable surface and not as an illusion, I was able to let go.

At such times I long for those moments in a really entertaining film when I am oblivious to it as a movie—not noticing the editing or the camera movement—and just get carried away by the experience. The film borrows my mind for a while, which leaves me blissful. Even better would be a moment when my mind just shuts down completely, but that's happened only once. It was in 1976 and I had gone into a New York City hospital for some tests. The sciatic nerve in my right leg had felt like molten lead for weeks and the neurologist wanted to find out what was going on in my back. In the days before there were MRIs and CAT scans, doctors did a myelogram.

No one said it would be fun to have injected into my spine some dye that shows up well on certain kinds of X-rays. It didn't help that I was freezing in the room where two men administered the test. All the tile and stainless steel made the space seem even more cold. The men kept talking to one another in a language I didn't recognize, much less understand. They must have been Steely Dan fans, too, since that was the music being piped into the room. I never liked Steely Dan. "You'll feel a little discomfort," one of the men said, as he rammed a big needle up my tailbone. Yes, discomfort. Finally, after the pictures, they wheeled me out. It was over, thank goodness. A while later, back in my room, I felt my mind slow down, come to a halt, and then go into neutral. Never having felt so relaxed in my life, I smiled. Still, the experience seemed odd, and I called the nurse.

When she came in, I said, "I'm not sure, but my mind feels like it stopped."

As she stared back at me, looking puzzled, I realized how funny it was to be talking about "feeling" my mind, but that was the best way I knew to describe what was going on. "What day is it?" the nurse asked. My mind didn't have an answer, nor did it care. "What month?"

The trees outside were bare and the sky was cloudy. "January?"

It must have been the wrong answer because she reached down and, with a clang, pulled the bars up on one side of the bed. I knew something was amiss. "Do you know who the president is?" She had walked around to the other side of the bed and was raising those bars. Watching her, I thought to myself, this is not good. Whoever the president was, surely he would be happy to see the big smile on my face. I felt wonderful. The world seemed absolutely familiar, and yet it was distant, apart from me. I was at home but without all the obligations of being at home. Given my euphoria, why was the nurse looking so unhappy? "Let me see your fingernails," she said. I held out my fingers and she looked at them, then squeezed each tip. I saw little white dots under my nails, and so did the nurse. "I'll be right back," she said, moving quickly out of the room. Let her go. Why did I call her? I'd never felt better.

Hours and hours later, after hordes of doctors, residents, nurses, and interns, my mind floated gently back to its nest. Evidently the oily dye had gotten into my bloodstream and gunked up my mind. Eventually, the stuff just washed away. I was a little sad, actually. It had felt so tranquil not to have a mind. For a brief while there were no obsessions, my mind was idling in neutral, and I was not seized with trying to figure out things like why the screen went blank in *Report*.

* * *

Yet I invite some of my mind's obsessions; they allow me to force connections among elements that don't seem to go together. Reading in his autobiography that Grandfather Stevens had taken a train out to the West End of New Orleans, where he saw his first movies, I created a link between movies and trains, or at least between movement and still photographs of trains. Mid-nineteenth-century photographs of people and landscapes were obviously representations of things that were frozen in time. No one looked at a still image of a house, or a person, or a body in a coffin, and wondered when it was going to start moving. A photograph of an immobile train was different. To look at it meant feeling the urge to ask questions about movement. Where had the train come from? Where was it going? When was it going to start moving again?

This connection between movement and trains leaped out at me the first time I saw the Andrew J. Russell photographs that recorded the building of the U.S. transcontinental railroad. One photograph in particular fascinated me, the one taken May 10, 1869, at Promontory, Utah, at the moment when the track was completed, connecting the two oceans. Central Pacific's Jupiter engine is on the left, its nose facing the front of Union Pacific's No. 119, which is on the right side of the photograph. When I first looked at this image, all I could think about was movement. The engine on the left has come along a track from the Pacific Ocean, the one on the right has traveled from the Atlantic. After the photograph was taken, did both engines back up or just one? How would they get one engine off the track to make room for the other one to move forward? The sense of Russell's photograph was of movement that had happened and was about to happen again, and this feeling pervades all his photographs of trains, at least for me. Presentiment must have gnawed at those who saw the same images in the 1860s. I would like to imagine that this longing for the enactment of movement was in part the force that gave birth to cinema, and that in less than two decades it was the moving pictures that came along to satisfy this desire for the representation of movement.

How appropriate that one of the first motion pictures seen by a paying audience, at Paris's Grand Café on December 28, 1895, was *L'arrivé d'un train en gare* (*The Arrival of a Train at a Station*). Finally, a deep craving had been satiated. As I go on concocting this story of origins, my mind creates a bond between me and my grandfather, who loved to move and who often rode trains. The journey-proud gene has manifested itself in me as a love of the movies, I tell myself. I like to move; in fact, I like anything that moves, so trains, movies, and moving all seem to bind me to my grandfather.

This linking of movies and trains, of movement and movies, helps me to understand how going to the movies serves an imaginative role. Imagining events is a way to assimilate them, even to make the unbearable into something bearable. When my children were young, I feared so much that they would die that I imagined it over and over. On television, if there was a report of a car accident, I would immediately visualize one with all my children killed. If my son got a cold, I would see him dying of whooping cough. Watching a daughter playing field hockey, I would see her kicked in the face, her neck broken. It was better to get ready for such a death in order not to be devastated were a child actually to die. Because it felt so stupid and sentimental, I never told anyone about these little movies in my imagination, and I certainly couldn't go around announcing how prepared I was if one of my children were to die. Imagining a death was a way to help prepare me for it.

Movies are ways of imagining movement, and imagining movement, like anticipating the death of my children, is a way to lessen the impact of movement. In this story of origins, one of the reasons that movies were invented was to help human beings cope with the way that movement itself had become such an overwhelming phenomenon, threatening and dangerous to the psyche. If the movies were not born when people looked at still photographs of trains, then surely they came into being when people stood in train stations and watched loved ones leave. Cinema was created, I told myself, to make it easier for the spirit to keep up with a body that was running amok in space and time.

I guess it worked. Movement seems pretty tame now, no longer as powerful a force to be reckoned with. The imaginative role for movies today often seems more to do with violence. Like imagining the death of my children, imagining brutality is a way to prepare for its impact. I know that my mind visualizes what it needs to assimilate, and I conjure up the movies that I need to see in order to survive.

Some madness may be at work in forcing a connection between trains and movies, but I blame the transcontinental railroad photographs of Andrew J. Russell. I also fault the Italian filmmaker, Antonioni, whose use of trains in *Il grido* (1957) and *L'avventura* (1960) inspired my lunacy. It's probably not Antonioni's fault; he was probably thinking of the trains in the paintings of Giorgio De Chirico, who once lived and worked in Antonioni's hometown. De Chirico isn't to blame either; his father was an engineer for a railway company. Fathers often inspire mad obsessions.

* * *

One of the mind's powers is its ability to read the minds of others. Because my mother said she grieved every time her father left home, I would have thought she'd never have anything to do with a man who might pick up and travel anywhere. Yet when she met my father, she knew he was a man who had already moved from north to south. As soon as they married, they left Jackson, Mississippi, and made their home in New Orleans. However much my mother thought she disliked men like her father who left home, I believe she was drawn to them. Or at least to my father. Her intuition must have sensed that my dad was a man who would be comfortable loving his family from a distance, maybe even as far as Africa! The people in my family move, they have the journey-proud gene. If they don't have that gene, they have the gene that enables them to intuit a wandering impulse in others, so that they can then marry someone who has the journey-proud gene.

* * *

Movies have minds, too, although it may seem weird to think so, since Hollywood producers often think of movies, particularly the scripts, as "properties." Which is the same as saying movies are inanimate objects to buy and sell, like automobiles. One of the main founding sites for the movie industry in Italy was the city of Turin because Fiat was already making automobiles there. Looking at some materials in film archives in Turin, I once found a photograph of a movie "assembly" room. Fifteen women, dressed identically, were standing behind a long table, and in front of each woman was a stack of film—multiple copies of one scene. The woman at the far end would hand one copy of her scene to the next woman, who would splice that first scene onto one of the copies of her own scene, then pass to the next woman the two scenes spliced together. The next woman would then repeat the process, as would the next, until the film reached the end of the table. All the scenes had then been spliced together into one film, not unlike a Fiat on an assembly line. Because the production process was like a manufacturing process, particularly that of the automobile, and because the camera was a machine, films were often thought to be merely industrial products—mindless and without artistic merit.

No, films are alive, capable of sophisticated mental processes. Some of them even have an "unconscious." Like slips of the tongue, jokes, and dreams that betray the human unconscious, an element of the movie erupts through the surface, revealing something that is different from what is presented by the rest of the film. Minnelli's *Meet Me in St. Louis* (1944), an otherwise wholesome celebration of family, rites of courtship, and the importance of home, also has a character, Tootie, who seems to have wandered in by mistake from some other movie. She tells lies, symbolically kills one of her neighbors, sings bawdy songs, and plays mean practical jokes. "Tootie's the most horrible!" her playmates say. At one point the girl decapitates a family of snowmen in her backyard. Her presence in the movie colors everything else, dissembling the sentimental view of the family and making it more ironic.

No doubt "unconscious" is not the perfect word to describe all those times when a shot or a scene or a character seems out of place, but it's a useful way to suggest what's going on when a part of a film seems odd and then turns out to be the key to what the film is really about. In Antonioni's *Zabriskie Point* (1969), an old man is sitting in a café in the desert. He wears a small Stetson hat and a plaid shirt; the camera looks at him in profile as he sits at a bar and takes a long drag on a cigarette, exhaling the smoke. Then he slowly raises a glass of beer to his lips. Patti Page is heard singing "The Tennessee Waltz" as the camera, outside the bar and looking in a window, zooms gradually toward the old man, as if caressing this moment. Yet, without a pause, the camera dollies back, pulling away a little from the very nostalgia it just embraced. This push–pull camera movement, which performs no narrative function and is otherwise gratuitous, is breathtaking, a balletic moment unlike any in the movies I recall. The image is so vivid, I can still recollect every element—the seductive words of "The Tennessee Waltz"; the weathered face of the old man; the caressing dance of the camera, in and then back; the slow way the old man exhales smoke into the air above his head; the careful manner in which he brings the glass of beer to his lips and then returns it to the bar.

What is even more interesting is that this moment is not at all typical of Antonioni. Patti Page's words are too full of nostalgia, the image is too close to sentimentality, the feeling of the scene is too unlike the rest of *Zabriskie Point*, which is ostensibly about the youth counterculture of the 1960s in America. The movie seems to celebrate their antimaterialist stance and the hope they represent for the future, but this moving-camera shot harkens back to the past. I can better understand the sequence if I see it as a rip in the veil of the film's consciousness. For a brief moment what is revealed is a deep and abiding affection for the past, something old and wonderful that has been lost. To understand the full meaning of this scene is also then to grasp why Antonioni places an intense lovemaking episode in a part of the desert that is millions of years old.

Films may seem to be made like automobiles, but many of the best ones have a crack in their exterior, through which another layer reveals itself and illuminates the meaning of the film.

* * *

The mind also has the ability to bury some secrets. When my twin sons were eight, the same age I was when my father left home, I went to their first ice hockey game. A few moments into the game, it was their turn to play, but when their skates hit the ice to come out of the box and onto the rink, my whole body shuddered and tears gushed down my cheeks. Because I felt so out of control that I feared standing in the bleachers, I left. Taking some deep breaths, I had a long talk with myself. What had happened? Suddenly, like being hit by a huge wave, I recalled how it hurt at age eight to play softball or football without my father there to watch. If you had asked me before my sons' hockey game if it mattered to me that my father never witnessed me playing a sport, I would have said no, and fully believed that I was being truthful. My mind had kept completely secret from me what I had felt at my childhood sporting events, but as soon as I stood at my own sons' game, doing what my father had never done, I experienced again the ache of not having my own father in the stands. After a few more deep breaths I went back in to watch my sons play hockey.

While my mind keeps things from me, it also finds unusual ways to tell me some things. A few years ago I was in the process of writing a paper on a film, and in the middle of the night woke up. Unable to go back to sleep, I tried to find the essay I was working on, but it seemed to have disappeared. That surprised me no end, since I was sure that the draft had been in my hands earlier in the evening. Exasperated, I drove to my office to see if I'd left the paper there, but on the way an eerie feeling descended on me. Trite as it seems, the hairs on the back of my head, above the neck, stood up. In my office I opened a cardboard letter box where I thought the paper might be, only to find a stack of letters from my father, all long forgotten. The one on top was a discourse on the pros and cons of going to Harvard. It seems—and I don't remember this—that Harvard had given me a small scholarship, and I had written for advice in deciding whether or not to transfer from my school in Texas. My Dad was giving me his opinion. Money was an issue, and he discusses those details, but he also says, "Never have been sold on any of the eastern schools. . . . Every school has some good in it to offer but it is strictly up to the student to obtain the most from what the school has."

Later in the same letter, after saying he doesn't like to give advice but will break the rule for a change, he adds, "It is sometimes good to be dissatisfied with what we have and do, but we can't always be changing just because it looks like it will be for the better. One must have an ordered life." "Ordered life," that was my dad. I read those words in the letter again and again, for they seemed to conjure up in me a whole lifetime of resentment. This measured, "orderly" letter about whether or not to go to Harvard, delivered in his meticulous handwriting, reminded me again of how difficult it was to be in touch with my father. Impassioned letters that I wrote to him, asking desperately for help and advice, wouldn't elicit a response for months. The letter that arrived back would never speak to my anxiety, but rather would present a cool and rational approach to the situation. Our communication system was interrupted by months and thousands of miles; I felt as if I was trying to engage in a shoot-out with someone I could only see through a telescope.

Learning at an early age that it was useless to write to my father about my problems, I chose to tell him what he wanted to hear—the good stuff. This letter that I had saved, surely because it was one of the few in which my father gave advice, now made me furious. All the anger I had hidden about my father suddenly spewed out at 3 A.M. in my office. Later, when I drove back home, I found the essay I had been hunting; it was in an obvious place on the kitchen table. Some part of my mind had ignored the sight of the paper and driven me to my office to find that letter from my father. That part of my brain had decided it was time to feel some old anger that I did not know was there, and it needed to get me to my office to start the process.

* * *

Movies lie to us about the way the mind works. I like to imagine alternate renditions of famous scenes, versions that would depict more faithfully how our minds really operate. What if Clark Gable went to the door in *Gone with the Wind* (1939) and stood there, staring at Vivien Leigh while she begged him not to leave. He's supposed to say, "Frankly, my dear, I don't give a damn." Instead there's a long pause. Finally, Vivien Leigh says, "What is it? Why are you looking at me that way?" Gable says, "I forgot what I was going to say." Then he leaves.

In *The Wizard of Oz* (1939), why couldn't Judy Garland say, as she opens the door onto the land of Oz, "We're obviously dreaming, Toto, because everything's in Technicolor."

I want Paul Muni in Hawks's *Scarface* (1932), ready for a shootout with the police who've surrounded his apartment, to realize suddenly that he's forgotten his ammunition.

Or why can't a character in a movie look up a number in the phone book and then, like me, forget it by the time he gets to the phone to make the call. Twice.

What about another performer in another film, after shopping at the behemoth Mall of America in Minneapolis, failing to remember where his car is parked?

If these misadventures of the mind were portrayed in movies, I would be pleased—but of course they're usually not. All too often the movie actor has perfect memory and perfect command of speech. Sometimes this can be exciting, I have to admit. In Polonsky's *Force of Evil* (1948), John Garfield is trying to get his brother, Thomas Gomez, to cooperate with those who run the numbers rackets. Garfield says, "Be calm, be sensible."

Gomez responds, "All right, I am sensible, I am calm. I'll give you my answer, calmly and sensibly, my final answer. My final answer is finally no. The answer is no, absolutely and finally no, finally and positively no. No. No. No. N-O."

Hearing Gomez's elegant use of words, and the rhythm of his dialogue, is exhilarating, like a sudden rush of adrenaline. Ordinarily such adept use of language would be daunting, intimidating to me, but one of the pleasures of moviegoing is that I identify with the heroes, and what they do and say I believe I can do and say. Or that when they do and say it, I'm actually doing and saying it myself. Dozens of other movies use words in a way that excites me about language, just as other films strike me as stunning with their visual beauty.

I am still haunted by the closing images in Visconti's *Death in Venice* (1971), a movie I haven't seen in twenty years, but that I remember vividly. The final scene of the film takes place on the Lido, with Dirk Bogarde as Gustav von Aschenbach, sitting in a beach chair on the sand, dandied up in a white suit, tie, hat, and excessive makeup—hair and eyebrows and mustache dyed black, face whitened, lips reddened. He watches intently as a young man, Tadzio, frolics on the beach. Then, left hand on hip, Tadzio walks out into the water. The farther out the young man walks, the more he becomes a phantasm, almost lost in silhouette, the sun in the distance making reflections that sparkle so brilliantly they blur the outlines of Tadzio's body.

When the water reaches his knees, Tadzio stops and, left hand still on his hip, turns halfway back, returning Aschenbach's gaze. The older man is overcome, and he tries to get up and go toward the boy, but Aschenbach realizes he is too sick. An immense contrast is apparent, as close-ups of Aschenbach's head are intercut with long shots of the distant Tadzio. The more the young man resembles ideal beauty, standing in the distance with a halo of light around him, the more Aschenbach's face looks grotesque in close-up. The black dye from his hair runs down his forehead and cheeks, making even more hideous his reddened lips and white-powdered face.

As the music rises in volume, Tadzio turns his back to Aschenbach and raises his left arm until it is parallel with the water, holding his fingers out as if they were holding something. The young man's sensuality, which had so troubled Aschenbach, now recedes as the boy comes to look more and more like an ethereal creature. The older man, reaching out again for the distant boy, or the idealized image of the boy, then tries once more to rise from his chair, but he falls back, dead. Watching this scene for the first time, I was deeply moved by the way in which the ugliness of Aschenbach's face is contrasted with the beauty of the young boy, as if flesh were being juxtaposed with spirit. The coupling of the two extremes is the basis of the tragedy.

Too much the academic, I wasn't content with the way the scene moved me; I wanted to analyze the causes. Only if I could rationalize my feelings would they seem legitimate. It was easy to find out what music was being played; the film's credits told me it was Mahler's Fifth Symphony, and listening to the whole piece, I realized that only the fourth movement was used in the scene. Now I had a name for the music.

Something about the way Tadzio moved, and stood, made me think of classical sculpture. His stances—left hand on hip in one, and arm outstretched in the other—looked so statuesque that I queried a few art historians and thumbed through a number of books with photographs of Greek, Roman, and Renaissance sculpture until I found two images that resembled Tadzio's poses. In one, a statue of David by the Italian Renaissance sculptor Verrocchio, David's hair looked identical to Tadzio's, and, even more important, David was standing with his left hand placed on his hip, almost exactly like Tadzio in the film. What caught my eye, too, was that the head of Goliath lay at David's feet. Intercutting Tadzio's body, left hand on hip, with the close shot of Aschenbach's face seemed to be a play on the ideas in the Verrocchio statue. The frame around the movie image had severed Aschenbach's head and made it resemble the head of Goliath at David's feet.

The second photograph I found, showing a Hellenistic bronze in the Vatican that was found in a shipwreck near Antikythera, repeated the pose of Tadzio when he raised his arm and seemingly pointed off into the distance. The caption under the photograph suggested that the statue was that of Perseus and that the outstretched arm once held the decapitated head of Medusa. This Hellenistic bronze seemed also to be a play on severed head and idealized figure, like Verrocchio's statue of David and Goliath.

In juxtaposing images of Tadzio's shimmering body with the grotesque face of Aschenbach, the ending of the Visconti film now seemed to allude to two pieces of sculpture. I don't know if Visconti intended these two poses to resemble the Verrocchio *David* and the Hellenistic bronze in the Vatican, but I do know that finding these allusions to David/Goliath and to Perseus/Medusa satisfied the part of my mind that wanted to find some rational basis for why I was so deeply moved by the scene. Discovering these associations did not give the same pleasure as experiencing the pathos of the last moments in the film—not by any means—but the images seemed now even more beautiful. Yet I also felt that my explanation was pretentious. Given a choice, I much prefer to be moved than to understand. What was most important, at least to me, about the ending of *Death in Venice* was the emotional power of the images. In such moments the visual world takes on the freshness and magnificence of Thomas

Gomez's language. I have a hard time getting my own mind to invent such astonishment for my eye and ear, so I'm grateful when the movies do it for me.

* * *

The same mind that wants to rationalize feelings is also fully capable of denying what is true, even when it's right in front of my eyes. My mind certainly kept from me an understanding of my mother's relationships with women. I didn't pay much attention to her friends until a few months after she died, and her sister, my Aunt Leontine, made a statement that stunned me. She said: "Your mother always liked girls better than boys." Hearing those words was like someone opening a curtain, pulling it back to reveal a crucial part of my mother's life for the first time. I realized then that her idea of fun was sometimes unusual, and that some of her best friends had been lesbian couples, and that, yes, she did like girls better than boys.

To be forty-two years old and just waking up to this realization made me feel stupid. How could my mind have kept this from me, and why had I let it? Unable to think of anything else, for weeks and months I replayed every scene in my childhood that might have been a remote clue about my mother's relationships with women. Each one, looked at anew, made me flinch, so obvious was it. I wanted badly to free myself of these images, but they wouldn't let go. How was it possible to witness all those moments and not realize what was going on?

With a jolt I recalled one incident, when I was fifteen. Having come home early from school, I walked down the hallway with a toothbrush and a stick deodorant in my hand. Passing my mother's bedroom, I saw her and a female companion in bed together. It was the middle of the afternoon. I stood there for a moment, said "Hi," and while talking to them raised my arm and applied the deodorant on top of my T-shirt. The totality of what I actually saw remains a mystery; only glimpses remain. My mind must have shut down and refused to let me see what was in front of me, or at least kept me from making any inferences from the sight of my mother and a woman in bed in the middle of the afternoon.

Now, almost fifty years later, thinking about this scene, I get angry for not being able to remember exactly what was in front of me. In my mind I look back at myself standing in the hall at that precise moment. It's summer, I can tell, for my skin feels sticky, and there are little drops of perspiration on my brow. The hall is dark. The front half of my body is lit by the light coming from my mother's bedroom, and, on the floor at my feet, there's a glint of golden light reflected off the oak floor. I am frantic to get inside the head of that fifteen-year-old person so I can see what he is seeing in front of him, there in my mother's bedroom, but I can only see what I now remember—the movement of white sheets, like sails when a tack is changed, and the hazy outline of my mother and the woman in the bed. I want desperately to make the whole scene, from beginning to end, appear in front of me, but it is too blurred. I hate my mind at this point, seeing it as an enemy that hides the truth. Yet I know the truth. I know because I am standing there applying deodorant on top of my T-shirt.

* * *

The least reliable part of my mind is my memory. It always tries to shape the past into a story that I like to tell myself. After my dad died, in my preferred narrative, I quit college and went to work in the oil fields to save money for school, wanting to put myself through college without anyone's aid. Besides, my mother said she had no money and couldn't help me. I believed this version of my past, but going through some old letters recently, I came across two from my mother, written to me at college. Detailing a sequence of days in which she had had to cover overdrafts in the checking account at my New Orleans bank, my mother wrote that she just wouldn't do it anymore. The other letter of hers to me started out, "Your letter was quite a blow this morning. The most I could help would be a couple of hundred or perhaps take over your car notes for a while, but that's all. You must learn someday (the sooner the better) to live within a limited income." The sentiments were ones that every parent has uttered, but the letter genuinely disturbed me. I did not relish reading it; the facts undermined my memory of the self-reliant self that I had created. These old letters had popped up to destroy my more appealing version of my past.

My memory also was that my Grandfather Stevens had liked my father, but after my Aunt Leontine died, I found in her papers a letter from my grandfather to her, dated January 19, 1936, sent from the Hillman Hotel in Birmingham, Alabama. "Can you help Gertrude find a home and job in Atlanta with you? I am so dissatisfied to have her go back to Jackson and to Perry. Isn't there ever going to be an end to that thing? It has gotten disgraceful. I don't see how her reputation can stand it any longer." What to make of such a comment? Given what I knew about my grandfather's religious beliefs, his unflinching certainty about what was right and what wrong, it seemed to me that from my perspective my father may have done little to upset my grandfather. Perhaps he had forgotten to say "sir" or had taken my mother to a movie on Sunday. Maybe they did nothing more than go out and drink a few beers or—who knows—maybe they did something much worse. This old letter contained sentiments that were impossible to interpret without knowing the situation, but on the surface it was clear that my grandfather had no use for my father, or at least had no use for the relationship between my parents. Reading these old letters, wrenched out of the past, is like seeing an Eisenstein film that has been revised so often by Soviet authorities—trying to make the film correspond to a prevailing ideology—that the current version of the movie makes no sense at all.

My mother and father were married six months after my grandfather's letter. Did that help my mother's reputation? Sometimes it's good to discover these letters—they reveal so much—and at other times I wish that they had all been burned. I certainly don't like being presented with documentary proof that forces me to give up my own version of history. While discovering these documents troubles me, their effect is also to make me want to invent a letter, one more to my own liking. I would even be willing to imagine one that contradicted my own memory, if what the letter said made me feel better about my mother and father. In Ophüls's film *Letter from an Unknown Woman*

(1948), Joan Fontaine writes a letter to Louis Jourdan that upends his life because she reveals to him a profound truth that differs from his memory. I would like to pretend my own recollections about the past are untrue, and that, like Joan Fontaine, my mother writes a letter that straightens me out. What I could do is make a little movie of her writing such a letter. The scene would be too wordy, but the actual statements are so important that I can't imagine my movie any other way. As we hear my mother's voice saying the words she is putting into a letter to my father, we see the events she is describing:

Sunday, May 13, 1945

Ed Honey,

I should have written before but everyone's been celebrating V-E day. It's like Mardi Gras here, and you know me, I just had to join in. Vivien said, "It's all over but the shouting, so let's shout!" I should be glad that part of the war is over, and I am, but I've also been so sad since you left that I can't be really happy, no matter what. I'm feeling awfully blue and lonely. In the middle of a big party at the office I had to go to the bathroom and cry. It's just been a week since Teddy and I saw you off at Southern Station and the thing I remember most was when you were stepping up on the train, holding your suitcase, and you turned around and looked at me and said, "Good-bye, sweetheart." I almost broke down, but I couldn't, for Teddy's sake. He was acting so grown up, I just couldn't give in to my feelings. I remembered all the times that Daddy walked out the door and said, "Good-bye, little Gertrude." I almost died then, too. I guess you're doing the right thing, and I know you won't stay in Africa forever, but so much can happen in two years and time has always scared me. I have no good basis for all my fears except an anxiety of the unknown future. It'll be so swell when you're back home with us.

Teddy hasn't said anything but I know he misses you. We came home and read the funny pages together after we put you on the train. He laughed just as hard as always. He's such a brave little soldier. He wanted to go out to a movie, and even though it was a

170 / MY REEL STORY

Sunday, I took him to the St. Charles to see "Waterloo Bridge." Honey, that was such a mistake! The movie is full of people saying good-bye to one another! Teddy didn't say a word, but my heart was just breaking. I was worried about him so much, I almost left, but I didn't want him to think that I wasn't courageous, too. I guess I shouldn't be telling you about it, maybe you'll be sad. I won't pick any more movies for Teddy to see! I was going to take him downtown to the Saenger to see "Sign of the Cross" this weekend, but I realized it was just because I wanted to see it. Remember? We saw it together when we were courting. Anyway, there is a scene in it that he's too young for, so I decided not to take him. Friday night he and Ralston went to the Mecca to see a Western, "Saddle Leather Law," and that was much better. He told me to tell you it had Charles Starrett in it because you both liked his movies.

Today is Mother's Day, and Teddy woke me up with a glass of orange juice and a piece of toast he made. I didn't ask him how he made the toast! He gave me the box of Whitman's you bought him to give me, and the card, and then he crawled into bed with me and we ate a few pieces of your candy. You're so thoughtful, darling. Pray for Teddy and me that we'll make everything a grand success. We'll pray for you, too. Write soon. I was hoping you might send a telegram or something to let me know you made it to Liberia okay, but I guess no news is good news. Say hi to Bill and Louise. Anyway, I love you, darling,

Gertie

My footage would end years later with me ecstatic to have found the letter.

I learned this little trick of perfecting my history while watching a Bresson film, *Une femme douce* (1969), in which a husband whose wife has committed suicide tells the story of their marriage. On the screen we're seeing the past while hearing his voice in the present, narrating the past, yet the two versions don't agree. What he tells us is not what we see, and even as he tries to justify himself, saying what a wonderful marriage they had, the images tell us just the opposite, and we know why the wife would have committed suicide. The husband wants so desperately to vindicate himself, to be freed of the guilt he feels for his wife's suicide, that he concocts a past that never occurred.

It's very comforting to tell myself another version of my own past, even if it means making up what happened. Movies do that all the time, and watching their images convinces my mind that its own projections are true.

8 No Touching

WALKING DOWN BOURBON STREET AT night in New Orleans's French Quarter, I passed in front of Rick's Cabaret, one of the new striptease clubs, just as two women stopped in front of a man who stood in the doorway. In the old days I would have called him a bouncer. He was well built, handsome, and dressed in a double-breasted suit; and no doubt it was his job to keep undesirables out. The two women, holding hands, were fat, and one was missing a front tooth. They looked to be in their early thirties. Each had multiple rings in nose and ears, and they were dressed identically in black shifts that exposed their shoulders and arms, which were covered by tattoos. The women waited and the man stared impassively. Finally, one of the women called out, "Are you hiring, baby?" The two women laughed, put their arms around each other, and walked on. The man didn't even smile. I kept going, but soon I turned around and retraced my steps several times. It was 1997, and I was sixty years old, but I was having trouble working up the courage to go inside a strip joint.

As I walked back and forth in front of Rick's, an earlier experience on Bourbon Street came to mind. I was nineteen and living by myself in the French Quarter because I had moved out of my mother's house in my old neighborhood. It was early morning of a weekday, and I was walking to my apartment. Tired men, their faces haggard, were using water hoses to clean off the sidewalks in front of the bars and strip clubs. Now and then, passing an open door on Bourbon Street, I would glance quickly inside at the people who must have spent the whole night drinking. It was February; what there had been of winter in New Orleans was over and the temperature was now mild.

A little Nash Rambler, bright yellow, had circled the block several times and then appeared again, parking near the curb. The man inside beckoned me, and I went over, noticing as I got closer that he was wearing eye shadow, a touch of rouge, and a little lipstick, too. When I reached the side of the Rambler, he took off his baseball cap, and long curly hair cascaded down his neck. "You're very nice-looking," he said. "How about coming to my place?"

With feigned politeness I said, "Thanks anyway," and went back to my walk. I didn't think much about this early-morning proposition; it had happened before. After all, this was Bourbon Street.

Like the neighborhood of my childhood, several miles away, the French Quarter was a place where everything was within a block or two—my barber, my grocery store, my cleaners, even my bar, Lafitte's Blacksmith Shop. It was enough on the edges of the tourist path that mostly locals went there. At my favorite nightclub, Al Hirt and Pete Fountain were playing together. I felt as if I had discovered them myself. Early in the morning I could walk two blocks to Café du Monde, feel the cool breeze from the nearby Mississippi River, and get a café au lait made with chicory-laced coffee.

The afternoon of the same day that I was propositioned by the man in the Nash Rambler, an old friend from college came to visit. He told me he wanted to see something different, "You know, the real New Orleans." Though unable to say it, he wanted something like a sex show. All my friend's epiphanies to date had taken place at the drive-in movie, or in the parking lot of the local Dairy Queen in his East Texas hometown. I told him we could go to the My-O-My Club, where men dressed as women and put on a floor show of suggestive songs, complete with a bump-and-grind dance. My friend was ecstatic.

That night we drove out to the West End on Lake Pontchartrain, the same site for entertainment and food where my grandfather had seen his first movies. The road outside the My-O-My Club was paved with oyster shells, so my car made a crunching noise as we drove around to find a parking spot. My friend was very excited. He was about to do the naughtiest thing he had ever done, and as we approached the club and walked in, I was afraid that his anticipation was going to make him spontaneously combust.

We stepped inside a space where the smoke filled the area above the heads of the audience sitting at tables. One act had just finished and people were talking, some at the tops of their voices. It was fairly dark and hard to see, but as we stood there, waiting for a table, someone screamed, "Baby!" and ran over to us. Who was this woman, dressed in a full-length green dress, cut low at the bodice, with curly blonde hair? As the figure approached, I saw a beard behind the makeup and realized it was a man—not just any man, but the one who had propositioned me earlier in the day. My college friend, startled that I knew anyone here, looked as if he were about to bolt out the door any minute. He had thought he would be able to hide in a corner of the My-O-My and take it all in as an observer, strictly an observer. What had he gotten himself into? The man, no, the woman, put her arm around me and called a friend over. They led us to a table in a dark corner and ordered rum and Cokes. As we sat down, I felt a hand on my thigh and then on my crotch. All my flight responses kicked in, but I thought leaving would be impolite, however silly that seems. I looked over at my college friend. Because his mouth was open and his eyes were bulging, I knew there was also a hand on his crotch.

I reached down and pushed my lady-friend's hand away. She gave me a pouting look. Trying to appear nonchalant, I looked around the club. My eye was drawn to a table about fifteen feet away where several women were laughing, drinking, and talking at the tops of their voices. Most of the people in the club were looking at them, wondering what was so damned funny. From the way their upper bodies swayed in slow motion over the table, it was obvious the women were drunk.

One person seemed a little familiar and I looked more closely. My mind didn't believe my eyes at first, but after a few moments of staring I was certain. It was my mother. Though my impulse was to jump up, grab my college friend, and leave quickly, charging full speed out the door, I couldn't take my eyes off my mother. She seemed deliriously happy, enjoying herself enormously. Pulling her arm from around the shoulders of one woman, she dropped it on the table and grabbed another woman's hand. With her other hand my mother was tearing a cigarette out of the corner of her mouth because she was laughing so hard it was gyrating in the air, about to fall out. Her body was thrown back, contorted in a paroxysm of laughter that had seized her in the middle of a drink, and now she was fighting to keep the liquid from rushing up through her nose. Despite myself, I chuckled, caught up in her pleasure. Now her head came forward, her body finally beginning to unwind from the laughter that had gripped it.

Retreating slowly in my chair, back into even more darkness, I motioned to my friend. A look and a beckoning finger were all the encouragement he needed, and we ran quickly for the exit, our two companions following closely. For a moment it appeared they planned to go home with us, but all they wanted was the money for our drinks. Throwing some bills at them, I rushed out the door, taking a deep breath of the fresh air outdoors. I felt refreshed suddenly, as if this was my first oxygen after I had been holding my breath for a while.

My college friend was talking animatedly about what had just happened to him. "I was scared, can you believe that!" Whether he was scared or not didn't really matter to me, and I didn't share his excitement. All I wanted to do was go back to my apartment, but my friend couldn't stop talking. "He had his hand on my thigh and then he just worked it up till he was caressing my nuts! I was about to punch him out, but I was afraid to move. Did your guy do that to you?" Though my friend was very excited, I wanted to point out that it was easier for him to be exhilarated because the man's hand was no longer on his crotch, but it didn't seem fair to make fun of the experience he had just had. He asked me why one man called me "Baby" and seemed to know me.

"Just being friendly," I answered, with a shrug, but my friend didn't look like he believed me. What would he say if I told him who had been sitting near us? I was happy to get away from the My-O-My Club, but as my friend and I walked across the oyster shells back toward my car, I realized that I was still smiling, thinking about my mother inside. To give herself over to fun the way she could, I envied that.

My mother loved a good time, so it didn't seem unusual to see her at the My-O-My Club. Very little about the woman ever surprised me. Or I never let her surprise me. What she did for fun, and whom she spent her time with, I told myself, just didn't interest me, not when I was a kid or in my teens or even later, much later. Being around her friends was always exciting, that was certain. They seemed so different from the other women I knew, like my playmates' mothers, who rarely worked and instead stayed home to cook and clean house, or, I should say, to supervise the maids who did the work. Some of them belonged to the Junior League, or to a garden club, but that's about all they did. My mother's companions were entirely different.

When I was nine, one of these lady-friends, Kit, took me for a ride in her little light plane. I had never ridden in a plane before, big or small. We took off from a small airport out near Lake Pontchartrain and climbed steadily above the lake. An outer door was next to my arm, and it leaked a little, so some of the cold air rushing by in the sky outside rattled the door and flowed inside over my jacket, chilling my arm. Thrilled doesn't even begin to describe how I felt. It was a cold wintry day, the wind was blowing, and little whitecaps churned on the top of the dark gray water below. Kit pushed forward on the stick and the plane dipped, diving for the lake, the water coming straight at us. My stomach turned a flip and my mouth stretched open as if I were about to scream, but instead I squealed with pleasure. The plane leveled off not far from the top of the lake, the whitecaps below rushing furiously past my eyes. I had no idea we were going so fast. When Kit turned and headed back to the airport, I almost cried at having to land, tears pooling in the bottom of my eyes and beginning to chill. Little memory of Kit remains, except that she wore black leather pants, like some I had seen on Marlene Dietrich and that seemed as exotic to me as the nude breasts in *National Geographic*. For years I confused Kit with Amelia Earhart. In my mind they were both heroes, both women, both pilots, and both wore slacks; they must have been the same person, or so I thought.

* * *

It's no longer necessary to visit the My-O-My Club, or walk Bourbon Street, to find sex. One recent night at my home in Vermont, I couldn't sleep, so I got up, heated some milk, and went to sit in front of the television, flipping through channels. Pay-per-View was presenting a preview of a show that I could order, and it teased me with the sight of a beautiful young woman slowly taking off her clothes, seductively wiggling her hips, and twisting her voluptuous body around. When she was down to her panties, she lay back on a recliner and moved sensuously around, tweaking her nipples with one hand and pushing the other hand down to her groin, which for a second she touched.

I marveled that such an explicit image was piped into my home, and that now on my local cable station I could see and hear things that I was never allowed to think, much less talk about, as a child. Not long ago I was at a Cub Scout meeting in a friend's home. Planning an outing, we were sitting around a dining table at one end of a large living room. At the other end of the room the television was on, and the young kids of the house were walking in and out, hardly noticing that on the television Debra Winger was humping Richard Gere in *An Officer and a Gentleman* (1982). Sex was out in the open, or at least the image of sex was out in the open.

When I see such scenes, I realize that I prefer my movie erotics to be like the breathtaking, sensual tracking and zooming shots in Jancsó's film *Red Psalm* (1972). Or in the few films, like Linklater's *Before Sunrise* (1995), that present talking to be as intimate as sex, which is the same as saying that sex is just one among several kinds of intimacy. To see such movies is to be reminded of the films I saw in the forties and fifties where sex in movies was hidden, which makes more sense to me than seeing Richard and Debra moan and bounce around in somebody else's living room. I'm not a prude; it's just that movie images of people having sex seem absurd, about as real as the childbirth scenes where a doctor holds up a newborn that is perfectly clean and weighs about twenty pounds. When I was ten and watching *The Big Sleep* (1946), I didn't pay much attention when Humphrey Bogart and Dorothy Malone locked the doors of her bookshop and went into the back room. After a fade-out and then a fade-in, they came out, traded a few innuendoes, and he left. I miss that image of sexuality; it seems much simpler than most of my real life experiences.

Not all movie sex was uncomplicated in the forties and fifties. I didn't see Wyler's *The Best Years of Our Lives* (1946) when it came out, but I did go when it was re-released in 1954. What stunned me—maybe because I was seventeen—was the way in which the film seemed so much about sex, but very indirectly. More than a few scenes take place with a man and a woman near a bed, some involving the woman undressing the man. In one sequence Myrna Loy brings Fredric March "breakfast in bed," but I was sure she wasn't just talking about the food. When the sailor, who has lost his hands in the war, stands by his bed and lets his girlfriend take off the harness for his artificial hands, exposing how helpless and vulnerable he is, I couldn't help wondering if what he was really letting her in on was what it was going to be like for her to make love to a man with no hands. Since nobody ever mentioned the sex I thought I saw in the movie, I never dared mention my own thoughts. It seemed clear to me that I had a dirty mind and had read these things into the film. To say anything would also mean acknowledging that, in the movie, passive men were being bedded by assertive women, which didn't fit my movie-influenced image of manhood. What made more sense was just to pretend, like the movies, that sex didn't exist.

In Vermont I looked back at my TV screen. The half-naked woman stood up, turned her body to the camera and pushed her underwear down and off, while swaying her behind at the camera. She then climbed up on a chair and turned her bottom to me until I could see the lips of her genital area. The woman said, "My name is Jeannie. Vote for me," and the image disappeared, replaced by words that told me how to order the Pay-per-View feature. Vote for you for what, Jeannie? I couldn't find out unless I was willing to pay for the program, whatever it was, but I was not that interested in finding out.

You're just a little too tame, Jeannie, a little too picturesque, pale by comparison to my introduction to sex, which happened when I was ten and my mother started letting me go with her to visit two women I found fascinating. They were window dressers at a department store in downtown New Orleans, designing and outfitting the windows with mannequined clothes and displays that would attract shoppers' attention. They were a happy pair. Jo was a large, almost athletic woman, with close-cropped hair sprinkled with strands of gray. The other woman, Edie, was smaller, even petite, with a huge grin; when she laughed, her eyes were hidden behind lids that almost shut.

One of the things I loved about visiting them was that they would come pick us up in their thirties Chevy coupe with a rumble seat outside in the back. The leather seat had been exposed so much to the weather that pieces were coming off and the whole surface was cracked and rough, like sandpaper. All the way to their home I would ride outside in this rumble seat, the wind blowing my hair and stinging my face while I sat there with an idiotic smile.

As soon as we got to their house, Jo would put on a huge pot of water, then cut a square of cheesecloth and drop into its center an assortment of mustard seeds, coriander, and cloves. Pulling the corners up and tying them together with a piece of string, she dropped the cloth ball into the water, along with some salt, cayenne, bay leaves, and a few lemon quarters. As the water came to a boil, a pail of crawfish or crab or shrimp was dropped in, and the house then filled with the acrid smell of the spices and seafood. So pungent was this odor that I could feel it tickling the hairs inside my nostrils.

I liked it best when we ate crawfish. A newspaper was spread over the white enamel table in their kitchen, and from the boiling pot Jo would ladle out the crawfish and make a huge mound in the center of the newspaper. After Edie made me a Shirley Temple drink, she pulled bottles of Jax beer from the refrigerator for the grown-ups, and we all dug in, snapping heads off and sucking out the juice, which sometimes was so hot with the cayenne that tears would stream down everyone's face. Breaking off the end of the tail, squeezing the meat into her mouth, my mother would snort with pleasure and almost always say, "Oh, God, that's the best thing I ever put in my mouth!" Then she'd take a swig of beer.

Jokes and stories whipped around the table like a silver ball in a pinball machine. Now and then my mother would make an effort to talk only about the food, but she was having too good a time, so her attempt was halfhearted. I would try to listen to the conversation, but everything was said and done so quickly that I wanted to say, "Tilt! I don't understand what you're talking about!" Instead I laughed, as full of pleasure as I was with crawfish.

Sometimes they got into heated discussions, over just about anything. The more intense the argument, the more they forgot I was there. Sometimes it was about movies. I hardly remember any of the titles they talked about, but I do recall how much my mother disliked all the movies where having a good time was made into something evil. She also hated the movies with what Jo and Edie called "bad" women.

"They're not bad," my mother would declare. "The movies make them seem bad so people will believe it's terrible to have a good time!"

"Gertie," answered Edie, "who cares? I like the bad women. How about Lana Turner in *Postman Always Rings Twice*? In that white skirt, she has the cutest little you-know-what."

My mother got angry. "Your mind is just in the gutter!"

"Gertie, it's just a movie!"

"I like to have a good cry when I go to a picture!" my mother said. "I want the girl to get the guy and live happily ever after!"

"The men are all numskulls," Edie said, and everybody agreed, laughing loudly.

Now my mother was getting noisier and noisier. "And the wives are all such Goody Two-Shoes!"

My mother always talked loudly and took defiant positions when she was drinking. There was no denying her point of view. When Edie, Jo, and my mother drank and ate too much, which happened some evenings, we would spend the night, much to my delight. Not only was I sure that they would sleep so late that I could skip school the next day, but the bedroom they let me use had a dresser with a drawer at the bottom that was filled with comicstrip booklets that were pornographic. They featured famous people, like movie actors, or characters that I knew from the Sunday funny papers—Maggie and Jiggs, Dick Tracy, L'il Abner, Flash Gordon, even Dagwood. Years later I found out the little pamphlets were called eight-page bibles, or Tijuana bibles.

The booklet I remember best was about Cary Grant, something about trying to prove he was not a "fairy." Cary had a huge penis, the size of a baseball bat, jutting straight out from his comic strip body, and he was always finding a time and place to put it into some woman's mouth or different holes in her behind, as his way of proving that indeed he was not a "fairy." Not knowing what sex was, I found the little books confusing. From these little eight-page bibles I got a glimpse of some strange behaviors by human beings, but they made no sense to me. I always thought that Cary was trying to pee into some woman's mouth or behind, which seemed really disgusting, but the pictures were fascinating, and I sometimes pored over those booklets late into the night, attempting to make sense of what the people were doing and saying to one another. It seemed important to figure out how Cary got his penis to grow so big. "Pussy," "cock," "prick," "fairy," and "cunt" were all new words for me, at age ten, so I had to figure out from the comic strip what each word meant.

Jo had a brother, and one weekend when we were visiting, I walked down the hall and passed his bedroom. He was asleep, but his door was cracked open and he was sleeping in the nude. His penis was all hard and big, too, just like Cary's, which shocked me. I thought the comic strip pictures were fantasies. As the brother slept, the penis rose and fell with his breathing. I wanted to stand there forever and watch it move up and down, but I was scared that he would wake up and see me.

When I got to the kitchen, my mother and the two women were whispering. Jo was making an up-and-down motion with her hand, imitating the brother's penis. Everyone laughed. They didn't know I had watched him, so they had no qualms about discussing what they had seen, although with somewhat muffled words that were supposedly vague, trying to shield me from the truth of what they were talking about. The way they giggled made it clear to me that they thought it hilarious what the brother's penis had been doing. To me, even at ten, the way that the women spoke about the brother made me certain that a hard, erect penis, whether the brother's or the ones I had seen in my eight-page bibles, was something you talked about in a hushed voice. Something was forbidden.

I had a wonderful time at this home; it was always titillating. People were laughing as they ate, drank, and joked, and I loved seeing my mother so happy, but a charge in the atmosphere made it feel a little dangerous, as if something unpredictable could happen at any moment. Getting close to my mother and her friends was very exciting, but I learned that I had to be careful to make a boundary, one that shouldn't be crossed, for fear of being electrocuted.

My mother was erratic: one moment she was joking about the penis of Jo's brother, and the next minute she was the refined Southern lady who would walk into any place in the world as if she owned it. "Was the trout swimming in the water last night, Alton?" she would ask her waiter at Galatoire's. "Good. Then I'll have the Trout Marguery."

"Right away, Mrs. Perry," Alton would say, "and your drinks." Alton knew she always drank a double vodka with a dash of water and lots of ice. Now and then he would surprise her with a Sazerac, a New Orleans blend of bourbon and bitters, with the glass first coated with absinthe. Alton was her favorite waiter because he always knew which drink to serve her, like the glass of Château d'Yquem she liked for her dessert. She often made me very proud of the way in which she had such a presence in the world, but there was a side that frightened me. One minute she was the restaurant queen, or hugging me, and the next minute she wouldn't make it home for dinner—or even for the night.

I never told my grade school buddies about going to my mother's friends; I wasn't sure why. What would I say? The little eight-page bibles made no sense to me and I was afraid if I admitted it, everyone would laugh at me. Surely they already knew about cocks, pussy, cunt, and pricks. I was the one in the dark.

* * *

What my mother and these women did together I have no idea. Whether or not they were lovers, I don't know. I do wish that my mother and I could have talked about her relationships with women, so at least she wouldn't have had to hide things from me, but I imagine it was hard enough being a Southern woman of her generation, having to conceal her sexuality from many people because it was so unacceptable. To be open with me was just impossible. She probably knew that I might not be able to handle this information. The forties and the fifties, when I was still living at home, were not times for sex talk. The only advice my mother ever gave me was not to sleep in the same house as an unmarried woman. That was adultery.

Perhaps everything would have been easier for my mother and me if sex had been represented more openly in the movies of the forties—we might even have been able to have a real conversation on the topic—but the Production Code restricted anything but a hint of sexuality on the screen. I remember seeing *Pitfall* (1948) and trying to figure out what Dick Powell was doing at Lizabeth Scott's apartment until 11:30 P.M. Was he trying to prove he was not a fairy, like Cary Grant? Nothing on the screen helped me. When I first heard from my friends about French kissing, I didn't believe such a thing was done; nobody ever did anything like that in the movies, or at least you couldn't tell it. Sometimes my mother would ask me to perform for her friends by showing how people kissed in the movies. I would purse my lips, keep them closed, and make a kissing noise. My mother and her friends thought that was hilarious.

The representation of sex in films has changed dramatically. Bizarre is how it seems now to recall all the fanfare surrounding Preminger's *The Moon Is Blue* (1953), which was banned for using vulgar words. I can remember how wicked I felt seeing the film and hearing, for the first time, characters on the screen use such lewd words as "virgin, "sex," and "mistress." Maggie McNamara says to William Holden, "But don't you think it's better for a girl to be preoccupied with sex than occupied?" How risqué, I thought. Later, in the mid-1960s, I drove all the way from Iowa City, Iowa, to Des Moines to see Sidney Lumet's *The Pawnbroker* (1965), supposedly because Lumet's work was significant, and I wanted to see his latest film, but mainly, I suspect, because I had read that a woman's breasts were briefly exposed in the film. Nothing like that had happened before in my moviegoing experience. Today my trip to Des Moines back in 1965 seems ridiculous.

* * *

For all her sexual difference, my mother was really a prude about such matters. When she wanted me to learn something about sex, she would send someone else to speak to me. My Uncle Alexis, the Russian designer, was the one appointed to discuss such matters when he visited. Knowing how much I admired him, my mother sent him to talk to me one evening when I was thirteen. It was a hot, sticky night, and I was sitting up in my bed, reading, when he came in and sat down in a chair across the room. "I want to have a talk with you," he said. I put my book down and nodded my head. "Young men begin a practice—"

Alexis's sentence broke off. Now I was intrigued. This uncle-by-marriage had told me once that he had been ordered by his father to burn the barn full of their horses in order to keep the animals from the Bolsheviks. Anyone with that much courage, I thought, shouldn't have a problem talking about anything.

He tried again. "It's normal, of course."

I waited, unsure what was so normal that it couldn't be named.

"The important thing to remember is, I mean, you have to put the behavior in perspective."

I tried to help. "Uncle Alexis, what are you—?"

He interrupted me. "Just don't do it very often, that's the important thing to keep in mind. Avoid overindulgence, intemperance, and excess in all things."

Uncle Alexis spoke Russian, French, German, and English. When he wasn't sure if he had the right word, he would repeat several synonyms, just to make sure the idea got across. "There's a wonderful English word," he said, "it's 'equipoise.' Think about trying to achieve equipoise. Never too much, or too little, of anything. Do you understand?"

I nodded. I guessed I understood; something about balance.

"It's why I wear gray, not too loud and not too somber." I did know my uncle's argument about gray clothes. He had adopted a dress code that he thought would set him apart from other men. Even the monograms on his shirts were done in gray thread. "What are you reading?" he asked.

"*Brothers Karamazov.*" I wasn't telling the truth, and my uncle knew it, but he just smiled. I didn't dare tell him the book was Maugham's *Of Human Bondage*. Alexis had no use for any British authors after Dickens.

As my uncle held his smile for a few moments and then walked out of my bedroom, I sat up in my bed and puzzled over what had just happened. What was he trying to tell me? His statements were so vague that it was months before I figured out that he was trying to speak to me about masturbation. My mother had sent him, but with what message? I wasn't sure. I couldn't imagine that "equipoise" was her word. As usual, her messages about sex were oblique and contradictory. The few times I tried to ask something of my mother, like what did the word "screwing" mean, she gave a clinical answer: "It's when the man puts his penis in a woman." Where does he put it, how does he get it in, and why in the world would he want to do that?

At the time, I learned very little about sex from my mother. Sometimes I wished that she liked movies the way my dad did, so that I could tell from them what she was thinking and feeling, but even if she had I doubt that I could have learned much from them about her attitudes toward sex. The movies were just too oblique. With my mother I had to make interpretations through the things she tried to hide from me. One time she brought home a recording of the song "Frankie and Johnny," playing it and singing along when she didn't think I was listening. When the record said "he," my mother would sing "she," as in "she done her wrong" instead of "he done her wrong." I realize now that she and her friends had changed the lyrics to make "Frankie and Johnny" into a song about two women, rather than a man and a woman, who have a lovers' quarrel. During this same period she brought home a recording of what I remembered as *This Is My Beloved*. Because I was never allowed to listen to it, which piqued my imagination, I was sure that something about the recording was taboo. One of the days when my mother was not at home after I returned from school, I sneaked the recording out and listened to it. I remember it as a spoken text of words written by Kahlil Gibran, with music in the background. Nothing much seemed very interesting, and I never played it again. Why was it such a big secret?

Remembering this incident recently, I began searching for the recording my mother owned, but the title didn't seem to exist. When I asked the librarian, she said she remembered the title as *The Beloved*. "One of my boyfriends gave me a tape," she said. "Gibran was really big in the sixties." I couldn't find *The Beloved* tape, but the librarian found the book that was the basis for the recording, which I then ordered. When it arrived, I opened the package immediately. "John Walbridge's new translation of *The Beloved: Reflections on the Path of the Heart*," the jacket said; "Kahlil Gibran's writings on love, marriage, and the spiritual union of souls." That didn't sound like what I was expecting, which was something like the eight-page bibles. Though I read the book, or tried reading it, the text hardly kept my interest, for the talk of love was much too sentimental and oversimplified. Who could get excited by a book that said things like, "Who among you would not cross the seas, traverse deserts, go over mountains and valleys to reach the woman whom his spirit has chosen." If my mother liked women, this sentiment was nice, but it was not what I was expecting.

I thought perhaps the text was uninteresting to me as a child because I didn't understand some salacious content, but now, as an adult, I couldn't find anything remotely bawdy. Then gradually it began to dawn on me why my mother hid the recording. When I read the story entitled "The Bridal Bed," I was certain what the recording meant to my mother. Here was the tale of an arranged marriage where the bride at her wedding party, immediately after the ceremony, seeks out her old lover and meets him outside in the garden. She tries to persuade him to run off with her, but he refuses, citing the fact that she is now married. She takes out a knife and stabs him. When he cries out, and the crowd from the wedding party comes to the garden, the bride says, "Look at this handsome young man. . . . He is my lover. I killed him because he is my lover. He is my husband, and I am his bride. We searched but could find no bridal bed worthy of our embrace in this world, which you have made so narrow by your customs, so dark by your ignorance, so corrupt by your lust. We have preferred to go somewhere beyond the clouds."

Now I understood. Of course. To my mother, romantic love was more powerful and important than social customs and norms. Gibran's text justified her own desire to break with such conventions in the name of love. A sentence on the book's flyleaf now made sense to me: "Gibran saw women as the particular victims of rigid social customs and expectations and of standards that made marriage an economic transaction." My mother thought of herself as just such a victim; and an economic transaction was what she had with my father, who sent her a check each month from Africa. I remember vividly seeing him through a doorway once, when he was home for a brief visit, counting out neat piles of cash on their bed. He was giving mother her monthly allowance and the bed was the right place to put it.

It was clear why keeping *The Beloved* to herself was so important. She must have feared that I might understand how passionate her feelings were, how committed she was to her desires, regardless of "rigid social customs." How desperate my mother felt seemed obvious. It was the 1940s, after all. New Orleans may have been more tolerant of homosexual love, but only marginally so. She was a Southern woman, bred and raised to believe that such love was wicked.

It didn't seem that way to me. I liked living with her when she had a new lady-friend. Those times were marvelous, for I caught the fever that she felt. Life seemed really exciting, the world was full of pleasures and possibilities. She would rise earlier than usual, fix me French toast for breakfast, help me pick out my clothes, and, with a kiss and a hug, send me on my way to school. I didn't mind as much that my mother was often away when I came home. Dinner was in the icebox, and I had my friends next door to play with. During these times when she had a new friend, my mother was very happy, she dressed more carefully, her smile had a special sparkle, and she laughed at every little thing. She didn't stay out all night that often, and when she came home, she wasn't, as she would say, "tight," or drunk. She would start talking about new topics, too, like how wonderful the New Orleans Symphony was and how she was going to take me that next Sunday to a performance of Tchaikovsky's *1812 Overture*. That was the only time she ever mentioned it or took me. New magazines, like *Mademoiselle*, appeared in the house, and, sometimes, new cuisine. Suddenly a recipe book appeared, and she would work for hours on a new dish. Now and then she would bring her friend over, someone I had never met before, someone she was very excited to have me meet.

While I loved those times, they never lasted for long. I realize now that the change came when she and her friend stopped seeing one another. My mother didn't suffer fools very well, and people eventually disappointed her, so she would break off the relationship. Sometimes

I think she did so out of guilt, either religious or because she felt that she was neglecting me, because one of the signs that a relationship had ended was that we would begin going to Sunday school and church every week. Knowing how little good it would do my mother, and how quickly the urge would fade, I hated being carted off to Sunday school and church. She was still miserable, seldom cooked me breakfast, rarely smiled, seemed dark and burdened, and was often still in bed when I came home from school. When she was up and walking, her movements were leaden, almost as if her skeleton was having a hard time dragging the rest of her body around. Tears would well up in her eyes for no reason that I could detect; but the surest sign of change was that she would find ways, often foolish ones, to criticize me. "Finish your food," she would say at the table, "or I'll take it back and give it to someone more deserving."

When she talked like that, I wanted her to find another lady-friend soon. I stood on the sidelines and cheered her on. Since she believed that life would make sense if she just found the right person to make her happy, I did, too. When she finally found someone she felt close to, I was thrilled. They were the happiest couple I knew. When my mother was lonely and depressed, her friend held her hand, and when my mother's friend went through some ordeal, like losing a business that her father had started, it was my mother who comforted her. My mother had settled down. There didn't seem to be any great passion about it; she had simply found someone to be with. When my mother became sick and went into the hospital, her friend became ill, too, and also went into the hospital. When my mother died, her friend died within a few months.

Her life wasn't perfect. She ate too much, smoked too much, and drank way too much, but she had a companion. I missed my childhood mother, the dangerous, exciting one. Though sometimes messy, outrageous, and unpredictable, she certainly was more fun.

* * *

I finally got up the courage to go inside Rick's Cabaret, but as I opened the door, I was almost blinded by the shafts of colored light that spun around the room. When my eyes adjusted, and I saw the young, beautiful woman who was stripping, I realized even more how ironic it was when the two ugly women asked the man at the door if he was hiring. Food was served at Rick's, so I sat down in the second row back from the stage and ordered a Caesar salad with shrimp. The waitress, herself hardly dressed, brought me tableware and placed it on top of the linen that covered the table. The posh decor made me smile. Rick's Cabaret was not like the strip joints I went to as a young man; they were a little seedy, the women older and pudgier, and you certainly couldn't order food and have it served at a table covered with a white cloth.

I had never seen such a beautiful woman doing a striptease. She was down to a G-string, working the edge of the stage just a foot from men sitting in the front row who stuffed bills into a garter around one thigh. Her free hand lightly caressed her breasts, then her crotch, and her hips undulated seductively as she gradually lowered herself so that only her feet and one arm underneath were holding her body up. Her position was almost identical to the plastic female figures used as tables at the Korova Milkbar in Kubrick's *A Clockwork Orange* (1971).

The little bulge of a muscle in the stripper's upper arm convinced me that she worked out, probably with weights, and her whole body showed the results, her skin stretched over taut muscles. She smiled, seemingly pleased at the effect that she was having on the men who reached out repeatedly to add a few bills to the dozen or so that were stuck on her. As she was bending backward, one man put several bills on her stomach, and she scooped them up with her free hand. Hardly noticing the loud music, I was enthralled by her beautiful young body and her movements. To keep from revealing my fascination I pulled out a notebook and began taking notes. This was an intellectual experience, after all, or so I told myself. I was just present at Rick's for information to use in some book, so I felt safe with a pen and journal in hand, and a lump of shrimp in my mouth. Or so I pretended. If people caught me watching the woman strip, I could always write something in my journal, or just look away and observe instead the large television monitor, hanging above the stage, which was showing a soccer match on ESPN. What the soccer match had to do with the dancing woman was not clear; Rick's just seemed determined to be a place where every need was met.

During a break in the floor show, a couple next to me hired one of the young women to come and strip for them. She brought over a big footstool, put it next to their table, and danced, peeling down to a G-string not much bigger than a stamp. While the stripper moved her body just inches away, the woman sitting at the table undid one of the man's shirt buttons and put her hand inside, caressing his stomach and chest. What she did was the most shocking act in Rick's, and I almost ran out the door. "No touching!" I wanted to shout. There's always someone who doesn't know the rules. Rick's was supposed to be safe. Voyeurs don't touch and don't want to be touched. That's why there are movies.

* * *

The subject of sex in the movies came to mind not long ago when I was looking again at two of the Andy Hardy films my father liked so much, *Love Finds Andy Hardy* (1938) and *Love Laughs at Andy Hardy* (1946). I would like to make a movie about my dad and these Andy Hardy pictures. The footage would begin with us talking about them.

"I can't imagine why you like films like this," I would say.

"What do you mean? They're swell."

"They don't make sense."

"'Give a Dog a Good Name.'" My dad, when pressured, sometimes quoted from a book he had memorized, Dale Carnegie's *How to Win Friends and Influence People*. It came out in 1936, the year he and my mother were married.

"What does that mean?" I ask.

"Pay attention to what's good in the pictures."

"What's good about them? They're repulsive, actually."

"Repulsive? No, they're charming."

"They're about the denial of sex. Look at Andy's parents—they're ancient. He's supposed to be nineteen or so, and they look seventy, at least. It's to make them totally sexless."

"You should learn 'How to Criticize and Not Be Hated for It.'"

"Look at Andy's love interest in one of the films, Lana Turner. I mean, this is a national sexpot, and here she looks silly, like she's playing dress-up."

"In that bathing suit," Dad says, "she looks pretty good to me."

"It looks like a sack on her, three sizes too big."

After Dad rubs his eyes, while mentally sorting through his Carnegie quotes, he says, "'If You Want to Gather Honey, Don't Kick Over the Beehive.'"

I'm determined to get him to see my point. "Bonita Granville, as Andy's great love in the other film, has about as much sex appeal as a concrete block. She even has a double chin."

"'Talk about Your Own Mistakes First.'"

My blood pressure is rising. "Out of spite one of Andy's girlfriends dates a man who is not only much older but turns out later to be her cousin. Now there's a sexy relationship! And what do you think when you see Andy dating that girl who's so big and lanky? He's so short, she's so tall, nobody could ever imagine them having sex together."

My dad smiles. "See, none of the people have sex, so they're not picture shows about sex."

"No, no," I say. "Since the films work so hard to deny sexuality, they're really about sex." When I hear these words come out of my mouth, I feel ridiculous.

My dad looks at me as if my nose just evaporated and says, "That's the most twisted thing I ever heard. Now I'm thinking you're the one with sex on the brain."

"Well, something is strange about these films, Dad. Andy's college girlfriend marries her guardian. There's gray in his hair and he looks twice her age. What do you make of that?"

Dad looks at a nearby wall, as if an answer is written there, or at least in a Dale Carnegie quote he can use. Finally, after a long pause, I say, "Do you really like these Andy Hardy movies?"

"I do. If the parents are older and wiser, that's good. Just enjoy the picture."

"It's not in me."

"I'd much rather see them," my father says, "than one of your modern pictures, where all they think about is—. I won't say the words. You know what I mean, all those different kinds of sex."

"It is embarrassing," I say.

"You're right about that, so we agree," my father says, "'Get the Other Person Saying Yes, Yes, Immediately.'" He winks at me.

I don't wink back, and after a moment he asks, "So you tell me what you think is a good movie."

A title pops into my head: "*Jeanne Dielman, 23 Quai du Commerce, 1080 Bruxelles.*"

"That's the title of a movie?"

"Yes."

My father asks, "What's it about?"

Now I wish I had cited some other film. "The answer won't tell you anything. It's not what the film is about, not really, but what you experience watching it."

"Okay, but tell me what happens anyway."

I say, "A woman lives alone with her son. Sometimes she entertains men."

"Entertains?" My father smiles. "So it's a film about sex—one of your modern ones where they show everything?"

"No, not really."

"What does this woman do other than 'entertain' men?" my father asks.

"She peels potatoes, cooks, cleans up, shops, takes a bath."

"That's it?"

"Yes."

"Nothing else happens?"

"At the end she kills a man."

"Why?"

"I think because he made her feel something, maybe he gave her an orgasm."

My father doesn't bat an eye, rushing to say, "That's it?"

"Yes."

"Nothing but sex and violence," my father says, with a big smile on his face, "one of your modern films." He winks at me again. "I should have known. Give me my Andy Hardy films any day."

"*Jeanne Dielman* is true to experience. The woman's life is banal, and she stuffs all her feelings."

"If you say so," my father says. "Principle number five is 'Talk in Terms of the Other Person's Interests.' Right?"

I'm beginning to get angry at my father. "No, it's not right."

"All those foreign films—who wants to see a movie that's true to experience? I hate that idea. I go to movies to get away from 'experience.' Do you actually enjoy this *Jeanne* movie?"

I'm not going to tell my father I don't go to movies for enjoyment, at least not his kind. I shrug.

"Tell me an American film you like."

"Sure," I say. "Ernie Gehr's *Serene Velocity*. It's an American movie."

"Catchy title."

"Don't make fun of something you've never seen; it's a wonderful film." I smile. "It's twenty-three minutes of a hallway."

My father winces and says, "You stop poking fun at me. Tell me some regular American films."

"*Best Years of Our Lives*."

"Now you're talking," my father says. "Especially the part where Fredric March and Myrna Loy tell their daughter that the secret of a happy marriage is to hate each other." My father smiles. "That's true to experience."

"That's not exactly what they say."

"Well, it's close," my dad says, laughing. He quickly adds, "Don't forget, 'Give a Dog a Good Name.'"

My movie footage breaks off abruptly.

9 Memento Mori

ON ANOTHER RETURN VISIT TO NEW Orleans I decided to take a guided tour of an old cemetery near the French Quarter, where people are buried above ground in vaults. The film *Easy Rider* (1969) has a scene that was shot in this graveyard, called St. Louis No. 1. Dennis Hopper, Peter Fonda, and two hookers drop some acid, and what follows is a psychedelic nightmare. The women disrobe, cry, and dance, while the men sit on the statuary and speak nonsense, even as the world spins about and sometimes appears in the exaggerated close-up of a fisheye lens. "How do I get out of here?" one of the hookers screams. Over parts of the scene, what's heard is the repeated "pow-pow" of a pile driver nearby and sometimes a young woman's voice intoning the Apostles' Creed, the Hail Mary, and the Lord's Prayer. It's madness, the stereotypical visualization of an acid trip.

My mother had once made a crack about St. Louis No. 1, looking at the grave sites and saying, "Don't they clean up real nice!" The Southern phrase means, "You look really good when you take a bath, comb your hair, and dress up." I remember her expression because it seemed strange to make a joke about the whitewashed vaults. The saying was too rural for my mother's vocabulary, but, like using "ain't" and "y'all," it was useful now and then for emphasis—or as a joke. Remembering the way my mother made fun of this cemetery, I thought I would visit it myself. Having heard that it was dangerous to go alone, I went on a tour with five people and a guide.

As we crossed Rampart Street and entered the "Campo Santo," as the sign said, the hot July day was interrupted by a brief shower, and the rain cooled the air, leaving small droplets of water on the tombs. As our group stopped just inside the cemetery, I saw that the little rectangular opening at the end of one vault was open, and I moved my face closer. Peering into the hole, sensing the moist darkness, I was transported for a moment back to the hiding place under my home, where I had peered out onto the world. For the first time I realized how much my secret place had been like a little tomb.

Our group's tour guide, a young woman in her thirties who was a little too enthusiastic about cemeteries, said, "Vaults above ground are common in France, so that's one of the reasons why early New Orleanians buried their dead this way, but much of the city is below sea level." She paused, looking at our group as if we should understand the implication of what she had said, but no one spoke, so she continued. "The water table in New Orleans was very high in the eighteenth century—it was before modern drainage systems—so burying people below ground didn't work." She paused again, as if surely we now understood, but still no one said anything. "When a flood, or a heavy rain, came along, the coffins would pop back to the surface, and nobody liked seeing their relatives floating around, so they started burying people above ground in these vaults." Now everybody on the tour finally understood, and we all nodded before following the guide as she began to walk again.

Looking around, I recalled that "Cities of the Dead" was a name given to these cemeteries, and it was easy to see why. The profusion of marble and whitewashed tombs resembled a cityscape. I had always presumed that these vaults, depending on their size, held only two or three members of a family, but the first vault I looked at had almost twenty names on it.

Before I could ask why, the guide said, "Some of these vaults contain the remains of several dozen people, going back to the eighteenth century. How is that possible?" None of us responded, so she went on. "When a family member died, the vault was opened and the coffin placed inside. The next time a family member passed away, they opened the vault again, pulled out the old coffin, and removed its contents—in this New Orleans heat, the vault acts like an oven, so it doesn't take long for the body to decompose. These ashes and pieces of bone were loaded back into the tomb, either pushed to the back or dropped into a *caveau* at the bottom. The body of the newly deceased was then put in the vault and it was sealed again, the same steps repeated generation after generation. Even today." I looked around at the other people in the group; we were all grimacing a little.

Near the end of my tour the guide stopped beside a large vault, saying, "This is the tomb of Marie Laveau, a famous voodoo queen of the nineteenth century. Well, we think it's the tomb of Marie, but it may be her daughter, who had the same name. She was a voodoo queen, too, almost as famous as her mother." The guide pointed to the base of the vault. "You can see that the faithful don't care which Marie is buried here." The ground was strewn with offerings—flowers, coins, lipstick, candy, even a glass of water; and the tomb itself was covered with × marks. Pointing down at one of the gifts, a half-eaten apple, the guide said, "The apple is not even brown, so someone left it within the last hour or so. This is no dead religion." Having presumed that voodoo was mainly a tourist gimmick, one of the ways to sell an exotic New Orleans, I was surprised to see all the gifts and the markings.

I asked, "What are the ×'s for?"

"When you ask Marie for a favor," the guide said, "you put an × on the tomb, at least that's what I understand. If the favor is granted, you come back and make two more × marks."

There were many more triple × marks than single ones. I was impressed. The group stepped away to look at a nearby tomb, and, since no one was watching, I picked up something at the base of Marie Laveau's vault. It was a small roll of paper, tied with pink thread. I pulled the thread off and unrolled the document, exposing three handwritten lines. The first said, "Death to—" The second and third lines contained the names of two men. I felt uncomfortable now, as if I were handling something illicit or dangerous. Did Marie Laveau grant this request? Quickly, before my companions could notice, I stuck the little piece of paper in my pocket. St. Louis No. 1 cemetery, the tomb of a voodoo queen, a little note asking for the death of two men—all these reminders of death disturbed me. The tour of the cemetery was over in a few moments, and as we all walked back to different parts of the French Quarter, I found myself thinking about the ways in which death has shaped who I am and what I think.

* * *

Flabbergasted when my dad left home to live and work in Africa, I decided that I would never again be so surprised by something terrible. The only other bad thing that could happen in my life, so I thought, would be to have my father die, so for the next twelve years I prepared for his death by imagining it over and over. A terrible car crash. Bitten by a black mamba. A Ford trimotor falling out of the African sky and crashing in the bush. Just as I would do years later with my own children, I prepared myself for just about any form of death. Sometimes the imagined events were so real to me that I flinched.

On April 2, 1957, sitting in a theater class at college, listening to the tenth person recite the same passage from Shakespeare's *Antony and Cleopatra*, I felt a hand on my arm and looked up to see the theater secretary. "There's an urgent phone call for you," she said. I knew immediately what had happened. When I reached the phone and picked it up, I heard my mother's voice say, amidst tears, "Your father is dead. He had a heart attack, and they couldn't get him into the hospital in time." Listening to my mother, I felt surprisingly calm, more relieved than anything. Having prepared myself so much for my father's death, the actual event seemed a little anticlimactic.

Where he was working in Liberia, West Africa, the embalming techniques were very primitive, at least that's what we were told, so the airline was reluctant to bring the body back, even in a sealed casket. After weeks of wrangling, they agreed, but the coffin had to be bolted to the outside of the plane as it flew back to the States. When the body arrived, almost a month after my dad's death, the local undertaker said that we should not unseal the casket. Nor should there be an indoor service, the odor was already bad enough. We would not want to see the body anyway; it would have decomposed badly after weeks in the African heat. We did not open the casket. I never saw my father's corpse. Only a graveside service was held. How could I ever know he was really dead? Later I began to think that we had been tricked. Surely my father wasn't dead; he must have had another family somewhere, and this was his way of getting rid of my mother and me. That was his last big secret.

Whatever enigmas surrounded my dad's death seemed insurmountable, and I went about the business of memorializing him. Taking his photograph to Jackson Square in New Orleans, I asked one of the artists there to do a pastel portrait, and then had it framed. I needed to honor him in some way, I told myself, and this was the best thing I could think of. It seemed absolutely certain to me that I was devastated by my father's death, but one night, not too many months after he died, I discovered different feelings when I went to see a Japanese movie, Kurosawa's *Rashomon* (1951), that was just being shown in New Orleans for the first time.

As the film opens, a hard rain is falling and two men are sitting under the Rashomon gate. As one of the men begins to speak in Japanese, these English words pop onto the screen: "I don't understand. I don't understand it at all!" Seeing these subtitles, I felt elated. My father wasn't with me, so I wouldn't have to listen to him complaining about the subtitles. As *Rashomon* progressed, presenting a tale told from several different viewpoints, I was even more glad my father was absent, for I wouldn't have to argue for a film that was more complicated and subtle than a Western with Fuzzy St. John. What pleasure I felt, watching *Rashomon* by myself.

* * *

Even though I was only seven years old when it happened, I recollect my Grandfather Stevens's death because I remember how my mother called me inside from playing in the yard, hugged me too tightly, and told me her father was dead. I kept shifting my glance over to the window, wishing I were outside playing. On the train to the funeral in Magnolia, Mississippi, I ran up and down the aisle, peering out different windows, first on one side and then the other. It was my first train ride, and I was too thrilled to sit still. After I had run by one man dozens of times, he asked me to stop, looked at me carefully, and then asked my mother's maiden name. When I said Stevens, he replied, "I thought so." If I don't actually recall this incident, my mother told the tale so often that I think I do remember it. She repeated the story because it fit her image of what the South was about, which was "blood."

My grandfather's wallet, the one he was carrying when he died in 1944, wound up in my mother's possession, and after she died, in mine. I took it out of her old cedar chest recently. The brown leather was worn and faded, and smelled like mothballs. Most of the contents were what you would expect—current identification and membership cards, a driver's license, an automobile registration certificate. Because he had just been transferred to Washington, D.C., by the War Production Board, there were also passes to the U.S. House of Representatives and Senate. One card scared me a little. "Work Wins Wars," it said, which sounded at first too much like "*Arbeit Macht Frei*," the Nazi death camp sign. In small type at the bottom, the card added, "Lumber fights for Liberty." Not surprisingly, another card certified my grandfather's membership in the American Poetry Association.

Several items in the billfold were peculiar. Even though this was his wallet in 1944, there was a little piece of paper on which he had typed: "Recapitulation of 1934's Work for the Southern Pine Association." Summarized carefully were his expenses, wages, numbers of inspections, violations reported. At the very bottom the note listed hours worked as "2035" and hours traveled as "1084." Here was more proof that my grandfather loved being on the road, but why did he keep in his wallet a statement that was ten years old? I can only imagine that it was important because 1934 was his first year again as a lumber inspector after the nightmares of the Depression and a heart attack. When he was almost fifty-three years old, his life had turned for the better and he was on the road again, traveling around the Southeast inspecting lumberyards. The year 1934 must have been the happiest one since the Depression began. In the wallet was also an identification card for the "Fire Proof" Skirvin Hotel in Oklahoma City, and on the back my grandfather had written, "Good etchers to follow up." Below that was a list of names that I did not recognize, except that of James McNeill Whistler. I shouldn't have been surprised. A man who wrote poems and books might easily have been interested in etchings, but the information was new to me. Here was a whole aspect of my grandfather that no one had ever mentioned.

Then I came across a thin piece of paper, neatly folded. Opening it, I found a carefully penciled design for what I took to be furniture.

Since my Grandfather Stevens often built pieces for himself and his family, the sketch was no surprise. But what kind of furniture? Was the drawing a side or top view? I couldn't tell. My grandfather's neat handwriting stipulated the dimensions of the object, along with an indication that there was to be a piece of plate glass, half an inch thick, over part of the side or top. The interior dimensions were twenty-two inches by sixty-six inches. The ends were gently curved. It was a skillful drawing, carefully shaded, and so precise it looked as if it had been made with drafting implements. What was this sketch, a long coffee table of some sort?

Later in the day I showed the drawing to my son, who was an apprentice to a custom-furniture maker. We were both intrigued by the fact that he was doing what my grandfather had sometimes done, building furniture. My son took one look at the sketch and said immediately, "It's a coffin." I was shocked and took the drawing back. I had misread a crucial part. The interior dimensions were not sixty-six inches but six feet six inches. Grandfather Stevens was six feet three inches tall. My son was right. It was a coffin, the section of plate glass for viewing the face of the corpse. I felt something heavy pulling me down in my chair. What was my grandfather doing with a drawing of a coffin in his wallet when he died? Did he build it? Or was this his instruction to his family about how he wanted his coffin to be made? Was the coffin built by someone else and used at his funeral? The drawing seemed macabre. Was this a final, perhaps futile, attempt to have control over his death?

I called an uncle, who was my grandfather's son-in-law, and asked if he remembered the coffin at the funeral. He said, "I wasn't even there. If I remember right, I was dodging bullets from German snipers shooting from the top of the Leaning Tower of Pisa." He had no idea what my grandfather's coffin looked like.

I called another uncle, my grandfather's son, and when I asked him about the sketch, he showed little surprise. All he could tell me was that his father had made several pieces of furniture. "I didn't know my father very well," he added. While I had him on the phone, I asked this uncle about the times his father was away so much, but he hardly recalled those days, or so he said. Then he took the conversation in another direction, although in his mind the ideas were connected. "I don't know much about having a family, you know. After Daddy had his first heart attack, he and Mother went off to Caddo Gap, Arkansas, and our family really broke apart. I was only thirteen or fourteen. The Depression had just hit and we were all in a mess. My older brothers and sisters, including your mother, all went out and found a job, but I was too young. My mother left me with a woman who took in boarders, somebody from their church, a good Christian woman, so she didn't charge me for the room. I still needed to eat, so I had to quit school and get a job. I'll never forget when Daddy got well and they came back to Jackson. Mother handed me an envelope with $2.75 in it and said, 'This is all we have, you're on your own now, son.' The money in the envelope was exactly what my landlady now wanted to charge me for room and board—a week! I was alone, with just enough to make it through a few days—can you imagine that?"

As my uncle talked, I thought back to the year of grandfather's heart attack and calculated my uncle's age. He was not thirteen or fourteen, as he said, but a month shy of seventeen when my grandparents told him he was on his own. It wasn't worth challenging him, since my real interest was in the coffin sketch. I asked if he remembered his father's coffin. Was it the same as the sketch? There was a long pause, and I interjected, "Were you home from the war?"

"Yes," he said. "Daddy died in 1946. The war was over and I had been home several months. No, Daddy wasn't buried in the coffin he sketched. I remember going to pick out the coffin."

Had my uncle said 1946? Someone rang his doorbell; he had to get off the phone. "I'll call you back," he said, and hung up. I checked all my records, including a copy of the telegram to my mother that brought the news of her father's death. My Grandfather Stevens died in October 1944. If my uncle was wrong about the year of his father's death, how could I believe his memory of the coffin? Maybe my grandfather had built his coffin and was buried in it. There was no one else alive who knew, and this uncle, who was eighty-two, seemed a little confused about dates. As with my own father, there was some mystery surrounding my grandfather's death, or at least about his coffin.

I have cousins who share this same grandfather. One of them is a good friend, so I called him and described the sketch. "What kind of person carries around a drawing of his coffin?" I asked. "A Stevens!" he responded. We both laughed. I knew he was talking about the piece of glass plate over the top of the coffin. We've often joked about our family, how they're all extroverts and think of themselves as the center of the universe, so it didn't surprise him at all that our grandfather would have sketched a coffin with a piece of plate glass on top where people could see his face. Or our grandfather may have hoped that as the coffin was being lowered into the grave, he might be able to look out one last time, to be the pure observer, taking in clouds and trees before the dirt was shoveled in on top of him.

After the conversation with my cousin, I looked again at the sketch. What came to mind were stories about monks who slept each night in their coffins to remind them of their own mortality. My grandfather must have been someone who faced death head-on, who did not turn away, someone who was so comfortable with death, who accepted it so completely, that he could draw his own coffin and keep the sketch in his wallet. His religion helped; he believed firmly that there was a life after death, a better life, one with God, but it was more than just a religious belief that led him to draw his coffin. Beds, coffins, furniture, they were all a part of living; nothing was to be feared or run away from. My grandfather may have faced his mortality by sketching his own coffin, but I don't think he ever built it, or the act would have entered family lore and the story told to me. Like the rest of us, he thought he had plenty of time.

* * *

Death and films are deeply connected, a fact that is very apparent when watching old home movies. In some of those I made as a child, my father appears as someone who is alive, but I know that he is dead. To watch any movie is to confront mortality. I learned this fact more than thirty years ago in an odd place, the windowless basement room of a university building in Vermillion, South Dakota. Dark and damp, like a cellar, it reminded me of the crawl space under my house in New Orleans. Projected on the wall of the basement room in Vermillion were movies that nobody had seen for sixty years or more. From 1896 to 1912 the only way to copyright a film was to print it onto rolls of photographic paper. Since most of the actual films had long since disappeared, the paper rolls at the Library of Congress were the only copies of these early movies. Because they were on paper, some of which was brittle, it wasn't even possible to look at them, much less project them as movies. The Library of Congress hired a man named Kemp Niver to restore the rolls of paper and to copy the images onto motion picture film so they could be viewed.

I sat in Vermillion with Kemp Niver looking at the first results of his work. The images, not seen for decades, reeked of death, at least to me. Watching some New York scenes, I saw the old Pennsylvania Station and the first Madison Square Garden, as well as the original Metropolitan Opera House, all buildings that no longer existed. The adults who walked in and out of these buildings, who rode the trolleys and elevated trains, who strolled along sidewalks in front of old brownstones, surely were all dead by now. Looking at these images of people and buildings now long gone made me very aware of the passing of time, and of a day years ago when I wasn't alive, but other things and people were. Someday I will die, I thought to myself, and someone else will be looking at images of me.

To watch most old movies is to experience this same sense of transience. The more outdated the ideas and the more melodramatic the plot, the more aware I am that the depicted world is dead, if it ever existed at all. When I see Ronald Reagan in *Kings Row* (1942), I instantly compare the young actor with the aged president he became. The past decays before my eyes as I compare the face on the screen with the more recent one in my mind. At one point the Reagan in the movie, upon waking up to discover that his legs have been amputated, screams, "Where's the rest of me?" The actor's outcry seems so melodramatic that I start to laugh, but then I recall that the aging ex-president has Alzheimer's disease. Where's the rest of him now? In comparing what might be said about Reagan today with what Reagan, the actor, said almost sixty years ago in a movie, I am aware that the past is dead, yet also linked mysteriously to the present.

Sometimes an old film deals with feelings and ideas that don't seem dead, which is also true of movies that are outrageous. When Divine in John Waters's *Pink Flamingos* (1972) watches a dog defecate on the sidewalk, then reaches down, picks up the turd, and eats it, all in one shot, I am stunned. For a moment I forget completely that the scene was shot over twenty-five years ago and that the past is dead— as is Divine, who died some years after the movie was made. But watching the act on the screen seizes my attention so much that only the present moment exists, and it exists with such intensity that the scene leaps off the screen and hits me in the face with its immediacy. Not all films remind us of death, it's true, but most do.

* * *

My grandfather's coffin sketch continued to be on my mind for the next week at home in Vermont, and I was thinking of it as I went to a concert. One of my colleagues, a musician and choir director, was retiring, and for his last public performance he was conducting a two-hundred person choir, and a fifty-piece orchestra, in Brahms's *A German Requiem*. The performance was in the gym of the college where I teach. I hadn't stopped to connect my thoughts with the concert, so when I sat down and opened the program, the first sentence surprised me: "Brahms had made plans to write a work in German on the subject of death and consolation as early as 1861." During a week when I was thinking about a coffin, I just happened to show up for a musical performance on themes that were already on my mind. "Blessed are they that mourn, for they shall be comforted" were the first lines the choir sang. I looked around, but I did not sense any mourning. We were not in a great cathedral but in a gym, festooned with the banners of colleges like Amherst, Bowdoin, and Williams. There were no Christian banners, indicating the stations of the cross or some other religious motif; this was not a great Protestant cathedral in Germany where *A German Requiem* was first performed. Had anyone in that church contemplated the experience of grief and death, or were they merely there to hear a musical event?

Caught up in Brahms's music, unable to comprehend the German words, I could easily fail to notice when the choir sang, "Lord, make me to know mine end, the measure of my days, and that I must pass on." This message seemed the same as the one my grandfather expressed with his little coffin sketch, tucked away in his wallet, but his act was private, not at all the public affair that was taking place in the gymnasium. The concert seemed to be more of a celebration of what composers, musicians, and singers can create. *A German Requiem* was a tribute to the living. When it was over, I went home and looked again at my grandfather's design. I had missed the point entirely. When my cousin said a Stevens was the kind of person who sketched his own coffin, he was more right than he realized. My grandfather, with his little sketch, was probably not confronting his own mortality as much as he was making one last attempt to create something that was beautiful and satisfying to him. That he never built it seemed now doubly ironic.

What I really loved about this little sketch was that it was handmade, an actual drawing that my grandfather did. I was holding a piece of paper that I knew he held, one that was touched by his pencil. I cherished the little drawing, not just because it showed me how my grandfather felt about death, and about the creative power of the living, but mainly because he sketched it with his own hands. To my mind if there was no future, no heavenly reward, at least there was a past and people with whom I felt connected. I did not have any icons in my home, or any shrines where I might genuflect and pray; all I had was my grandfather's wallet, his identification cards, the slogans, his list of people who made great etchings, and his sketch of a coffin. If I couldn't acknowledge my own fate, the way my grandfather had, I could savor his desire to design and build a handsome coffin. To make something to be proud of, that was an impulse I understood.

I found a person skilled in paper restoration and sent my grandfather's sketch off to be cleaned and to have its stains removed. Framing the drawing, I then hung it on the wall of my living room, next to some keepsakes there that speak very clearly of death.

* * *

The other reminders of death on my living room wall are hair wreaths. My wife and I have been collecting these for years, jokingly saying that we have the largest private collection in the world. Created in the mid-1800s in different parts of North America, the wreaths were made by gathering several locks of hair from family members, then weaving the strands together into a horseshoe shape that from a distance looks like a garland of small flowers. The effect was heightened by the inclusion of little colored stones, pieces of ribbon, and braid. Up close the collage effect breaks down and the components are obvious. Visible are different kinds of hair—straight, kinky, curly, white, red, brown, blond. I wouldn't be surprised if some of the locks were from a family dog or cat; maybe even a beloved horse. I look at these wreaths and find them a little morose, even macabre. After all, these strands of hair are from humans who once walked the earth, but who are now dead. Which hair belongs to an aunt, which to an uncle, which to the oldest living family member, and which come from children? Since making the wreaths was women's work, which of the mothers or wives or sisters took the time to collect the hair, to weave it over wax molds, and then to dip those into a vat of hot water? Probably full of starch, the hot water melted the wax and fixed the shape of the hair. Now the wreaths hang in shadow boxes on my wall, while the people's bodies have long since decayed in the ground.

Not really sure why they were so fascinating, I had collected quite a few of these hair wreaths before I realized that they reminded me of movies. The people who gave their hair were now dead. The people and buildings in the movies I saw in Vermillion were dead, too. All movies show something that has since changed—the actors have gone on to other movies, sets have been torn down, old buildings have been replaced, some actors have died. Hair wreaths and movies speak of loss, change, and death; they're both implicitly acts of mourning.

Mourning is something I know very little about and do even less of. I understand grieving; I do that almost automatically. Mourning seems more deliberate, an assertion that the dead once lived, that they were important, and that their death is a loss. I don't recall seeing anyone wearing mourning clothes, but I do remember embroideries, prints, photographs, paintings, and mementos that were kept in my family to preserve someone's memory. My mother held on to her father's wallet for thirty-five years. My Grandmother Stevens, until her death, carried around a little note she found in the papers of her husband, my grandfather. It read, "I have loved one woman and have devoted my life to her and our children. We earn so little and get so much." She had the last sentence carved onto his tombstone. Why did my grandfather write down such sentences? Was he trying to remind himself, or convince himself, or what?

As far as I can recall, nobody in my family did it, but I have read about some families where members kept strands of hair, putting them in a locket, or in a mourning ring, or even in the back of a brooch whose front was a photograph of the deceased. As long as the hair was worn, the dead person was still in some sense alive. All these mourning objects were also memento mori, a reminder of death itself. Because I seldom make this kind of effort, and because I don't mourn very much on my own, and rarely as a part of a community, I don't think much about life after death. To design my own coffin never occurred to me, and the pastel portrait of my own father has long since disappeared. I live and I die; that's the whole story. It matters to me, and to a few people close to me, but not to the rest of the universe.

* * *

Mourning is not a favorite movie subject, and only Bruce Conner's *Report* (1967) and Vertov's *Three Songs of Lenin* (1934) come to mind when I think of mourning films. What strikes me about these two films is how both break with everyday realism, almost as if it is impossible to mourn within the mold of representational filmmaking. By using repetition, by juxtaposing actual documentary footage with staged scenes, and by weaving discontinuous images together with discordant sounds, both films remind me of the braiding and weaving in my hair wreaths. Feelings about death are so intense that some kind of reiteration seems to be called for, like the days I and others spent after JFK's assassination watching some scenes over and over on television—the landing of Air Force One, the motorcade in Dallas, Jackie's roses strewn over the backseat of the president's limousine, the swearing in of Lyndon Johnson, Oswald's arrest, Jack Ruby shooting Oswald, the funeral cortege in Washington. Seeing these images dozens of times seemed to help us to grieve and maybe even to mourn.

* * *

During college, I thought a lot about death because I worked in a funeral home. An ideal job, it came with a free room above the business, and often, sitting at a desk during a long night's vigil, there was plenty of time to read and study. All I really had to do was to be ready in the middle of the night to go pick up the body of someone who had died. Now and then I also helped with funeral ceremonies, like walking down front to close a coffin lid during a service, or driving the hearse. "Never put your arm on the window ledge," my boss told me. "It looks disrespectful." During my free time I would go into the room where the embalmer was working on a corpse. Clamping the jaw closed so that it would be that way when rigor mortis set in, he then made incisions on both sides of the groin to pump fluid into one artery and blood out the other. I eyed the genitals and the shape of the body, watching with some admiration the way the mortician would apply makeup to the face to give it some inkling of the living person. Human beings these were not, I told myself repeatedly. I saw only a carcass.

That the feelings of dread and curiosity at a funeral home would lead to something unusual, like practical jokes, I should have guessed. The embalming room had a sign on the wall: "We're the only people who wash our hands before going to the bathroom." Sometimes the funeral home would receive a corpse that was unidentified, and that by law we had to keep for thirty days. The excitement for the month was to move the corpse around and put it in surprising places, like standing in my closet one day when I opened the door. I jumped back several feet until I realized who, or what, it was. Another morning the body was in bed with me when I woke up.

Sometimes we had to work very hard to suppress our laughter. The wife of one dead man, who was extremely well endowed sexually, kept saying over and over again, "I'll never find another man like him!" Hearing her words, it was very difficult to keep a straight face. Another time a second worker and I walked down to a coffin during a funeral service, one of us to close the lid and one to put flowers on the top of the coffin. "Your fly is unzipped," my colleague whispered to me as I held up the wreath of flowers. It was too awkward to reach down and zip up in front of the bereaving audience, so I waited until I had marched up the aisle, only to discover that my zipper was okay. What a cruel joke; all that embarrassment for nothing.

The worst prank ever played on me was when they let me turn on the motor that pumped embalming fluid into a body. The embalmer, as he was leaving the room, told me, "Just turn the pump on. I've got to make a phone call." The body was of a young man who had died from a heart attack just a few blocks away. He was brought straight to the funeral home, his flesh still warm. When I flipped the switch on the pump, and turned around, the upper part of the body, including the arms, rose slightly off the embalming table and the eyelids fluttered open. Frightened, I ran out of the room, only to find the embalmer and others in the hall, doubling over with laughter. They knew how a warm body would respond, and I was reacting just as they were sure I would.

After a few weeks in the funeral home, except when little children were brought in, I no longer reflected much on death. I wanted to feel fear at the sight of the corpse; I wanted to be reminded so strongly of my own death that I would tremble and then live each day as if it were my last. It didn't happen. Over time the job became routine. Another carcass to pick up, clean up, dress up, put in the ground. The only touching, human moment was when the embalmer's father died. After we took the body into the preparation room, and left it there, the embalmer locked the door and kept us out. He wanted to prepare his father's body himself. Most of all, he said, he wanted to do the makeup on his father's face. When he was done, he came out of the room with a manila envelope that, I think, contained his father's personal effects. Perhaps today, if he is alive, the embalmer still has his father's wallet.

* * *

I didn't really learn much about death in the funeral home, except ways to avoid its emotional impact. Working at a funeral home, feeling death becoming mundane, was like watching deaths in a movie. Peckinpah's *The Wild Bunch* (1969) was the first movie I remember where the deaths were really vivid; blood flew everywhere. Now that film looks mild, as each successive movie has tried to make death more and more gory. No doubt my great-grandchildren will find the deaths in *Natural Born Killers* (1994) and *Pulp Fiction* (1994) pretty tame.

When movies try to make death more meaningful, and not just grisly, the effort is often swallowed up in sentimentality, as if the only way to think about death is with feelings that are overwrought and misplaced. Butch and Sundance choose to depart life in a hail of bullets! Gregory Peck is killed as he storms a Nazi machine-gun bunker! Ali MacGraw dies in Ryan O'Neal's arms! A young bride, Debra Winger, is called away much too early by the Grim Reaper, leaving children, husband, and mother! Dramatizing death is not the same as facing the real thing head on.

I want to watch death in the movies for the same reason that I imagined my father's death while he was away in Africa, and for the same reason that I imagined the death of my children. If I see enough examples of fake deaths in the movies, won't I be better able to deal with death when it happens? It might be true only if there were more movie deaths that made me confront the reality of dying; but they're rare. The brutal indifference of the murderer in *Henry: Portrait of a Serial Killer* (1990) frightened me a little, and the dark humor of some of the deaths in Scorsese's *GoodFellas* (1990) felt oddly real. I well remember being moved in Powell's *The Red Shoes* (1948) when the heroine, Vickie, dies in a way that is simultaneously silly and tragic, stupid and heroic.

Since the days when my movie heroes were about to be sucked down by quicksand, I don't often recall being affected by a death in a film. Those like Janet Leigh's shower murder in Hitchcock's *Psycho* (1960) are memorable because all the resources of cinema are used to create an event that can take place only on the movie screen; yet I feel manipulated. What's usually more interesting are the moments leading up to a death, and what follows. Much more harrowing than Susan Hayward's gas chamber execution in Wise's *I Want to Live!* (1958) are the previous six minutes, virtually devoid of sound, as the filmmaker cuts together a number of close-ups: Hayward fingering a religious medal; the telephone that might ring and stop the execution; the cyanide pellets poised above the acid; and, most menacing of all, the tube sticking out of Susan's blouse that will be hooked up to a stethoscope so the doctor can tell when her heart stops beating. The horror of the gassing is made even more vivid afterward when the reporter, who has been writing about the woman, turns off his hearing aids and the world grows absolutely silent. Hayward's actual death is much less poignant than the moments before and after.

Why I want so much for movie deaths to have the same impact as actual deaths puzzles me, yet I do. It would be much easier to think of movies as figures of speech, which are never literally true. When my newscaster says, "The White House announced today . . . ," I don't conjure up an image of the White House with a huge face on the front, and lips that move and speak. Would that I could accept movies as tropes, too. Instead I want movies to be more real than life itself, to profoundly move me. Yet, on the other hand, I also want movies to be almost totally untrue to life, to seize me with something that is richer and more complex than my own life. This contradiction haunts my movie watching.

Most of the time, in actuality, movies help me run away from the reality of death. My mother was in an intensive care unit for six weeks before she died, and I was allowed to see her for only ten minutes out of every hour. Tending to her dying, I could fulfill finally that dictum of my father's as he walked out the door for Africa, saying, "You go home and comfort your mother. You're the man now." Staying in the waiting room for fifteen hours a day made for a brutal schedule. To prepare myself for those ten minutes every hour, I had to do all those things that are called healthy, like eating nourishing food, getting a good night's sleep, staying away from alcohol, getting exercise. Now and then for my own sanity, I felt I had to get away, and I would skip one of the ten-minute visits and slip off to a movie.

The first time I went, I saw *Apocalypse Now* (1979), but that was a mistake. How could I watch a movie with so much violence and death? When the skipper of a boat was felled senselessly by a wooden spear, I walked out. A few days later I tried *Alien* (1979), thinking that a science fiction movie would be so engrossing that I wouldn't think about my mother, but I didn't stay there long either. Not only was the main computer called "Mother," but there was a constant sense that something dreadful was about to happen, almost as if the ship were pregnant with horrible violence. I couldn't take it and left before the ending.

After a few weeks I went to another movie, *Breaking Away* (1979), which I thought would be perfect. It's a simple film with a plain story, some bike riding, even a little romance, but at the very end of the film there is a bike race. I was sure the hero of the film was going to win, or the film would make no sense, but as the cyclists pedaled away and it seemed that my hero might not win, I got so anxious that I had to leave. All the way back to the hospital my skin tingled as if I had the hives, but the stinging stopped when I entered the intensive care waiting room and felt again the dread of death.

As my mother lay dying, I began grieving not only for her death but other deaths, too, those yet to come and those that I had never really grieved for, like my father's. It was in the intensive care waiting room that I thought about my father's death and realized how peculiar was my memory. That some parts of my story were absurd hadn't occurred to me before. Do airlines really carry caskets attached to the outside of planes? One of the evenings while my mother was in intensive care, I went back to her house and looked through the materials she had saved about my father's death. I was shocked to read that his body actually came back on a ship, the SS *African Glen*. My mother had also kept the program for the funeral, which was inside a little Episcopal church, so there had been a service indoors after all, not just the graveside service I remembered.

We did not open my father's casket, of that I am certain. Today I would give anything to have seen the corpse, however decomposed and rank, just to have one final image of my father and to know that he was the one in the casket. Just because the undertaker suggested keeping the lid sealed didn't mean I had to agree. I acquiesced just to dramatize my father's death, which is also why I thought the airline had brought his body home in a casket attached to the outside of the plane, and why I didn't remember the service inside the church. Desperate for my father to be someone unique, I had made extraordinary everything associated with his death; I refused to let myself believe that his dying was simply that, nothing more or less. Sitting in my mother's house and fingering the souvenirs of my father's funeral, I grieved for him; his passing no longer seemed dramatic. The next morning, when a nurse came in to feed my mother through a tube into her stomach, an effort that even the doctor said would not sustain her for long, I was sure that she was going to die soon. After her death I would grieve again for her, and for my father, in the death of every other loved one.

* * *

Death can be overcome by imagining that some people are still alive, like my father. I will resurrect him and make a movie of us living together in New Orleans. The footage will begin with my search for a house to buy. A place is for sale on Coliseum Street, just a few doors down from where my parents lived when I was born. The Greek Revival and Italianate features are like those of the other homes I cherish in New Orleans. Two-story, with windows that stretch from floor to ceiling, this is the kind of home I always thought I should have lived in as a child. I take my father to see it, but on the way he stops in front of a nearby house, one that's also for sale, and also on Coliseum. He reads a plaque on the fence out front and breaks into a little dance. "We have to buy this house!" he exclaims. It's an attractive home, but not like the New Orleans houses I love, so I shake my head.

"No, *this* is the place we have to buy!" announces my father. I read the plaque and understand. My father has not lost his connection to Africa, and the plaque tells us that this house was once the home of Sir Henry Stanley, the journalist who trekked across Africa to find Dr. David Livingstone. I don't really like this house as much, but I buy it.

Now and then after we move in, I overhear my father saying, when he thinks no one is listening, "Dr. Livingstone, I presume?"

The house may not be my idea of an old home in the lower Garden District, but I still throw myself into the task of furnishing and decorating. A mover arrives one morning with my grandfather's bed, the one he made in his garage in Dallas, Texas, and I laugh when I see it. "Why don't we just put it together right here?" I ask.

The mover stares at me as if I have spoken in Swahili, and he says, "You mean, right here, in the front yard? It'll get wet."

I don't know myself what I'm thinking, and I stop chuckling, trying to compose myself. "Of course, you're right," I say, but I still wish he would put it up in the front yard. The mover takes the bed in, puts it up in my bedroom, and leaves, while I sit on the porch. Stretching the entire length of the house, the porch is one of my favorite things. My father insists on calling it a veranda, and we sit there often. Before he gets up in the morning, I drip some French Market coffee for him and heat a pot of milk. The coffee odor is so strong it staggers me, but I love it, and so does he. On the porch we sit in our rockers, taking pleasure from our coffee; in the afternoon we come back to the porch and drink iced tea and eat ladyfingers, my father's favorite cookie. A simple, happy life is what we enjoy.

A few days after we move in, I try taking my father to a movie downtown, but the Canal Street theaters we went to years ago are almost all closed. The only one still open, the Joy, was built after my father left for Africa, so we only went there a few times when he came for his annual visits. The experience now is terribly different. Entering, we are confronted by an armed guard who takes our tickets. An unpleasant smell, like rancid butter, so saturates the lobby that I am afraid I will throw up. The movie that's playing, *Men in Black* (1997), will start in a few minutes, so we go in and sit down. It's late afternoon and the theater is almost deserted. Way above us the ceiling has several huge rings that must be water stains from a leaky roof. My father grimaces, and I look down to see what he is making a face about. His shoe is stuck on a wad of gooey cheese, left on the floor by someone eating nachos. My father doesn't say a word, he just looks disgusted, but I go and get him some napkins so he can clean the bottom of his shoe.

While the picture runs, I steal a glance at my father now and then. He looks more puzzled than anything; not even the special effects give him much pleasure. His face lights up only once, and that is when Tommy Lee Jones makes his car climb up the walls and ceiling of the Holland Tunnel in order to get around some traffic. My father looks transfixed, his mouth hanging open.

At the end of the movie, shaking his head, he says, "What was that supposed to represent?" It feels as if it's my fault he doesn't like the movie, even though he is the one who wanted to come. As we leave the Joy, Canal Street is dark, and I suddenly remember that the street is no longer safe at night. Walking toward the Mississippi River to get a streetcar, we are being followed. A little frightened, I try to see who is there without completely turning my head around, but that is impossible. Finally, getting up the courage to look back, I spot a middle-aged couple. Something about the way they hold hands makes me feel a little safer. Canal Street, once the heart of the city, is now almost deserted at night. We pass the site of D. H. Holmes, one of the largest and most famous stores of my childhood, but it is boarded up. Near the old entrance, where New Orleanians used to meet "under the clock," two men are seated on wooden crates playing chess on a cardboard box between them.

After this trip to the Joy we don't go downtown. Because the theaters in suburban shopping centers are too far away, when we go out to see a movie, we go to the Prytania Theater, which is close enough to walk. My dad likes that. The Prytania often runs foreign films and revivals of older pictures; nothing pleases my father more than to go to a movie that he saw fifty, sixty, or seventy years ago.

I also buy heavy drapes for the sitting room of our house, and a thirty-six-inch television, so the two of us can rent videos and watch them at home. The first night we look at *Fury* (1936), and after my father gets over the initial shock of watching a movie on a television screen, he is delighted. It's the first movie he saw in New Orleans, when he and my mother moved here after getting married. My father is still amazed that Spencer Tracy, who started the film as someone sweet and affable, turns into a vengeful monster after a mob almost kills him. I tell my father that the movie was directed by Fritz Lang, who, having fled Nazi Germany, knew a thing or two about the psychology of mobs. My father looks at me rather strangely. Hearing any information that's not in the film destroys the illusion for him, so he'd just as soon not know anything about the director.

From then on he picks the videotapes we rent, so we spend most evenings watching old Westerns with people like Bob Steele, Hopalong Cassidy, Wild Bill Elliott, Roy Rogers, Gene Autry, and, naturally, Ken Maynard. I try to be patient and understanding, but one night I tell my father, "I don't know what you see in these films."

He stares at me rather blankly for a minute until he realizes that I am serious. "What do you mean? I love them. Where else can you find a world where everything is simple, where good and evil are black and white, and where the good guys always win?"

In such bliss my father and I spend our nights and days. Often we garden. I have sketched out a plan for landscaping the house, mainly with camellia bushes that have flowers of different colors, shapes, and blooming times. We'll have camellias from late autumn through spring. Dad works on a vegetable garden, planting butter beans, corn, and tomatoes, but after a while he seems to lose interest. Something's going on with my father, I don't know what. He won't look me in the eye. Finally, one day, he speaks. "Why don't we go on a trip somewhere?"

I try to stay calm; if I disagree too much, he'll get adamant. "You're ninety-two years old, isn't it time to settle down?"

"Don't ever get too attached to anything. Or any place."

It's hard to keep from showing my father that what he says not only saddens me, but makes me furious. He's well aware that I created this whole movie just to be with him. Not knowing what else to do, I try to smile a little, and he smiles back. The conversation is over.

I sit on the porch a while, stunned and speechless. Then I see that my father is staring at our neighbor, a widow who has also been putting in a vegetable garden. He watches her a long while. She's an elegant woman who always wears long sleeves when she comes outdoors because, as she later tells us, her skin is very sensitive to the sunlight. Her head is covered with a sun hat with tiny holes in the wide brim that create little points of light on her face, like stars. What skin I can see is milky white, and her face is framed with little ringlets of red hair, peeking out from under the hat that she holds on her head with a ribbon tied under her chin. Her smile is broad and radiant, and she giggles easily, with a little too much gusto for me, but her laughter causes her head to move around so quickly that the little points of light on her face look like a meteor shower. When we first moved in, she came to the fence and introduced herself, and after that we exchanged greetings once in a while. She must sense that my father is staring at her now. She's walking to the fence, looking down at my father's tomatoes.

"You have to pinch the suckers or the tomatoes won't get very big," she says, pointing at my father's tomato plants.

"Is that right?" My father doesn't move. He's not good at being corrected by anyone, and he knows what to do with tomato suckers, but he senses that she knows that he knows. The woman turns and goes back to her own work. "Nice lady," my father says to me. I expect him to say anything but that.

The next day he goes to the fence and talks to her a long time. They compare notes about different kinds of tomatoes, or so he tells me. Within a month my father is spending more time talking to her about his garden than actually working in it. The woman's name is Frances Evelyn, but, as she tells my father, friends call her F.E. He invites her over and they sit on his veranda, sipping tea and laughing, while I work in the yard. He doesn't call her F.E., but Frances, and she doesn't call him Ed, but Edward. They seem to want to redefine each other. I ignore their game and continue to call her F.E.

My father deserves a little company, so I don't object, but then one day he suddenly says to me, with tears in his eyes, "I told Frances I love her and I want her to marry me. She didn't say anything!" My ears refuse to hear what he says. I didn't resurrect my father from the dead in order to have him fall in love with some widow whose name is a set of initials.

At first I am angry at him. "What are you talking about? She's half your age!"

"She's fifty-five," my father says.

"And how old are you? She's closer to my age than yours!"

My father frowns; he doesn't like to be reminded of his age. "I saw her first."

I am aghast, and I rip off my gloves, throw them on the brick sidewalk, climb the wooden steps, and pound my way into the house. It's cool inside, and I go to my room, throwing myself across my bed like some adolescent who's just been disciplined. Within a few minutes I calm down. Giving my father a hard time will not work, I know that much. I get up and go back outside. Sitting on the porch, he eyes me, not sure what to expect. When I take a rocking chair next to him, he looks away and says, "Don't try to tell me I haven't done it in a long time; I know that."

I hadn't really imagined that my father was thinking about having sex, but I latch onto the idea. "That part of your anatomy probably doesn't work anymore."

"I went to see a urologist," my father says. "The drugs he gave me didn't work, so he taught me how to give myself a shot. It worked fine the second time I tried."

"How come it didn't work the first time?" I try not to conjure up an image of my father in the bathroom, sticking a needle in his penis to give himself an erection.

"I don't see so well down there."

It's true, the man has a large belly. Before I can speak, my father goes on, "My bifocals work fine for distances and up close. I'll just get trifocals."

My mind is filled with all the other conversations that I would prefer to have with my father, but while I am deciding which one of those to pursue, my thoughts are interrupted by a voice calling out, "Edward!" F.E. is standing at the fence, waving. My father is up, out of the chair, and at the fence in an instant. I've never seen him move so fast. F.E. and my dad talk. Soon, they hug awkwardly across the top of our wrought iron fence, and then she turns and goes back into her house. My father comes back toward me with a big grin on his face.

"Will you be my best man?" he asks. I don't answer, but he doesn't notice. He bounces inside the house, while I sit in my rocker, feeling as if someone is reaming out my chest with a catheter.

The wedding is set for a week later; it'll be in F.E.'s yard, but only a few people are invited. My father and I will be there, along with a niece and nephew of F.E.'s. He's already warming to the niece and nephew, selling his bedroom suite to the nephew without asking me if I want it. He tells me he wants to sell the house, too, but I won't let him and the deed is in my name. While furious at my father, I don't say anything, even though it's clear he'll soon be spending more time with F.E.'s niece and nephew than with me. Waking that morning, the day of the wedding, I know that I can't go through with it.

"What?" he screams at me when I tell him I won't be his best man.

"Daddy, I don't want anything to do with this wedding. I hate the whole idea."

"You're so selfish," my father says.

Yeah, I think to myself, trying not to say what I really think, which is, "When you left before, for Africa, all I did was smile and pretend it didn't matter. 'Who needs a father?' I told myself. Well, this time you won't get my blessing."

My father is getting mad, and he's about to speak, but I know what he is going to say, so I beat him to it by saying, "You little shit!"

I walk out of his room and let him finish dressing. After he leaves and goes next door, I watch the wedding from our front porch. He and F.E. are standing under a huge magnolia tree, facing a female justice of the peace. It looks like F.E.'s nephew is best man. F.E. has put her stereo speakers in her windows, and out of them is coming some crap—Montovani or Lawrence Welk conducting, Liberace playing the piano, maybe even Perry Como singing. When the ceremony is over, my father and F.E. walk toward a big motor home that is parked out front at the curb. My father bought it so they can go on an extended trip. He's planning to take F.E. back to Kokomo to show her where he grew up and to meet the children of his brothers and sisters. After that the newlyweds are going to visit Wabash College, where my father went to school for one year, and then they're driving out to Yellowstone National Park and up through the Canadian Rockies, stopping off at Banff. Finally, they're going to New York City to see some plays, staying at the Commodore Hotel. I don't tell my father that the Commodore no longer exists.

As F.E. and my father near her gate, I climb down my steps and walk toward the motor home. Whether I'm going to hug him goodbye or hit him with my fist is not clear. As I get closer, Dad hardly notices me, so wrapped up is he in helping F.E. into the front seat of the motor home. They're tittering. My father goes around the front of the motor home to get in on his side. For certain he sees me out of the corner of his eye, but he doesn't turn his head. He's wearing a brown gabardine suit, something I've never seen him in before. The shirt is gray. His face seems transparent, almost as if there is no blood in his skin, and he looks fragile. When a huge grin envelops his face, some dimples appear that I don't remember he had.

Seeing how frail and happy he seems, I lose my desire to do anything except watch. He ignores me, but F.E. waves, trying to be friendly. I stay still, feeling as if this is an event seen from someone else's body. The color of the motor home is ghastly, a kind of baby-shit yellow. The vehicle starts to move away, taking with it all feelings about my father, F.E., their wedding, their trip, their ugly motor home. In his rearview mirror my father's face looks straight back at me, with no expression. Let him go, I say to myself, good riddance; fathers leave.

As they pull out, I notice that the back of the motor home has a shade hanging inside a big picture window, and dangling on the end of the drawstring for the shade is a little gnomelike creature, a Smurf. With a stupid smile and unruly hair, it swings wildly from side to side as the motor home drives off.

Staring intently at the little creature, certain that it reminds me of something, I finally realize that it looks like the doctor who told me my mother had cancer of the esophagus. He and I were outside her room in the hall of the intensive care unit.

"Inoperable," he says. "I'm sorry."

I ask, "What are the options?"

"To be perfectly frank, none. It's gone too far."

"What about radiation? Chemotherapy?" Though he just shakes his head, I say, "I once heard there's someplace in Asia where they remove the esophagus."

"Nobody I know thinks it's a good idea. Her last months would just be even more miserable. The CA is in her brain."

"CA?"

"Cancer." The doctor isn't looking me in the eye anymore, just down at the stack of papers in his hand, thumbing a corner as if he's splaying a stack of playing cards.

"What about some new experimental drugs?"

"None."

"What about drugs the FDA hasn't approved yet? I don't mind taking her to Mexico or somewhere."

The doctor tries to smile a little, as if he is very sympathetic, but the look is perverse, and he knows it. Turning his head away, he says, "I've checked and double-checked, called other oncologists at the best medical centers; it's always the same answer."

I don't believe what he's saying. "There's always something to try." I laugh. "Acupuncture!"

Now the doctor stares at me, not appreciating at all my humor. "No, nothing."

I return his stare. "There's always something."

The doctor shakes his head, then walks away.

After standing for a moment in the hall, I go back inside my mother's room, but I don't tell her what the doctor said. I wish I could, but we have an understanding, she and I. We only talk about the food.

10 Crossing The River

I FLEW BACK TO NEW ORLEANS AGAIN, but somewhere over Tennessee I realized that for the first time I wasn't sure why I was going back. In earlier trips there had been people to see and special places to visit, but now, nothing, almost as if someone had switched a magnet off. Little about the city attracted me anymore. After each previous visit to some particular site—my old neighborhood, Bourbon Street, a cemetery, the *batture*—some enticement of the place had evaporated, and now nothing in the city felt compelling.

Like it or not, I arrived back in New Orleans, and, the morning after my plane landed, went out and walked aimlessly around, without a plan. Strolling through the Garden District, I felt a little pang at the sight of a particularly beautiful wisteria vine, its flowers hanging down like huge lavender tears. I was drawn to one house that was raised off the ground and fronted by a long porch with tall French windows. Inside were rooms with extremely high ceilings and crystal chandeliers. The front door of leaded glass broke light and vision into complex patterns. Maybe a few things were appealing as I walked the streets, but not much. Being back in New Orleans felt like visiting an old lover, someone I was really passionate about once, but now I couldn't figure out what used to be so exciting and wonderful.

Nothing was left to do but wander around. After a few hours I wound up at the edge of the French Quarter, not the Bourbon Street part but the area closer to the Mississippi River where there were galleries, shops, and restaurants. Because Café du Monde, the large coffee shop, was crowded with tourists, I crossed the street and walked around Jackson Square. The perimeter was lined with people peddling various wares—music, paintings, magic tricks, individual charcoal portraits. Here and there, behind a small table, a man or a woman was offering palm readings and predictions of the future, using tarot cards. One of the men attracted my interest. His face, a beautiful caramel color, seemed so peaceful, and he was not dressed in some eccentric costume like many of the others who offered spiritual advice. I had an urge to sit down at his table, but I hesitated, a little frightened. What if he hypnotized me, took all my money, or touched me in some way I did not want? Even worse, he might see inside me and reveal something otherwise hidden, or he might predict a future that I did not wish. Yet I felt lost in New Orleans, and this was the first time that day I sensed a strong urge to do anything; so I got up my courage, walked over, and sat down on the opposite side of a little table in front of the man.

"I'm Raja," he said, smiling, and held out his hand.

"Ted," I responded. We talked about his fee, which seemed fair to me.

"Is there anything particular you want to know about?" Raja asked.

"Yes," I found myself saying. "I want to understand something about me and movies, and why I am in New Orleans."

Raja smiled, but didn't say anything. Then he draped a cloth over his little table, and, on top of the cloth, placed several stones, two bracelets, and a piece of agate with a dark eye-shaped center. While shuffling a deck of tarot cards, he said that he would talk to me about health, finances, love, and how to achieve equilibrium in life. I cut the deck of cards, and then, as Raja directed, picked eight that I placed face down in a circle around the agate eye. As I turned each card back over, he used it to tell me about myself, about my past and future, and also about life, at least his philosophy of life. What began as fortune-telling quickly became a treatise on every aspect of existence, even diet. "Supplement your food with garlic, organic alfalfa, and wheat grass," he suggested. "That's all you need."

Claiming to read my inner and outer auras, Raja preached to me. I listened carefully for a while. Nothing he said was new—I had read it all elsewhere—but this was the first time a gentle, kind human being had looked me in the eye and, with the utmost sincerity, said such things as "You can elevate your consciousness only if you learn to tame your emotions." Raja's message seemed very anachronistic, given how many of my friends had proclaimed the need to "follow your heart." Though impressed with his sincerity, I didn't really believe that in 2003, as he said, I would be a part of a spiritual healing community somewhere in a valley surrounded by low hills. "Maybe Pennsylvania," Raja offered. Even when he stated correctly the number of my children and grandchildren, I still couldn't bring myself to accept that he had any special powers. Believing him would be nice, particularly when he promised that I would live until late in my eighties, yet I couldn't conjure up much faith in what the man said. Finally, Raja stopped talking. I had turned over all eight of the cards, and he had told me everything he would.

"What about my two questions?" I asked.

"Yes," Raja said. "You want to know about New Orleans and the movies?"

"I do."

Raja looked at me for a moment. "You're seeking guidance," he said.

That's pretty obvious, I thought to myself. Looking at him, I said, "Well?"

"You're seeking guidance," Raja repeated, smiling.

I wanted to pin him down and get some guidance, but I was sure he would give me a cliché about looking inside myself, so I didn't say anything; I just got up, paid him, shook his hand, then left. I hadn't learned much, but at least I had overcome my fear of psychic readers.

Strolling again, this time toward the Mississippi, I saw a ferry crossing the river to the city of Algiers, on the west bank. A slight mist was falling, there was a breeze, and a ferry ride across the river and back might be invigorating. When I was five or six, my father had taken me for rides on this same ferry, but I never knew why. Maybe he found them relaxing, or he just wanted to feel what it was like to get away.

When the ferry docked at the end of Canal Street, I got on. In a few moments we pulled out and began pushing through water that was muddy and churning wildly. Because the river turns a corner at this point, the currents were going in various directions, some upstream, some down, some toward the bank and some toward the center of the river, almost as if the water didn't know what it was supposed to do. I sat on the stern of the ferry and watched the skyline of downtown New Orleans recede, its tall buildings getting shorter and shorter. The city was slipping away from me, not disappearing but losing intensity as it became a wide-angle long shot—a CinemaScope rectangle that seemed flat and meaningless. The rain clouds cut out the sun, and the buildings, drained of color, were dark boxes. For a moment I felt like my students when I show them an old movie. "It can't be any good," they groan, "it's just black and white." Yes, I thought, there's no color to New Orleans. If the buildings had been white instead of dark, I would have sworn that I was looking at the St. Louis No. 1 cemetery—a City of the Dead. I traced the tall buildings with my gaze, trying to make some connection, wanting desperately to feel something. The teacher's worst nightmare: I'm standing in front of a class of a hundred students, the movie of New Orleans has just ended, and my brain is blank. It doesn't seem like New Orleans any more, just a skyscape no different than a dozen other cities. Yes, the old Jax Brewery building is now a shopping center; there's the aquarium; I can make out the long thread of a mall called RiverWalk, full of trendy shops; and I can see the top of the Harrah's casino—but nothing I see is really unique. The Marriott, The Double Tree Inn, the Hilton, the Sheraton—they could be anywhere. I might as well have been looking across the Mississippi at St. Louis, or across Lake Michigan at Chicago, or across the harbor at Baltimore.

New Orleans didn't seem so special, and I didn't care if I ever saw the city again. Movies, too, seemed distant and unimportant; it didn't matter to me if I ever saw another film. For a moment I felt the way I did in the hospital when my mind went slack. When the ferry reached the dock in Algiers, it seemed like another country.

I felt the urge to look up. The sky seemed luminescent. Teetering precariously close to the edge of the deck above me was a toddler in a huge white sailor cap that almost covered his eyes. Without thinking, my arms reached out, ready to catch him. In an instant of my imagination, I shot a movie in which I actually saw him fall off into my waiting arms, and the people on the ferry applauded. As I called "Action!" the miniature skyline of New Orleans exploded in a shower of concrete and steel, and in its place appeared filmed images of me being a hero. I kept people from chopping up other people with machetes, stopped others from sticking needles in their arms, assassinated a tyrant as he was giving a pompous speech about racial purity and national sovereignty. I filmed myself able to explain to the dying why they had lived; I supervised the destruction of yet another nuclear-tipped ICBM; I gave mountains of food to the hungry. The movie I imagined beyond New Orleans made me exhilarated; I saw clearly that there were things for me to do, causes to espouse, plans to implement, roles to assume. As I heard imaginary ovation, pumping me full of adrenaline, the father of the toddler ran over and jerked him back from the edge of the deck so quickly that the little boy screamed. All my self-righteous images vanished; my movie was over. A sharp drizzle stung my face and suddenly a large pelican flew out of nowhere, surprising me, then a cormorant zipped by, skimming the tops of the waves.

My reverie was interrupted further when I heard laughter and looked over to see two couples. They must have boarded in Algiers. One of the young men was standing against the railing, his arms raised and outstretched, and the other three young people were laughing at him. It made no sense. What was funny about standing with your arms raised and spread out? Then it dawned on me that the young man was mimicking the postures of Leonardo DiCaprio and Kate Winslet in the movie *Titanic* (1997), standing on the bow of the ship with their arms outstretched. I should have known; *Titanic* was the current rage with adolescents. New Orleans's parting shot was a movie, damn it. So much for guidance.

The snob in me reacted quickly. I wanted to say to the young man, "Look, if you must try to impress your friends by mixing up movies and life, do what Gene Kelly did in *Singin' in the Rain*, when he wanted to find a way to tell Debbie Reynolds he loved her. He took her onto a movie soundstage, switched on some big Klieg lights, illuminated a glorious sunrise on a painted cyclorama, turned on the fans until the wind blew Debbie's dress and hair, then danced and sang his heart out." I wanted badly to say, "Young man, be like Gene Kelly, use your imagination! Be in one movie while pretending to be in another movie."

Better to keep quiet, I thought to myself. They probably had never seen *Singin' in the Rain*. One minute I didn't care if I ever saw another movie, and the next I was arguing for the superiority of *Singin' in the Rain* over *Titanic*. My body couldn't flush films out of my brain the way it could the gunk from a myelogram gone awry. As the ferry moved back across the river, getting closer and closer to New Orleans, the tall buildings seemed more and more imposing, threatening to topple over toward me, and I wanted to run back under my old house to look at the city through a rectangle carved out of the bricks. New Orleans was always better as a movie anyway.

About the Author

Ted Perry is the Paris Fletcher Professor of the Arts at Middlebury College in Vermont, where he teaches courses in film and video. At the Museum of Modern Art in New York City, he was Director of the Department of Film. Perry has taught film and video courses at the University of Iowa, at the State University of New York at Purchase, at the American Film Institute's Center for Advanced Film and Television Study, and also at the University of Texas at Austin, where he was director of graduate studies. At New York University he was chairman of the Department of Cinema Studies, Director of the 1994 Salzburg Seminar on Film, as well as trustee emeritus of the American Film Institute. Perry was also Visiting Henry Luce Professor of Film Studies at Harvard University.

A native of New Orleans, Louisiana, Ted Perry studied at Baylor University in Texas and at the University of Iowa, from which he received the M.A. and Ph.D. degrees. His writing has produced a number of articles and books, most of them on Italian cinema, but he has also written and directed plays for the stage and documentaries for television. A frequent lecturer, he has spoken here and abroad on various aspects of film.